As Mad
As A Hatter!

Author of

The Ingenious Mr Pedersen
Listers – The First Hundred Years
Dursley and Cam in Pictures

Co-author of

Aspects of Gloucestershire History — Dursley
Cam Hopton Endowed School

As Mad As A Hatter!

Puritans and Whitefieldites in the History of Dursley and Cam

DAVID E. EVANS

Alan Sutton
1982

Alan Sutton Publishing Limited
17a Brunswick Road
Gloucester

First published 1982

British Library Cataloguing in Publication Data

Evans, David E.
As mad as a hatter.
1. Dissenters, Religious—Gloucestershire—Dursley—History
I. Title
287'. 142419 BX5202.D/

ISBN 0-904387-90-9

Typesetting and origination by
Alan Sutton Publishing Limited.
Photoset 11/11 Caslon
Printed in Great Britain
by Page Bros (Norwich) Limited

Contents

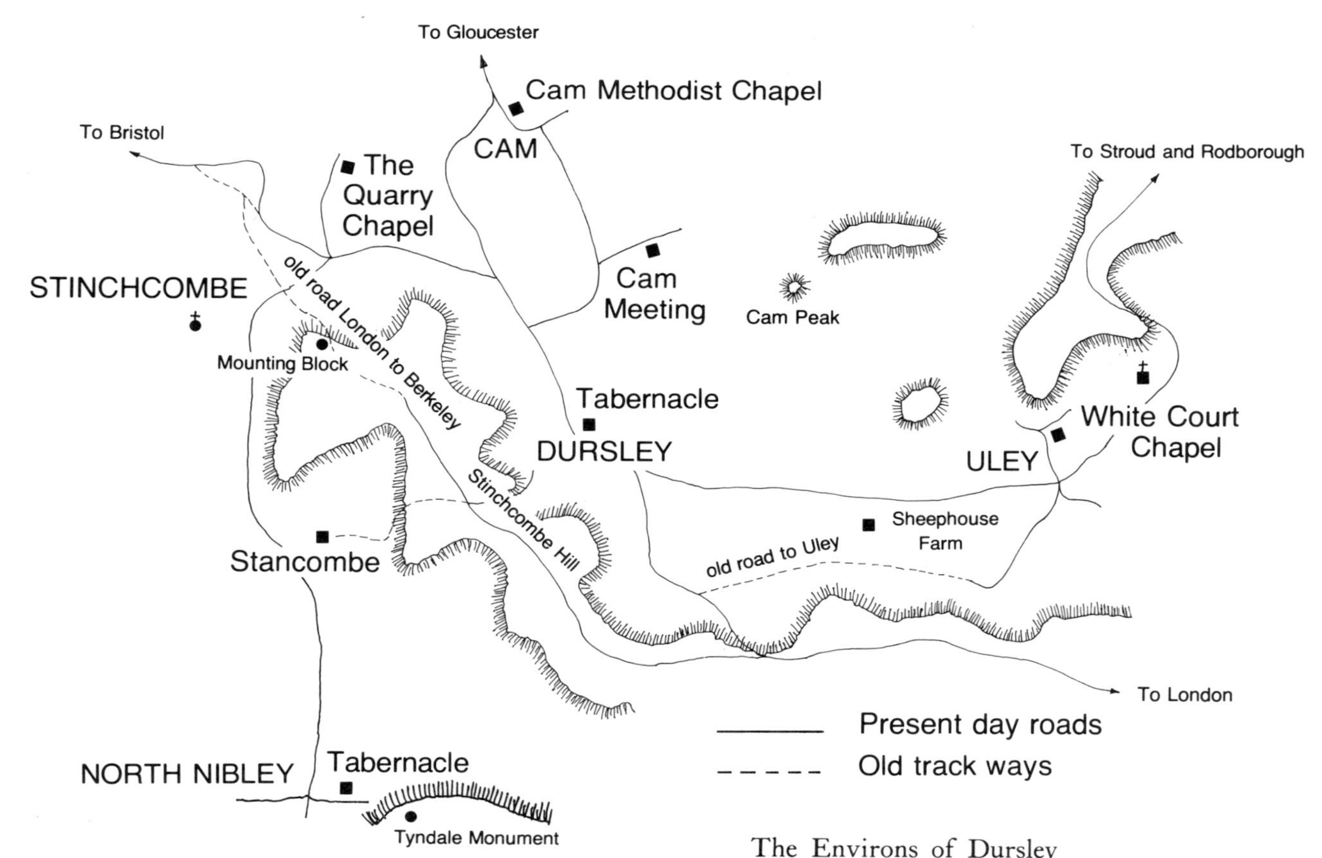

The Environs of Dursley

Foreword

by the Revd. Glyn Jenkins B.A., B.D.
Minister of Dursley Tabernacle United Reformed Church

Very few churches have people with the initiative, perception and ability of David Evans: initiative to 'grasp the nettle' of writing a book of this nature; perception in seeing church life against the backdrop of history; and ability to marshal the facts and complete the exercise.

Some people may call him 'as mad as a hatter' to contemplate such a task. yet he has good pedigree in the pages of the New Testament for many of the early Christians were called 'fools'. He has not only contemplated the task; he has seen it through. It is a task which has demanded the three R's: Resolution, Research and Risk. No-one can doubt the author's resolution because this book has been a book close to the heart and faith of the writer. Research is a long, fascinating but painstaking art, fraught with disappointments but enlivened by the constant discoveries which make everything worthwhile. Risk is part of living in today's world – it is more than economic risk. In this book, David Evans is not just folding back the pages of unwritten history, he is allowing his personal faith and commitment to the Living Christ to bring out and assess the contribution of the generations.

The real concept of the Christian life is the world on our doorsteps. Every town and village in this country is a storybook of life and a microcosm of society. This is the world of tradesmen and craftsmen and cleaner-women. This book is about such people. In the orbit of life, every generation has something vital and responsible to offer. Today's generation is no different. The Dursley of today is a place where people work and where people are unemployed; where the regular shopping is done and the children are taken to school; where the engineer tests his engines and the manufacturer makes his three-piece suits. Here the doctor ploughs his round and the farmer looks for healthy crops. Around us is a mixture of life with high and low wage-earners, locally long established families and the many 'immigrants' from the Rhondda valleys, Italy, Poland, the Midlands and the North. But still Dursley is small. I have personal memories of being driven round some of the housing estates on my first visit to Dursley. After emerging from Highfields Approach I could not believe that that was one of the biggest estates in Dursley. After the over-spill areas of some of our cities, Dursley appears small and slumbering. If you wanted, you could quite happily live your life away in this quite beautiful and desirable place, because most facilities are close at hand. The natural boundaries of Stinchcombe Hill and Long Down protect its life. Yet this book will show that the church, although serving the immediate needs of people, is not by nature insular and parochial. Every parish minister knows how easy it is for people to think in a narrow, local way. Clashes on the streets of Bristol and violence in Northern Ireland may be, for some, a distant scene. The history of our church proves that there has always been an awareness of wide concerns and an outward vision.

In the year of this book being published the local church is having to address itself to such issues as the World Disarmament Campaign, the Brandt report on World Development, Christian Lifestyle, and Church Unity. Visitors to the Tabernacle have included thirty young people from the Covenant Mission Church of Sweden, a minister from the Presbyterian Church of Korea and a speaker from the Corrymeela Community in Northern Ireland.

All this shows that the Church of today needs the past to help correct the present and focus the future. The task in front is no bigger than the power behind us. It was that power that led the crowds out onto Stinchcombe Hill to hear the great preachers. That power also sustained the Church through periods of decline and self-questioning. The same power leads the Church forward to look beyond local loyalties to a better future and a bigger vision. The Church's task has always been to point people away from itself to its Lord, who is the Lord of all people. Before you is part of the story as it happened and is still happening in Dursley. Read on, and with God's power, we will all see ourselves as part of that story – the last chapter has always yet to be written. . . .

The Parsonage,
Dursley.
1982

Author's Note

Dursley is small as towns go. One hundred years ago it was very much smaller and so was Cam. Neither however was so small that the Victorian incumbents at their respective parish churches of St. James, St. George and St. Bartholomew were unable to live in newly built houses of considerable size, none of which are used by today's incumbents who have neither the wealth nor the servants to run them. This was more than just a local characteristic and for many parish priests, life in the Victorian era was one of considerable leisure allowing time for pursuits outside the religious. Many researched and printed the histories of their parishes. The Rector of Beverstone, some five miles from Dursley on the Tetbury road, was one who did this.

The Revd. John Blunt, for such was he, delved in to the pasts of his parish and those of Dursley, Cam and Uley and published his results in 1877 under the title *Dursley and its Neighbourhood*. He wrote at a time when relationships between the various religious denominations were frequently uncordial. John Blunt shows his bias for, from reading his book, it is possible to reach the conclusion that the three valley parishes had no-one who dissented from his particular view of ecclesiastical life, or, at least that any such were insignificant and of no importance. Such was not the case.

To understand why Nonconformity flourished in our valley, as in others in this part of the Cotswolds, two points need to be known. The first is that for hundreds of years there have been no great landowners living here so that the subervient forelock touching yokel — autocratic or paternalistic squire relationship is unlikely to have existed. Instead there have been successions of independent or semi-independent farmers and woollen cloth workers – fulling mill owners, weavers, shearmen, dyers, card makers and the like. These of varying levels of prosperity, or lack of it, and their families and perhaps a workman or two, made up the communities with a few gentlemen of independent means on their small estates.

The second point to remember is that because of this ability to control much of their working day, there was an inclination in some to want to carry this into the area of religious observance. This was to be found less in the Established Church than in the societies of worshippers who dissented from it. Thus in the eighteenth century, when detailed records become available in Dursley and Cam, we find Presbyterian and Methodist groups of considerable size supported by these same mill owners, weavers, card makers and the rest.

When they came to build meeting houses they were not tucked away in back streets but set boldly in obvious positions. The one exception was the Water Street chapel, but this was because it was erected at the bottom of the garden of the imposing house in Long Street occupied by its minister.

By Parliamentary Act, those who dissented from the Anglican Church were for long debarred from civic office, but locally, in spite of this handicap, they played a prominent part in town life.

This book complements in some degree that of John Blunt. It is concerned with those people who were unable to accommodate themselves in the main stream of Anglican life and who were either forced from that church, like those who came to create Cam Meeting, or who, because of indifference or antagonism, broke away, such as the followers of George Whitefield and John Wesley.

Central to the book is Dursley Tabernacle United Reformed Church, early adherents to which were frequently called 'meetingers' or 'Whitefieldites'. A key man in the nurturing of the society which eventually built it was John Dando, hat maker in eighteenth-century Dursley. He was therefore a Methodist, though of the Calvinistic variety, not the Wesleyan, and the early Methodists with their great vitality and enthusiasm were often thought to be 'quite mad' by their contemporaries. In concentrating on the church he helped to build, the other churches of the area are not ignored and much previously unpublished material relating to Cam Meeting, Dursley Methodist Church and the Parish Church of St. James is included.

One final point. The United Reformed Church Year Book, and its Congregational predecessors back to 1861, give the date of the beginning of Dursley Tabernacle as 1710. There can be no doubt that this is incorrect. No date can be set firmly for the first gathering of the society which gave rise to the Tabernacle but there is every likelihood that it was in 1742.

David E. Evans,
Dursley.
1982

Acknowledgements

I acknowledge with gratitude the help I have received from the following people in a variety of ways;–

Miss Valerie Rodway of Cam for deciphering my handwriting and converting it into typescript.

Miss Joan Kingham for reading the typescript and offering valuable suggestions.

Mr. Charles Howarth of Uley for his expertise and patience over much of the photographic work.

Mr. Alan Sutton for seeing this book through its printing and publishing stages.

Mr. Arthur Hancock of Kingswood, Bristol, for advice and the loan of material relating to Kingswood Tabernacle.

The Revd. J.W. McMinn and the Elders of Rodborough Tabernacle for permission to photograph the portrait of Thomas Adams.

Mr. Derek Archer, Editor of the Gloucestershire Gazette Series of Newspapers, and his staff for courteous permission to search through past editions of the Dursley Gazette, and to print Gazette photographs.

Mr. D. Billett; Mr. F. Booth; Mr. J. Bosworth of Cirencester U.R.C.; Miss E.M. Bretherton of James Forbes U.R.C. Gloucester; Mrs. R. Cowley; Miss C. Cuff; Society Stewards of Cam Methodist Church; Revd. S.J. Davies of Uley; Mr. J. Dando of New Zealand; Mr. & Mrs. O. Evans; Mr. J.D. Foy of S.W. Gas; Mrs. L. Griffiths; Mrs. M. Gunston; Mrs. N. Head; Mrs. M. Henderson; Master G. Jenkins; Revd. & Mrs. G. Jenkins; Mr. R. Jones; Revd. R.J. McKelvey, Principal of The Congregational College, Manchester; the late Miss G. Kendall; Mr. and Mrs. T. Larkham; Mr. J. Lunt; Mrs. D. Marshall; Mr. D. Mills; Mr. R. Montgomery; Miss M. Newth; Revd. & Mrs. F. Nunn; Revd. Dr. G. Nuttall; Mr. D. Owen; Mr. J. Palmer of Wotton Under Edge United Church; Mr.

P. Page of solicitors Page & Co, Bristol; Mr. F. Perry, J.P.; Mr. F.C. Penley of solicitors Penley, Milward and Bayley; Mrs. J. Pickford; Mr. & Mrs. C. Pyle; Miss J. Skipp; Revd. B. Short of the Unitarian Historical Society; Mrs. J. Smart; Mr. R. Sparrow; Mr. & Mrs. B. Stamps; Mrs. M. Talboys; Mr. E.H. Williams; Mr. R. Wintle; Mr. B. Woodcock; Mr. R.N. Woodward of Wotton-under-Edge.

The Librarians of Manchester Central Library; Gloucester Central Library; Dr. Williams's Library, London; Memorial Hall Library, London; the National Library of Wales, Aberystwyth; John Rylands Library in the University of Manchester;

The Keeper of the Public Record Office, London;

The Archivists of Gloucester Record Office; Cheshunt College, Cambridge; Hampshire Record Office; Cheshire Record Office; Bristol Record Office;

Mr. A.G. Esslemont of the United Reformed Church History Society Archives;

Revd. Charles Surman, archivist of the United Reformed Church whose index of ministers was of great value;

Past writers of minutes and other documents and past photographers, whose patient recording of events has provided such a wealth of information.

Mr. A.H. Bruton and Mr. E.C. Montgomery whose historical 'milestones' booklets triggered the quest which has resulted in this book.

Mr. Herbert Edwards for permission to print the memoirs of soldier William Clark.

The many people who have loaned photographs and whose names are by them.

Part One

Puritans at the Church of St. James, Dursley, and the rise of Cam Meeting.

The chief end of man is to glorify God and to enjoy him for ever
(Assembly of Divines *Shorter Catechism* 1648)

A Map of Dursley and Cam

Note. It must not be assumed that all the places shown co-existed at any one time.

Boulton Lane Chapel and School	17.	Rectory, old	6.
Bull Inn	25.	Rectory built by Canon Madan	5.
Cam Meeting	2.	St. James's Church	18.
Castle Farm	13.	St. George's Church	1.
Dando's hat shop	12.	St. Mark's Church	27.
Harris's cloth mill	4.	Tabernacle, original	7.
Hill Road Chapel	8.	present	11.
Howard's cloth mill	21.	burial ground	9.
King's workshop	26.	Twemlow's house	20.
Market Place and Town Hall	16.	Victoria Schools	14.
National School	19.	Water Street Chapel and School	22.
Oaklands, later Rednock	3.	Wesleyan Methodist Chapel	15.
Parsonage	10.	Woodmancote Green	24.
Ralph's house	23.		

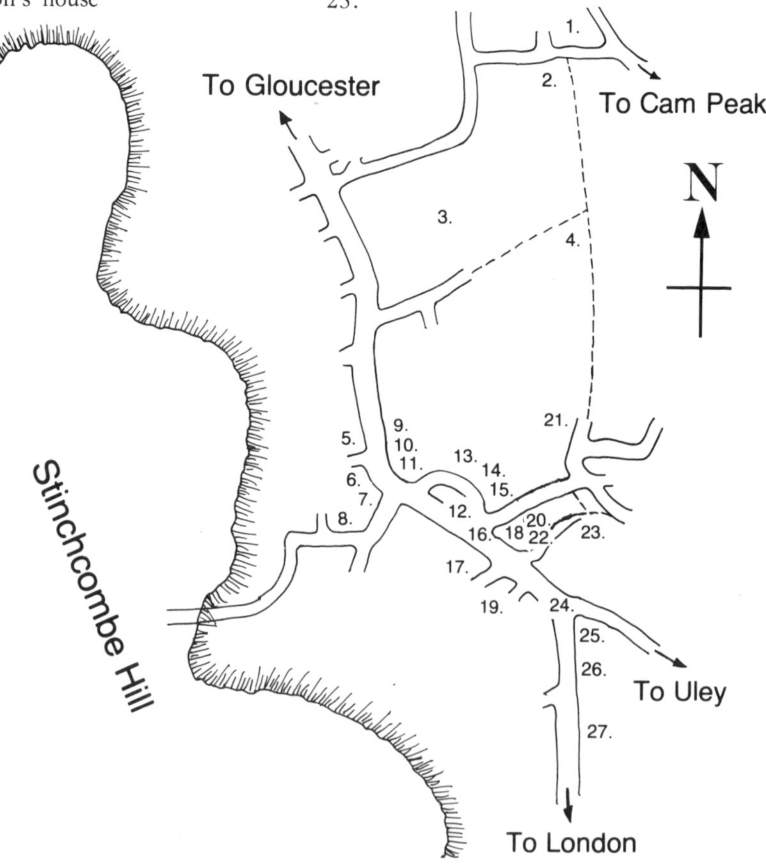

1

Puritans and the Parish Church

> Instead of their old Rectors and Curates the Dursley people had to receive as a pseudo pastor some ignorant layman . . . who dubbed himself a minister and got into the old clerical nest by the help of the few leading Puritans of the neighbourhood and who dealt out to them in Church, one long winded homily as a prayer and another as a sermon, each being chiefly conspicuous for bad taste, red hot politics and maledictory theology.[1]

So wrote the Revd. John Blunt of Joseph Woodward, parish minister in Dursley 1647–62. To understand the presence of Mr. Woodward we need to go back further in time.

Henry VIII's break with the Roman Catholic Church set the church in England moving slowly towards theological positions adopted by the new Reformed Churches of Europe. The trend was checked by the accession of Queen Mary but continued under Elizabeth. The new Church of England was not homogenious however, and during the reigns of the first two Stuart kings extremes of opinion created great strains within it. On the one hand there were those who looked back to the traditions of one thousand years of churchmanship in England and who believed that the Anglican Church should return to its rituals. In opposition were those who felt that the church was in danger of re-incorporating 'popish practices' which were described as 'Roman varnish such as paintings, crossings, crucifixes, bowings, cringings, altars, tapers, wafers, organs, litany rails, images, copes, vestments'[2] and candles. These people challenged the church to move in the opposite direction, to purify itself still further even to the extent of adopting the Presbyterian system, as set up in Scotland, which meant abolishing much of the church's super-structure including bishops and archbishops.

In the churchwardens accounts for Dursley there is evidence of the Puritan attitude, for in 1618 'a new table borde' was given to the church by Widow Morse. In all probability this was used as a communion table in the body of the building around which communicants would sit. The date coincides with the arrival of the first curate in actual pastoral charge, Samuel Hallowes. Samuel Burton, the rector (1607–34) was also rector of Dry or Long Marston,[3] where he was buried, and Archdeacon to five successive bishops of Gloucester. Probably he spent little time in Dursley but one assumes he must have shared Hallowes' outlook.

In 1633 William Laud became Archbishop of Canterbury, an appointment that brought little joy to Puritans as it seemed likely that his preferment by the King, Charles I, was an attempt to re-introduce Roman Catholicism. The Book of Sports was reissued. This had first been issued in 1618 and laid down what was lawful recreation for a Sunday.

> . . . for his good people's lawful recreation his Majesty's pleasure is, that, after the end of Divine Service, they should not be disturbed, letted or discouraged from any lawful recreations; such as dancing, either of men or women; archery for men, leaping, vaulting or any such harmless recreations; nor from having of May-games, Whitsun-ales, or Morris-dances, and setting up of Maypoles, or other sports therewith used, so as the same may be had in due and convenient time, without impediment or let of Divine Service; and that women should have leave to carry Rushes to the Church for the decorating of it, according to their old custom; withal prohibiting all unlawful games to be used on Sundays only, as bear-baiting, bull-baiting, interludes, and – at all times, in the meaner sort of people by law prohibited – bowling.[4]

It is curious that bowling should have been considered so wicked. Such was Puritan opposition to the re-issued book that some 800 clergy refused to read it in their churches as directed – and were deprived of their livings.

Their attitude to the book can be seen from the following passage from the writings of Richard Baxter, one of the most eloquent Puritan preachers of his day. He was born in, and is talking of Shropshire, but it is not hard to visualise Dursley's town centre and Parish Church while reading it. The town's name of the time – 'Drunken Dursley' – makes it just possible that what is described happened here to.

> I cannot forget that in my youth in those late times, when we lost the labours of some of our conformable godly teachers for not reading publicly the Book of Sports and Dancing on the Lord's-days, one of my father's own tenants was the townpiper, hired by the year (for many years together), and the place of the dancing-assembly was not a hundred yards from our door, and we could not on the Lord's-day either read a chapter, or pray, or sing a psalm, or catechise, or instruct a servant, but with the noise of the pipe and tabor, and the shouting in the street, continually in our ears; and even among a tractable people we were the common scorn of all the rabble in the streets, and called Puritans, Precisians, and Hypocrites, because we rather chose to read the Scriptures than to do as they did (though there was no savour of Nonconformity in our family). And when the people by the book were allowed to play and dance out of public service-time, they could so hardly break off their sports, that many a time the reader was fain to stay till the piper and players would give over; and sometimes the morrice-dancers would come into the church in all the linen and scarfs, and antic dresses with morice-bells jingling at their legs. And as soon as common-prayer was read, did haste out presently to their play again.[5]

Archbishop Laud allowed no latitude of views and ruthlessly insisted that clergy accepted the central authority of the Church and uniformity of religious practice. Thus in 1636 in accordance with his demands the communion table in Dursley Parish Church was removed and the altar at the east end used once more.[6]

Over the years the differences of opinions on many issues within the Anglican Church coalesced and coincided with the two sides in the struggle for civil power between Charles I and Parliament. Broadly the Puritans were Parliamentarians, favouring elected government, while the High Church party were supporters of the monarchy, which in the case of Charles I meant absolute power in the hands of the King. On 3 November 1640 the King summoned a new Parliament in order to obtain finance for the continuing war against the Scots. The Long Parliament, as it came to be known, consisted of 128 Parliamentarians and seventy-five Royalists and as such was in no mood to be dominated by an autocratic king. Conflict was inevitable and, after two civil wars, culminated in the execution of Charles on 30 January 1649.

In mid 1645 Parliament decreed that a 'Directory for Public Worship'[7] was to replace the Book of Common Prayer in Churches. Every incumbent was ordered to read the Directory openly in church on the first Sunday after he received it. If he continued to use the Book of Common Prayer he would be fined £5 for the first offence, £10 for the second and for the third, given a year's imprisonment.

The Presbyterian Directory was the result of several years deliberations of the Assembly of Divines – a gathering of ministers of religion set up by ordinance of Parliament in 1643 to consider remodelling the liturgy, discipline and government of the Church of England. It began by paying tribute to the Book of Common Prayer but stated that this had been misused 'disquieting the consciences of many godly ministers and people' and therefore was being replaced. It stressed that the new Directory was only a framework based on 'divine institution' and 'rules of Christian prudence' – elaboration of it was left to inidividual ministers.

The Directory laid out an order of church service.

Call to worship.
Prayer.
Reading from scripture – about a chapter at a time, in turn from all canonical books of the Bible with perhaps an explanation.
Long prayer. Intercessions with God, propogation of the gospel, conversion of the Jews, fall of Anti Christ, the cruel oppression and blasphemies of the Turk, the King's Majesty, conversion of the Queen, Parliament, nobility, judges, gentry, pastors, teachers, schools, the weather, wars, temptation of Satan, were all suggested topics.
Preached word on a text of scripture.
Prayer and Lord's Prayer.
Psalm.
Blessing and dismissal.

It ended with advice on the sacraments, sanctification of The Lord's Day, the marriage ceremony, visitation of the sick, burial of the dead, public fasts, and many other observances.

Powers of checking that parish ministers complied with the decree were given to the Committee for Plundered Ministers. This curiously named Committee had been set up by Parliament three years previously to eject 'scandalous, insufficient and malignant' clergy and in their places settle other ministers – mainly Presbyterian in outlook – many of whom had been deprived of their livings at the hands of Royalist forces and whose assets had been plundered. Generally the Committee allowed the clergy they ejected an annual sum equal to one fifth of their former incomes.

In Dursley in 1645 Hugh Robinson D.D.[8] was found wanting and removed from the parish. He suffered, it is said, the indignity and discomfort after his arrest of being made to ride to Gloucester Gaol facing backwards on his horse.

Hugh Robinson, son of Nicholas Robinson, Bishop of Bangor, matriculated from new College, Oxford, in 1603 and was from 1613 to 1627 headmaster of Winchester School. His scholastic duties did not however prevent him from collecting a number of widely separated benefices and therefore their incomes – Llanbedr-y-Cennin, 1613, Trefriw 1618, Bighton (Hants) 1622 and Dursley, 1625. He is also said to have become Archdeacon of Winton and Canon of Wells. It is doubtful if he visited these places often, except perhaps to receive yearly tithes. His cousin was Godfrey Goodman who became Bishop of Gloucester in 1625, and it has been suggested that this explains why Robinson was given the rectory of Dursley, and later, in 1634, the archdeaconry of Gloucester.

Parliament, which felt that parishioners should have value for money, decided that Robinson was a 'great malignant' and stripped him of all his benefices. The fact that he was also clapped in gaol suggests that he was one of those who refused to abandon the Book of Common Prayer. Some, at least, of Dr. Robinson's parishioners appear to have tried hard to get him reprieved. The churchwarden's accounts for 1646 contain references to having petitions drawn up and printed in Gloucester and London and payment of 'Attorneys fees at Glouc & att Strowde before ye Committee' which could well relate to the unfortunate man. Payment of 10*s.* to 'William Bristow for going to Doctr. Robinson' was also made but all to no avail.

Gloucester gaol was notorious for its appalling conditions and it is perhaps not surprising that Robinson soon bowed to the national situation, 'joined himself to the puritans, espoused the cause of Parliament, took the Covenant' and in 1646 published *The People's Plea fully vindicating the Power and Proceedings of the Parliament*. These acts seem to have rehabilitated him in the view of the Committee for Plundered Ministers, and he was allowed a living in Hampshire. He died on 30 March 1655 and was buried in St. Giles-in-the-Fields, London, being described as 'an able divine, excellent linguist (and) well skilled in ancient history.'

The position in Dursley Parish Church, vacated by Hugh Robinson, was taken up by Joseph Woodward, a tanner's son from Upper Cam.[9]

In 1640, still a young man, he was appointed Master of Katherine Lady Berkeley's Free Grammar School in Wotton-under-Edge. 'While filling this situation he was amiable and obliging, but far from serious in his conduct and spirit. He was the companion of ungodly and dissolute men and lived without God in the world.'

Unlikely material perhaps for what was to follow, but as sometimes happens, Joseph mended his ways, left his old companions and sought the company of Wotton's 'godly Puritans'. The change in him was profound and affected his attitude to school work. He abandoned the latin prayers for the soul of the school's long dead patroness and 'prayed in living language for living men'. He introduced scripture reading, the singing of psalms and other 'pious exercises'. Then aged about twenty-three, he went to Oxford and gained B.A. and M.A. degrees.

At the age of about thirty he felt compelled to take up a religious life and was ordained. He preached for the first time in Upper Cam Parish Church taking for his text Acts IV v.20 'For we cannot but speak the things which we have seen and heard'. Evidence suggests that this was in 1647. Such was the impression he made that the members of the pastorless church in Dursley called him unanimously to be their parish minister. The strength of the call seems to indicate that there existed in the town a large number of people who looked for a return to the more puritan, pre Hugh Robinson, days of some years before.

His appointment was confirmed by the Committee for Plundered Ministers on 7 May 1647. 'Whereas Dr. Hugh Robinson, Rector of the parish church of Dursley . . . having another benefice hath relinquished his interest of and in the said Rectorie. It is therefore ordered that the said Rectorie shall from henceforth stand sequestered to the use of Joseph Woodward, a godlie and orthodox divine and that he doe forthwith officiate the cure of the said church as Rector and preach diligently'.[10]

The prospect for Joseph Woodward was not inviting as the town's moral condition was low. It was his son who said that the town was known as 'Drunken Dursley' at that time. Maybe he saw the situation as a challenge, for in spite of being tempted by an offer from Wells at double the stipend he would receive in Dursley, Dursley he chose. He energetically threw himself into his duties and refashioned the Church's organisation on Presbyterian lines. Services would have been simple with great emphasis on the preached word and extempore prayer. The alter would have been replaced once more by a communion table around which communicants gathered – an arrangement still to be seen in Deerhurst Church. His ideas offended some members of the Church and they 'refused to pray and sing and receive the sacrament'; others withheld the promised contributions to his stipend. Greatest cause of offence to some was his insistance that he would admit to the Lord's Supper only those he had examined regarding 'knowledge of Christian truth' and with those whose conduct he was satisfied.

The story is told of one of his parishioners who refused to be examined and declared that if bread and wine were not given him he would take them. 'A solemn impression' was produced in the town when on the sacrament day he went to church to carry out this 'impious resolution' – and fell dead on the threshold!

The opposition Woodward received made him ill and he decided to leave.

> Several persons came to Dursley with a design to take him to another place where he had better prospects and he was much inclined to go with them but the very persons that opposed and slighted him before, when they found he was likely to leave them, came and begged his pardon, promising a better carriage for the future and so he consented to stay. . . .

His troubles were not at an end, however, as seven men 'resolved to ruin him' in a way unspecified but seemingly using false evidence.

In 1648 Woodward was one of sixty-four Ministers in Gloucestershire to sign what was, in effect, a Presbyterian manifesto. The ministers of London drew up a testimony declaring the Presbyterian system of church government to be the most agreeable to 'Jesus Christ revealed in scripture'. They also testified to the truth of the Solemn League and Covenant and against the 'Errors, Heresies and Blasphemies of these times and the Tolerations of them'. Thirteen counties including Gloucestershire, Wiltshire and Somerset supported the London pastors, many of their ministers signing 'concurrent testimonies'. If they were trying to influence Charles I in the last tragic phases of the attempt to get an agreement between King and Parliament, they failed. Within six months Joseph Woodward was grieving at the news of the execution of Charles.

The Parish Registers record the baptisms of children of Joseph and Ann Woodward – Ann 12 October 1647; Joseph, a 'sunn' 19 May 1652 and Josiah, 22 February 1656. Joseph junior in 1678 became headmaster of 'the public school' in Dursley and in 1683 was licensed to minister in the parish of Stinchcombe and preach in Dursley Church. Later he became the Revd. Dr. Woodward of Maidstone, Kent.

The following passages show the character of Joseph Woodward (Sen), M.A., the 'ignorant layman' of the Revd. John Blunt, quoted at the beginning of this chapter.

> Besides the toil of a school, he preached twice every Lord's-day, expounding in the morning and catechizing in the afternoon, before the sermon. Every Tuesday he expounded for an hour or two; and carried on a lecture every Thursday, usually without any assistance from other ministers. On Lord's-day-evenings he repeated to his scholars and many of his auditors at his own house; and at funerals, he either preached or expounded. He was always very plain and warm in maintaining the foundations of religion. Twice a year he kept a public fast, besides many in private. Every Monday after dinner he used to visit ten families to instruct the ignorant, reprove the scandalous,

comfort the dejected, &c. He was very diligent in instilling the principles of religion in the younger sort, and collected money for teaching poor children to read. He himself also was very liberal in works of mercy. He was a very strict observer of the Sabbath; and used on that day to rise very early.

Dursley was very much altered by his labors of many years there, and became one of the most wealthy and best trading towns in the neighbourhood. Some of them having told me, that they cleared a thousand pounds a year by the trade of clothing, in the time of his residence there. His presence in the streets, made the youth grave, and the aged circumspect. It made the sober to rejoice, and the guilty to hide themselves in corners. He seldom went to church but with a multitude with him. For his house, being distant from the church the length of a long street, (Parsonage Street – the Rectory is now 100, Kingshill Road) every one got their families ready as he came by, and stood in their doors, and so fell in with those that followed; so that he literally 'went with the multitude to the house of God'. And every one's zeal seemed inflamed by the flame he beheld in his neighbour; so that I have heard that there was the most composed and affected congregation that could any where be seen'.

The comments about a school and scholars will have been noticed. Maybe it is to Joseph Woodward we should credit the first Sunday School in the town.

'Puritan' now is synonimous with 'dour killjoy' but this wasn't its meaning to such as Joseph Woodward. They saw and expressed inner joyfulness and pleasure in religious observance. Sunday was a day to be looked forward to, when the normal weekday cares and work could be put aside for public worship, private prayer, reading of the scriptures, singing psalms and meditation upon the words and activities of God. It was this reverent joy and delight in the things of God which caused Parliament in the Commonwealth period to abolish Christmas. Excesses of merrymaking and personal indulgence were considered to have so debased the significance of December 25th with irreverence and paganism that it was considered better not to have it at all. To compensate, the second Tuesday in December was declared a public holiday but like many ideas of the Puritans, this one was not accepted by the populace in general.

To strict Puritans, marriages in Church had no scriptural basis, they were purely civil contracts. Dursley parish registers contain eleven such marriages, each made before a Justice of the Peace, in the period January – September 1654, after enabling legislation had been passed in the previous year by the Barebones Parliament. For example, on 6 September 1654: 'Arthur Vizor and Edith Mills both of the parish of Dursley were married according to an Act of Parliament in that behalfe and ? (supervised?) by Thos. Boards one of the Justices of the county'. Each parish had its registrar. Thus; 'We the inhabitants of the Towna nd parish of Dursley . . . whose names are hereto subscribed have elected and chosen Maurice Lewis of ye said Town to be Register according to the late Act of

Parliament' There follows a list of names and the date of 22 September 1653.

Under Joseph Woodward, parish affairs were not neglected. Church accounts for the years of his ministry have numerous entries for stone, wood, tiles and lime for repairs to the fabric of the church, almshouse, church house and graveyard. There are also entries for timber and ropes for the bells and bell loft which indicate that at least some of the bells were used.

Some items in the accounts reflect national events such as numerous notes concerning relief to destitute Irish folk who passed through the town from 1653 onwards, the year in which the Cromwellian Act of Settlement in Ireland came into full effect.

In 1657 relief was given to men 'taken with man of warr' and by the Spaniards, men caught up in Cromwell's naval attacks on Spanish possessions, and from 1653 to 1658 there were large annual payments 'for ye good and maimed soldiers of Upper Bench Marshalse'. In 1656 1*s*6*d* relief was paid to four travellers 'with a pass from his highness' Oliver Cromwell by then Lord Protector.,

Joseph Woodward, earnest and pious, of 'large soul and public spirit', did not however take kindly to any attempts of his parishioners to desert or question his ministrations for he is declared to have been 'a great enemy to the "sectaries" taking much pains to oppose and silence them'.

These 'sectaries' were Quakers. The ideas of George Fox first appeared in Gloucestershire at Tewkesbury, in about 1655, and quickly spread to other parts of the county including Dursley. Of great humility, strength of faith and independence, Quakers soon became a source of great vexation to authority, refusing to pay tithes, remove hats in 'steeple houses' or before magistrates and in any way compromise their beliefs, whatever the penalties. Conflict between them and authority was frequent and though often harshly treated they usually emerged with nobility. In Dursley, Joseph Woodward had Quaker problems. On one occasion in 1657, one, Deborah Harding[11]

> after the Priest (Woodward) had ended his sermon, would have given a christian exhortation to the people, but they fell on her with an uproar, some crying 'Kill her', others 'Strike her down', others 'Tear her in pieces'. The Magistrates to secure her from the rabble sent her to prison. After some time, an Uncle of hers interceeding on her behalf, they would have winked at her escape through a back door which when she refused to comply with, they sent her to Gloucester Gaol.

The first prison Deborah Harding found herself in may have been in Dursley itself. The town's church wardens' accounts note that in 1649 2*s*.2*d*. was paid to 'Ye Master of Bridewell' and in that, and in the following two years, there are payments made towards a new 'House of Correction' or Bridewell.

Church wardens changed at the beginning of each May and yearly the parish account books record the items handed on. On 2 May 1654, for example, apart from a 'linen cloat' and pewter ware for the communion table and various deeds for parochial buildings, there were listed

> 2 Books of the Paraphrases of Erasmus on the Epistles and Gospels
>
> 3 copies of Foxe's 'Book of Martyrs'
>
> A 'Directory of Public Worship' (bought at Gloucester in 1645 for 1*s*.6*d*.)
>
> A 'Book of Homilies'

Foxe was a contemporary of Bishop Hooper, burnt at the stake in Gloucester in 1555, in the reign of Queen Mary, for adhering to Protestant principles. Foxe published a history of Protestant martyrs and it became in time venerated second only to the Bible. In many early Nonconformist chapels after the 'Glorious Revolution' of 1688, it was the only item, apart from the Bible, allowed on the communion table. In Dursley Church, in 1653, Walter Danford was paid for setting up a desk for the Book of Martyrs and a year later two blacksmiths were paid a 1*d*. a piece for making chains to secure the copies listed above.

2

Cam Meeting and Water Street School

The death of the Interregnum's great leader, Oliver Cromwell in 1658 and the flight of his son and successor, Richard, in the spring of the following year, resulted in a collapse of political stability in the country. The accession of Charles II to the English throne was looked for and, following his declaration made at Breda promising religious liberties, Puritans in general were enthusiastic at the prospect. Presbyterians indeed believed that in return for their support, the King would agree to a monarchy limited by constitution and would agree to making Presbyterianism the order of the Established Church. Joseph Woodward in Dursley was as happy as most at the prospect of the restoration.

By the middle of May 1660, a few days before Charles returned, Puritans had to accept the fact that many of their expectations would come to naught. They clung, however, to the hope that they could be accommodated within the national church if it returned to episcopy. In Dursley, as required, the new King's Arms were put up in the church, probably with a comment underneath urging obedience and on Coronation Day the bell ringers excelled themselves.

In the elections for the new Parliament in 1660, the Puritans fared badly and it quickly became clear that the staunch royalist Anglicans, who now predominated, had no time for toleration. With power once more in their hands, they pursued the idea of a uniform episcopal pattern of religious observance with single minded thoroughness, even vindictiveness.[1] In quick succession, Puritan members of Parliament fighting unsuccessfully against them, two Acts were passed. On 24 December 1661 the Corporation Act became law and under this all elected to, or selected for, municipal office had to take Anglican Communion, renounce the Solemn League and Covenant (a covenant drawn up in 1642 between English Parliamentarians and the Scots to abolish prelacy and establish presbyterianism in England, among other items), and declare it unlawful to take up arms against the King.

The Act of Uniformity followed a few months later. This required every minister and schoolmaster to give 'unfeigned assent and consent' to everything in the revised Book of Common Prayer – its thirty-nine Articles of religion, rules, rites and ceremonies and its set prayers. It also required every minister who had not been ordained episcopally to be so ordained and required every minister to vow to make no attempt to bring about change in the Established Church. If these requirements were not met by St. Bartholomew's Day, 24 August 1662, the ministers (and schoolmasters) would be deprived of their livings on that day, one month before the year's tithes were due to them, and without compensation.

In Dursley, Joseph Woodward[2] did not live to see St. Bartholomew's Day. In the summer of 1662, aged only about forty-five he died of tuberculosis. Before his death he had decided what his actions would be if he saw August 24th. Writing to James Forbes, holder of a preachership in Gloucester Cathedral he said, 'With submission to the will of God, I desire to live a little longer that I may bear testimony against episcopy and the new conformity'. By this time Woodward had been joined by Henry Stubbes,[3] a minister some ten years his senior, who had taken over the pastoral duties of the sick man. Between him and the Woodward household a deep bond of affection developed, a bond made the stronger by the compassion of the elder to the dying, younger minister and by their common resolutions over the coming black St. Bartholomew's Day.

Henry Stubbes was born in Upton Cheney near Bath of Scottish ancestry. In 1633 he entered Magdalen Hall, Oxford and received an M.A. degree in 1630. He became Rector of Partney, Lincolnshire, but his Puritan views found no favour when Archbishop Laud came to power and he and his wife and baby soon fled to Ireland. In 1641 the Irish Rebellion caused him to return to England where successively he was incumbent of the churches of Saints Philip and Jacob in Bristol, Chew Magna and St. Cuthberts, Wells. While in Somerset he was an assistant to the commissioners appointed by Parliament to eject scandalous clergy. At the restoration of the King in 1660 the former vicar of St. Cuthberts returned and Henry settled in Dursley. Here, on 24 August 1662, refusing to bend his conscience, he was ejected from the living. In this, nationally, he was joined by about 936 clergy of whom seventeen were ejected from churches in Gloucestershire – among them Avening, Kings Stanley, Thornbury, Wotton-Under-Edge, Beverstone, Stroud, possibly Slimbridge and probably Frampton-on-Severn. These joined as outcasts those already 'silenced' in 1660, when the Anglican clergy evicted as 'scandalous' many years before claimed back their livings – some thirty-one in Gloucestershire. It is estimated that by the Act of Univormity, 'This straight waistcoat for men's consciences' the Established Church lost some 1760 of the most able and devout of its ministers.

Ejection of 'aberrant' ministers had taken place in other times and had been effective. This attempt, however, to find a solution to problems within the Church by ejection was a failure, for such was the hold Puritan ideas had in the lay population that neither a Parliamentary Act, nor the malice with which those who refused to conform were harried in the quarter

Ejected !

The 1662 Act of Uniformity resulted in many good men leaving the Anglican Church. This could well have been the scene at Dursley Rectory as Henry Stubbs bids farewell to his parishioners.

century after its enactment, was able to destroy them. It is appropriate to pause at this point and consider why men like Henry Stubbes acted as they did. By abiding by their consciences, each exchanged a secure income, usually a vicarage or rectory that was his and his family's home, the prestige that Parish Minister carried and the satisfaction of a calling that could be carried out well and openly, for a future in which nothing was certain except indefinite, and possibly extreme hardship.

Henry found deprivation early for in November 1662, Colonel Birth, M.P. and formerly a prominent officer in the Parliamentary Army of the Civil War, wrote to him to sympathise. The letter which was intercepted, reveals that Birch, in an attempt to alleviate Henry's lot, was prepared to allow him £5 p.a. payable quarterly.

Simply the issues for people like Stubbes were:-

1. Although prepared to accept an established episcopal church they could not contemplate one with a hierarchical structure, with courts and canon law that differentiated between priest and bishop, and stressed the priestly character of the ministry.
2. Although prepared to take an oath of allegiance, they would not commit themselves to anything which put the monarchy above the law.

3. They could not accept re-ordination by a bishop if previously they had been ordained by some other means. Ordination was the recognition by the Church that a man had been called by God to be a minister of the Gospel. For a man to be ordained a second time meant that he accepted that everything he had been doing in the name of God to that time had been invalid.

   The famous comment by John Howe, one time chaplain to Oliver Cromwell, ejected from Torrington, Devon is worth repeating. Seth Ward, then Bishop of Exeter, asked him 'Pray sir, what hurt is there in being twice ordained?'

   Howe replied 'Hurt, my Lord, it hurts my understanding; the thought is shocking, it is an absurdity since nothing can have two beginnings.'[4]

4. The Directory of Public Worship had left much to the discretion of the officiating minister – it was just an aid to public worship. The revised Book of Common Prayer was unacceptable because its rigid structure for worship, forbidding extempore prayer and reducing preaching to insignificance, seemed to deny the possibility of the intervention of the Holy Spirit in worship.

The Act of Uniformity by making it impossible for the Established Church to accommodate these views not only drove their holders out, it further isolated Anglicans from the great Reformed Churches in the rest of Europe.

17 May 1664 saw the Conventicle Act on the statute book. This decreed that anyone attending a 'conventicle' or assembling together in numbers of more than five persons, in addition to the members of the family, for any religious purpose not conforming to the rites of the Church of England would be fined £5 or given three months imprisonment for the first offence. For a second offence the punishment would be doubled and for a third, transportations – but not to Puritan New England. This was open to, and received abuse, as it provided powers of forcible entry and search by two Justices of the Peace and 'full and perfect conviction' by the mere recording of an offence by a Justice, which could be proved by hearsay evidence.

The Five Mile Act was passed on 30 october 1665. This enacted that no non-conforming minister or teacher, except while travelling, was to come within five miles of a 'city, town-corporate or borough' sending a member to Parliament or any place where he had formerly preached or taught. Penalty for each offence £40. Also no-one was allowed to have pupils or teach who did not attend Anglican worship or who had not sworn an oath of obedience to the King.

Henry Stubbes was caught up in this punitive legislation, and that which was to follow, with its accompanying persecutions: What sort of man did Dursley lose?

'Of all men I ever knew, he seemed to me one of the most humble. His preaching, his discourse, his garb, and all his behaviour spoke pure humility. Never did I hear from him a word of ostentation, much less of envy at the precedence of others' He was 'a grave divine wholly given up to the service of God' and as 'a plain, moving and fervent preacher, he was eminent for the great work of converting sinners'. Richard Baxter preaching his funeral sermon said "I scarcely ever knew a man, who served God with more resignation and devotedness, in simplicity and godly sincerity, living, like the primitive christians, without any pride or wordly motives; and in whose case I had rather die'.

Records of the activities of Nonconformist ministers are not profuse for obvious reasons, but references in diocesan surveys and other documents give glimpses. Henry Stubbes seems to have spent his time between London and Somerset, evading the law and preaching in illegal conventicles. Episcopal returns for 1669 reveal that he was known to minister to groups of Nonconformist lay folk at Chippenham, Grittleton, Sherston, Abingdon, Doulting and Winsham near Crewkerne; at Bath Easton he used a barn; at Glaston a barn fitted out with a pulpit and seats; at Camely near Bath he even managed to use the Parish Church. One can imagine the anger of the authorities at the audacity of such a man and at their apparent inability to stop his activities and those of so many like him. These ejected ministers in some cases seem to have been well organised and to have formed team ministries. Thus at Charlton-cum-Pretinentys (near Malmesbury), where there was an underground church reportedly 300–400 strong, in turn preached Henry Stubbes, Benjamin Flower and Mr. Hancock, almost certainly Edward Hancock ejected from St. Philips, Bristol, 'an earnest moving preacher'.

Benjamin Flower, on one occasion described by an irate vicar as 'the Bishop of Chippenham' with 'his nest of vipers' and 'squadron of irregulars',[5] had been displaced from Cardiff in 1660[6] and ejected from Castle Combe in 1662.[7] His early schooling was at Wotton-under-Edge[8] and dates suggest that he was probably taught by Joseph Woodward.

In 1672 – probably under the Declaration of Indulgence issued by the King – Bishop Pritchard of Gloucester, gave Henry Stubbes the parish of Horsley, a poor living worth only £8 p.a. and one that had been ministerless for some years. There he ministered until 1678, although the King's Indulgence was revoked in 1673, using the parish church and only those parts of the Anglican liturgy with which he agreed 'not withstanding the censure of the rigid'. In July 1678, aged seventy-three, he died of a fever while in London and was buried in what became the great London burial ground for Nonconformists – Bunhill Fields. Although probably never a rich man Henry tithed his income when alive and at his death he left £4 a year each to Dursley and Horsley – chargeable on lands at Horsley – for the purchase of Bibles and primers. In Dursley this bequest operated until at least 1757 when fourteen 'Mr Stubbes books' (i.e. Testaments) were distributed but by 1877, according to the Rev. J. Blunt, it had been lost.

He gave £200 to Bristol and a similar amount to London to be used annually for the poor to buy bibles and to assist the widows of poor ministers. It is also said that he gave £50 to Uley to be used to teach poor children to write. He left eight published works. His will contains many biblical references and in it he exorted his wife to read frequently Jer. 49 v.ii Ps. 68 v.5 and Heb. 13 v.6.

Bunhill or 'Bonehill' Fields where Henry Stubbs rests. It is said that some 120,000 people were buried in the grounds before they were closed in the 1850s.

The loss of these grave divines, Joseph Woodward and Henry Stubbes, within a few months of each other in 1662, must have been of great moment to the religious life of Dursley. No doubt though, most parishioners adapted quickly to the new Rector, who was also Rector of Walton-on-the-Hill, Surrey, and his curate, who was in actual pastoral charge. There must, however, have been some lay men who in all conscience were unable to accept the change back to episcopy, the change from the simple acts of worship of the late Puritan ministers to the grander richer services of the new priests. Possibly to avoid trouble with authority they did as many Presbyterians are known to have done, they became partial or occasional conformists, attending parish communions occasionally to retain membership of the church but also gathering together to praise and worship God in their own way at other times. It is possible that for many years proscribed meetings were conducted by Francis Haine, said to have been ejected in 1662 from Thornbury Church. Evidence for this comes from

1672. On March 15th of that year Charles II issued his Declaration of Indulgence. Under this, all except Roman Catholics were granted liberty of worship providing the place and the preacher or teacher were licenced. A special office was set up in Whitehall to deal with applications for licences and in June Francis Haine received his as an Independent preacher and one for his dwelling in Dursley to be used as a meeting house.

It is of interest to note that early in 1673, a barn of Charles Eliot at Stinchcombe was licensed as a meeting house for the use of James Forbes ejected in 1662 from Gloucester Cathedral.

This freedom for Nonconformists to worship as they wished lasted only for eleven months. It had been authorised by the King against the wishes of Parliament, which believed that Charles was intent on easing the plight of Roman Catholics. In 1673 the King, embroiled in a war against the Dutch, had to turn to Parliament for financial assistance and, as a condition of giving this, the Declaration had to be revoked. Once again the full weight of the country's legal and ecclesiastical system fell on those who refused to accept the authority of the established church, and again they had to endure heavy fines, ill treatment and imprisonment. Estimates suggest that between 5000 and 8000 Nonconformists died in prison in the reign of Charles II for conscience sake.

Persecution was most intense in the bigger towns and cities in Gloucestershire, though the north Cotswold villages didn't escape lightly. Cirencester, Bristol and Gloucester have many records of confinements in the appalling gaols of the time, mob violence and monstrous fines, so that in some cases meeting of Nonconformists were held in woodlands, or, as at Castle Green in Bristol, rooms used for preaching had escape doors built into them by which ministers could evade sudden search parties.[9] Some idea of the general situation that existed between 1667 and 1689 is conveyed by the following passage:-

> Great were the sufferings of those who resided in Gloucestershire. The most eminent cavaliers (magistrates) rode about armed with swords and pistols, ransacking their houses and abusing their families in a violent manner. At the house of Mr. Helme, at Winchcombe, the bed whereon his children lay was not spared; and their outrageous conduct so frightened his wife as to throw her into an illness which threatened her life. Mr. Warren, who possessed the parsonage at Rendcombe, was with his wife and family penned up into an upper room of his house, and so harassed night and day by the violence of the assailants and the noise of the hautboys, (a musical instrument like an oboe), that he died in the place . . . .
>
> One pious minister was assaulted as he was entering his pulpit. Another was violently pulled out of his house; his wife, children and goods were thrown into the street, none of the parish were allowed to give them entertainment, and he himself was haled to jail.[10]

Greatest persecution fell on the Quakers. For being a Quaker Thomas Atkins – a chandler or dealer in candles, oil, soap etc. in Dursley – was brought before Bishop Nicholson at the time of his visitation to Dursley on 16 September 1662. Atkins, who with his wife Mary, had come from Ross-on-Wye, was fetched from his house by two constables. Part of the long examination went as follows:

> *Bishop*. You must be conformable to the laws of the nation.
> *Thomas Atkins*. I am conformable to the Law of God.
> *Bp*. But I will make you conformable to the law of the nation too.
> *T.A*. I am made by the hand and power of the Lord God already, and I hope thou nor no man shall ever make me conformable to that which I know to be a sin against God.
> *Bp*. You are a very stubborn fellow, but I will make you submit or else I will send you back from whence you came.
> *T.A*. I am not subborn, as thou thinkest; I am a man that feareth God, and I fear not what man can do unto me.
> *Bp*. I will make you bow, or I will make you fast enough.
> *T.A*. My hope is in the Lord, and thou shalt never make me bow to that which I know to be sin against the God of my life, and if thou shouldst be permitted to tear this Body to pieces, yet I fear thee not. I desire thee to shew me that Scripture, where thou canst prove, that any true Christian, that lived in the eternal fear of God, ever persecuted any man for conscience sake; or that any of the saints of God ever threatened any as thou dost me: if you canst, shew it.
> *Bp*. Those whom you call saints would persecute more than any man, if they had the power in their hands.
> *T.A*. Thou canst not make that appear, neither by Scripture, nor present example of those that live in the same life.
> Several other threatening words the Bishop uttered as he went down stairs, and so passed away to the steeplehouse, leaving Atkins on this occasion free to return home.[11]

Thomas Atkins seven years later gives us a glimpse of Dursley's Presbyterians. George Fox in his Journal for 1669 records that while at a meeting of Quakers in Nailsworth he talked with Atkins and his wife 'Whoe lived not farr of Naylesworth, a shopkeeper, and they tolde mee there was a separate meetinge of ye presbyterians and they tooke an oath of there people y' they shoulde neither buy or sell or eate or drinke with friends (Quakers) on a Sunday.' On one occasion a woman prominent in the group fell ill and the Doctor 'could doe for her noe good'.

Evidently the woman's condition became critical on a Sunday, for two or three of her companions went to Mary Atkins shop and after pretending to buy, asked Mary's help. In doing so they confessed they had broken their oaths. 'Soe Tho. Atkins wife tooke ye woman in hande and cured her. And soe ye Lord broake ye wicked bonds of ye presbyterians asunder yt they had had ensnared there people with'.

George Fox was in the area again in 1677 when he recorded that on 26 December he went with friends to Stinchcombe to a Quarterly Meeting where they had 'good service'.

Records are almost silent on persecution and prosecutions in our local area and maybe it was an oasis of relative calm in the country. It was a thinly populated valley, the combined population of Uley, Dursley, Cam and Stinchcombe amounting to only about 2500 souls in 1676.[12] It was remote from the cities and had no large country estates, the owners of which were usually high Anglicans; rather there were many lesser men of substance, clothiers and the like, who judging from later years, probably sympathised with, if not acutally supported, Nonconformity.

In following generations the one great landowning family, the Berkeleys, were uniformly 'whig' in political outlook and it is possible that George Berkeley, head of the family 1658–1698, was also of this sentiment. If so, this would also have helped towards a more tolerant attitude.[13] It seems probable that, providing local Nonconformists did not make themselves too conspicuous, they were largely left alone.

Nonconformists were sometimes in a curious situation. Although so detested and harried by High Church men, more moderate Anglicans saw them as allies in the fight against the Roman Catholics which many felt the Stuart monarchs were attempting to re-habilitate. Such was Henry Compton, Bishop of London from 1675. He began moves to unite Anglicans and Nonconformists against Rome and, in 1676, conducted a survey in every parish in England of people over the age of sixteen in an attempt to estimate religious allegiance.

Locally the results were:

PARISH	CONFORMISTS	PAPISTS (R.Cs)	NONCONFORMISTS
Dursley	800	nil	4
Cam-cum-Stinchcombe	669	nil	10
Uley	300	nil	25

Whatever the accuracy of these figures they indicate that by this date there were probably more Nonconformists in Cam-cum-Stinchcombe than in Dursley. Possibly the Vicar of St. George's Church, Cam, 1664–81, John Barnsdale was sympathetic. Barnsdale had signed in 1648 the same Presbyterian 'concurrent testimony' as Joseph Woodward. He was Vicar of Frampton-on-Severn in 1662 and it is almost certain he was ejected as a Nonconformist. As sometimes happened he either sincerely changed his mind or found life, with perhaps a family, too harsh and so later conformed. Apart from the fact that some of these Nonconformists were Quakers and some Presbyterians we know nothing of them – except that one of the latter, Lydia Purnell, in 1673 gave a communion plate, still in existence, engraved 'The gift is smale, the love is ale.'

We now loose sight of these people until 1690, after James II had fled, and Mary his daughter and her husband William of Orange had come to the throne. Toleration of Nonconformist religious worship was then declared to those groups who registered their meeting houses, and whose ministers took an oath. In this new found freedom another national survey

This pewter plate is believed to have been used in Communion Services by local Presbyterians while under persecution. It is inscribed 'the gifte is small x The love is all Lydia Purnel 1673' and measures 24.5 cm. across. *(Photo. David E. Evans)*

was conducted. This time, in 1690–2, it was of Presbyterian and Independent causes in an attempt to set up a fund to help poor ministers in those denominations. This revealed that locally there were three gatherings, without ministers –

> Att Berklie A new meeting once a fortnight, give 10*s*. a time
> Att Cam A new meeting, give 10*s*. a time
> Att Wotton-under-hedg (sic.) A new meeting, give 8*s*. poor, great opportunity for service.

It also revealed that the Presbyterian and Independent ministers of Somerset, Wiltshire and Gloucestershire had already set up an association and had talked of raising a fund 'but trading soe dead, taxes so high, and ye poverty of professors soe great that it greatly discourages'.[14]

Quarter Sessions record that in 1690 a Quaker meeting place was licensed in Stinchcombe and in the following year another at Stancombe.[15] The 'new meeting' in Cam may indicate a revived cause or a pooling of resources of several house groups in Dursley and Cam now that larger gatherings were permissible. Whichever it was, the meeting grew in confidence and by 1702 was sufficiently strong to consider both calling a permanent minister and erecting a chapel. Land for the meeting house, the present Cam Meeting, was given by clothier William Hicks and his first wife, Mary.[16] It was part of a field called Woolpens and the first trustees included James Forbes of Gloucester, by then influential minister of Barton Street Independent Chapel; Isaac Noble, 'much blessed' minister of Castle Green Independent Church, Bristol; John and Thomas Pope, clothiers of Cam, Nathanial Hicks of The Quarry, owner of Upper Cam corn and fulling mill;[17] John Phillimore, Gent, of the Vennings also called Cam Manor, owner of Cam or Corriet corn and fulling mill;[18] and his son, also John. The new meeting house was registered at County Quarter Sessions in 1703.[19]

The minister was Joseph Twemlow, member of an old Cheshire family. He was about thirty when he arrived in 1702[20] and is recorded as being Presbyterian. His family tree, compiled in about 1870,[21] shows him as having a younger brother Nathan, also ordained. Probably this is the Nathaniel Twemlow mentioned in Cheshire Presbyterian records of the early eighteenth century. Joseph's arrival marked the end of a forty year struggle in the area for survival of a distinctive way of looking at man's relationship with God, a way not acceptable to the Established Church.

Water colour of Cam Meeting by E. Moris and dated 1899. The chapel originally had two doors symetrically placed. The extension on the left housed schoolrooms and stables and was built in 1895. *(Pastor and Deacons of Cam Meeting)*

Very little has been written about the history of Nonconformists in Gloucestershire, but in the *Victoria County History of Wiltshire* (Vol. III) – there appears a detailed analysis of its emergence in that county, which with its wool trade was similar to mid-Gloucestershire. One conclusion was that those Nonconformists groups which survived into the eighteenth century did so because of the devotion and steadfastness of a few families over several generations, rather than because of outside leadership or ministerial preaching. Probably the same can be said of the local situation which crystalised into Cam Meeting.

Joseph Twemlow's thirty-five year pastorate seems to have been lively and happy for by 1715 his congregation is recorded as 800 hearers, of which 50 were of sufficient standing to be county voters in Parliamentary elections.[22] His hearers must have been a sizable proportion of Cam's population, perhaps the majority, and formed one of the largest Nonconformist groups in the county at that time. One of the fifty people wealthy enough to be a county voter must have been the Nathanial Hicks whose name appears in the list of trustees above. In his will he left £5 p.a., chargeable to his estates, to be used 'for teaching children of the parish of Cam aforesaid to read and write, to cast accounts and to learn the Assembly of Divines Shorter Catechism.' An indenture of 1739 relating to this bequest instructed the trustees to pay the minister of the Protestant Dissenting meeting house at Cam for the time being for ever, upon condition that he should teach the children in the said meeting house, every Lord's day in the afternoon between Lady Day and Michaelmas yearly, and expound to the congregation the shorter catechism of the Assembly of Divines, who met at Westminster in or about the year 1642 or 1643, and should hear the children give an account of their having learnt it in the words of the catechism'. If he defaulted the trustees were empowered to give the money for 'pious uses' among the congregation, excluding the minister.[23] It is probable that Cam was Twemlow's only pastorate, as he is recorded as being ordained at Cam on 7 May 1707.[24] He was, however, no isolationist. In 1718 he was in Thornbury with six others, including Isaac Noble, buying a 'ruinated barne, toft or tenement in a street called Nelme Street'. The barn was pulled down and on the site was built a Presbyterian Meeting House, forerunner of the present Thornbury United Reformed Church.[25] He was also well known to the Independents of Gloucester. In 1726 their church book recorded:-

> 26th October. A Meeting of the church to seek the Lord . . . on account of the dispensations of divine providence in our own church and the neighbourhood that God would . . . set a fit person over the congregation at Bristol (Castle Green) and would . . . spare strength and bless Mr. Twemlow that he fill up our vacancie by succeeding (i.e. prosper?) the ministry of this church to the edification and conversion of many, whether by stated or occasional sermons . . .[26]

Pastor in Gloucester at this time was Thomas Cole, and his church was very outward looking, holding preaching services in many villages in the county. It seems from the extract that Joseph Twemlow had agreed to help in village evangelism.

Twemlow and Cam Meeting exercised influence over a considerable area locally. The congregation each Sunday converged on the meeting house from places as far apart as Berkeley and Uley, in which places houses were also licenced for Presbyterian worship in 1702 and 1703.[27] Baptisms recorded for the decade from 1702 include frequent entries for Cam, Dursley, Uley and 'Coley' but also mentioned are 'Tedbury', Slymbridge, Nibley, Nailsworth and Berkeley.[28] Some of the Uley baptisms are noted in the Anglican registers of that parish, all with the comment that the parents were 'Dissenters from the Established Church of England'. Sometimes Joseph Twemlow was mentioned by name.

> Nehemiah, ye son of John and Mary Smith, was born Jan 25th 1709 but not baptised by me, John Jackson, but Mr. Twimlow, dissenting Teacher in the meeting house of Cam was they say the man. . . .

John Jackson later became curate of Dursley. One curious entry, in June 1705, from an annoyed rector reads:-

> A son of Henry Hill jun. and Margaret his wife, both Dissenters . . . buried by report in ye churchyard of Uley but noe notice given me of ye time of ye said buriel.

To help the poor and needly of the meeting house two separate funds were set up at the end of 1704. For one, collections were made quarterly at the 'doors of our assembly' and administered by trustees. For the other, collections were made at every sacrament or communion service, which seems to have been held bi-monthly at this period. This money was divided out by the members at the following 'lecture day'.[29]

It is likely that the chapel at Cam when new built was typical of the period and similar internally to the style still to be seen at Monks Chapel, Corsham and the old Baptist Chapel, Tewkesbury – pulpit on a long wall, (at Cam near to the present tablet to 'A. Baines'), communion table set centrally in front of it, seats on three sides round the table and three galleries likewise. With a little imagination one can picture a Sunday morning scene at the Upper Cam meeting house in the 1720s – an austere building, filled with soberly clad Presbyterians, a fervent preacher, Joseph Twemlow and a long service probably on the following lines:-

> Unaccompanied singing of a psalm
> Short prayers asking for God's presence
> Exposition of a passage of scripture lasting perhaps half an hour
> Sermon
> Long prayer during which congregation stood and in which written petitions for the needs of members were handed to the minister in the pulpit.
> Psalm

The original internal arrangement of Cam Meeting may have been similar to that still existing at Monks Chapel, Corsham, Wilts, seen here, though on a larger scale.
(Photo. David E. Evans)

The interior of Cam Meeting as it is now. It was refashioned in 1818. Before this the pulpit was on the long wall on the right. The uppermost plaque above the pulpit is a memorial to Joseph Twemlow. *(Photo. David E. Evans)*

Cam Meeting — a view from the pulpit. *(Photo. David E. Evans)*

Short Prayer
Benediction[30]

The old chapel was substantially altered in 1818 when new windows were put in and the interior galleries, seats and pulpit was remodelled to create basically what exists now.[31]

In 1703, the house of John Sanacker in Dursley was licensed at Quarter Sessions as a Presbyterian meeting house.[32] In the following year the house of Thomas Young, also in Dursley, was similarly licensed but simply for Protestant Dissenters – a term which included Presbyterians.[33] It seems likely that the houses were used by Twemlow to begin regular preaching in the town, repeating on Sunday evenings sermons he had preached earlier in the day at Cam Meeting – a practice followed for some seventy years by following ministers.[34] The issuing of these meeting place licences indicates that Presbyterians had a following in the town. Its strength is unknown but it may have had some connection with riots that took place in the Autumn of 1702, the year Twemlow settled in the area.[35] It may be just coincidence too, that Queen Anne had come to the throne in the March, a monarch who set about undoing much of the religious toleration that had existed in the previous reign.

In September and October 1702, David Powell, the curate at St. James, was attacked on several occasions by a stone throwing mob, which numbered up to 200 people, as he was going to the parish church to take services. Sometimes 'the tumult and noyse did continue whilst Mr. Powell was in the church'. So loud was the noise in the churchyard that once the curate had to stop the service. The constable of Dursley, John Sparry, seems to have had sympathy with the crowd for when a warrant of arrest was delivered to him from Justice Wagstaffe, he at first refused it, saying 'he knew of noe Wagstaffe but was a fool . . . (and) if the Sheriff and the Chancellor and Wagstaffe came to suppress the ryots and if they struck one blow he would strike two'.

At some time unknown but possibly 1710, Twemlow moved into a house at the top of Long Street, Dursley, almost certainly now 30 Long Street. In 1718 he bought 'three old decayed houses or cotts' fronting Water Street whose joint grounds abutted his own garden. These he had demolished, and built a schoolhouse for 'teaching poor children of Protestant Dissenters to read, write and cast accounts'. This building was also used on Sunday evenings and one week day night for preaching the gospel.[36]

Perhaps the idea of founding a school came from an earlier Anglican charity school. John Jackson M.A., curate of Dursley, in February 1710, shortly before he left the town, preached a sermon urging 'the pious instruction of poor children whereby those poor souls who would otherwise run up and down "like wild asses colts as they were born" (Job XI v.12) should be instructed in the principles of christian religion and that schools should be opened for that purpose'.[37]

His appeal did not go unheeded for in April he was able to report to the Society for Promoting Christian Knowledge (S.P.C.K.) that a school for thirty poor children had been erected and opened, supported by local subscriptions.[38] By May 1711 Jackson had been replaced by Edward Turner of Cam, as curate and he reported that the school was in a sorry state because of mismanagement. He set out to 'animate the subscribers' and was so successful that by Easter 1712 he had sufficient money to pay the master and mistress and clothe the children. To this end he requested of S.P.C.K. '20 blew capps' to be 'sent by Skipton ye carrier from ye Kings Head in ye Old Exchange (London)'. He also requested spelling books and useful tracts 'to dispense in that great town (Dursley) to encourage ye subscribers'. In 1714 more caps were ordered, this time with 'red strings'.[39] The school flourished for several years but in or about 1716 was abandoned. The Revd. Turner's letter advising the S.P.C.K. of this is ambiguous but seems to imply that 'all or the greater part of the principal inhabitants' turned against it[40] – a reaction of a Presbyterian cause growing in strength ? It is possible that at about this time Twemlow started his own school in his house in Long Street as it is likely he tried out the school idea before going to the expense of erecting a building for one.

For over 150 years Twemlow's School in Water Street provided education for local children. As with Cam Hopton Blue Coat School, dating from the same period, it survived because it was amply endowed and did not depend on the vagaries of annual subscriptions. For the Water Street

Water Street Meeting House-cum-School, Dursley, c. 1930. Above the far door was the date 1715, put up in about 1900. As the building was not erected until at least 1718, it may be based on information, now lost, that Joseph Twemlow's school began in his own house in 1715.

School the first endowment came from Josiah Sheppard, cloth factor of Blackwell Hall, London, then the clearing house for the country's wool cloth. He died in 1734 leaving in trust over £2000.[41] To get some idea of values in today's terms, this, and following figures should be multiplied a hundred fold. Three trustees were appointed by the High Court of Chancery, among them Joseph Twemlow. The money was invested in Old South Seas Annuity Stock. In 1745 the portion of the stock relating to the school, nominally £100 but sold for £89, was used to buy Withibees or Withibeers, six acres of land in the Wanswell – Hinton area of Berkeley. The short fall of £11 was made up by Mary Sheppard, Josiah's widow, and Mary Stevens.[42] In the following year eighteen acres of land called Cuttercrofts were bought in Hamfallow using £200 given collectively by Mary Twemlow, by then a widow; John Sparry, clothier of Dursley and possibly the same man who was parish constable at the time of the 1702 riots; Thomas Bayley of Coaley; and Silvester Hitchings and Edward Whatley respectively of London and Bristol.[43]

The incomes from the lands, which remain today (1981) with the trustees, were used to pay the schoolmaster and general school expenses.

Mary Twemlow died in 1759 and was buried beside her husband in St. George's churchyard 'without shew or funeral pomp'. In 1740 she had relinquished her trustee responsibilities, assumed at the death of her husband in the previous month. The trustees appointed in September 1740 were:-

*Daniel Fowler the elder	Cam	Gentleman
Nathaniel Hicks (cousin)	Cam	Yeoman
*John Pope (cousin)	Cam	Clothier
John Sparry	Dursley	Clothier
John Morse	Dursley	Gentleman
Onesiphorous Elliott	Dursley	Clothier
Charles Egby	Dursley	Salesman
*William Taylor	Dursley	Broadweaver
George Dauncey	Uley	Broadweaver
*John Garlick	Uley	Plaisterer
Thomas Wilkins	Uley	Broadweaver
*George Minett	Coaley	Yeoman[44]

(* Identifiable as members of Cam Meeting)

In 1760 the trustees included John Purnell, Esq., John Barnes, Surgeon and Richard Oliver, Gentleman, all of Dursley. The school was held in high regard.[45] Under the trust terms the schoolmaster had to be a Protestant Dissenter and in 1740 he was Daniel Young. Apart from reading, writing and figure work he had to teach the forty children in his charge the Assembly of Divines shorter catechism.[46] This Presbyterian catechism had been produced in 1648 'to be a directory of catechising such as are of weaker capacity' and was commonly used to instruct children in Dissenting or Nonconformists churches for nearly 200 years. It began.

Q. What is the chief end of man?
A. Man's chief end is to glorify God and to enjoy him for ever.
Q. What rule hath God given to direct us how we may glorify and enjoy him?
A. The word of God, which is contained in the scriptures of the Old and New Testaments, is the only rule to direct us how we may glorify and enjoy him.

Daniel Young and following school masters lived rent free on the premises and had to keep them in good repair. Any profits he was able to make he could keep.

In the following years trustees came to include representatives of other churches of Nonconformist outlook, as these appeared on the scene in Dursley and Uley, and their ministers were frequently the schoolmasters. Few records of the school survive, and those that do are account books giving mainly running expenses and school masters' salaries.[47] In 1781 £2.4*s*.6*d*. was spent on quills and paper for scholars and £7 on the half year salary of the master. In 1822 books to the total value of £2 were presented to children for good behaviour. In 1826 the school had about 30 boys and the master received £35 p.a. By 1830 this had risen to £22 10*s*. for a half year.

An inspection in 1872 by Her Majesty's Inspectors brought the disturbing news that the school was condemned as inefficient in its size and lack of playground. A meeting of Trustees was called in December to consider the situation and came to the conclusion that the school was 'capable of being made increasingly beneficial to the inhabitants of the locality'. It was decided to approach the managers of the Wesleyan School in Boulton Lane to see if an 'efficient undenominational school' could be established in the area by 'appropriating the endowment of the Water Street School the building or procuring a convenient and eligable schoolroom'. Any surplus money could go towards supporting a schoolmaster. The then master, the Rev. James Williams of Cam Meeting, and the Rev. Jason Jenkyns of the Tabernacle were asked to investigate, but nothing appears to have come of the approach. In January 1877 on the resignation of Mr. Williams as school master the position was advertised in *The Schoolmaster*.[48]

In the next ten years the school declined and in 1887 it was recorded that the schoolmaster had resigned, all the pupils having left. The old school was never re-opened as such but let out by the Trustees for town meetings. One long letting was to the Anglican National School by the parish church. That school's log book reveals that in September 1892, the infants moved into the Water Street buildings while their own and the schoolmaster's house were demolished and new schoolrooms erected. They stayed until August the following year. Their teachers and Rector Gresley found the premises an improvement on those vacated, but the schools' inspectors were not happy and were very critical of both facilities and teaching. In 1918 the buildings were sold and subsequently became a fish and chip shop and

The National School 1899. The school buildings are now used as a Parish Centre by St. James's Church. In this picture are Mrs and the Revd Gresley and the Revd Webb.

(Lionel Ayliffe)

Members of Cam Meeting on Stinchcombe Hill c. 1900. Back centre with beard is the Revd David Truss *(Mrs F.D. Trude)*

builder's workshops. A fire in the 1960s gutted the building and the ruins are now a bottle gas store. Nonconformists have never placed as much value on their buildings as some other branches of the Christian Church but it is sad that these mute, maimed walls make up all that remain in Dursley of the physical heritage bequeathed to us by our Puritan-Presbyterian ancestors.

It is a consolation though that the spirit of Joseph Twemlow lives on in his Trust. With the cessation of schooling in Water Street, an arrangement was made in 1887 under which fees would be paid to enable boys to attend Mr Hunt's school in Prospect Place. Cost to the Trustees – £5 p.a. per boy or £40 p.a. for 10! This arrangement continued until the First World War. In 1921 Dursley Secondary (later Grammar) School was opened on the Rednock Site and the Twemlow Trustees then paid fees of children to attend this. The Trust was reorganised in 1947 to provide grants to children of Free Church parents attending further education establishments and it is in this form that it continues today.[49]

Joseph Twemlow resigned the pastorate of Cam Meeting-cum-Water Street in 1738[50] and died August 1740. He has been followed by a succession of ministers of diverse gifts and qualities who have served this Dissenting cause well. Nicholas Martyn (1738–44) and Thomas Hornblower (1745–66) were almost certainly Presbyterians[51] like Twemlow, but thereafter, as happened to many English Presbyterian churches in this period, Cam Meeting became Independent or Congregational in outlook.

The Revd Owen Griffiths outside Cam Meeting Manse at the bottom of Cam Pitch. The right hand end facing up the Pitch, later became a Co-op shop and was demolished in 1980. This picture was taken about 1910 *(Miss V. Taylor)*

Brian and Betty Stamps, the present pastor of Cam Meeting and his wife, outside the chapel, January 1982. *(Photo. David Evans)*

In 1978 a new chapter opened when, after some time without a minister, Mr. Brian Stamps, headmaster of Slimbridge County Primary School became pastor. Brian, for seventeen years an Anglican Lay Reader, received a request to take a service or two at Cam Meeting and found that it was near to closing. After careful consideration he offered his services and now he, and his wife Betty, are reviving and giving good heart to one of the county's oldest Nonconformist causes. Its buildings date from 1703, but spiritually it can be traced with certainty back to 1647 and the establishment of Joseph Woodward as Rector of Dursley, and more tenuously, to some two decades before this to Dursley's Puritan inclined, pre Hugh Robinson, clergy. Today it is in the Congregational Federation of Churches.

Bishop Bensen of Gloucester surveyed his diocese for Nonconformists in 1735[52] and the figures he obtained were updated in 1743[53] and 1750.[54] The results, in families, for our locality were:

Year	*Dursley*	*Cam*	*Stinchcombe*	*Coaley*	*Uley*
1735	250 Pres* Meeting Hse & School	250 Ind*	15 Pres		20 B* 40 Pres
1743	250 Pres	400 Ind	15 Pres	9 Pres	16 B 77 Pres
1750	100 Pres	300 Ind	15 Pres	9 Pres	16 B 77 Pres
Population – (individuals) 1743/50					
	20000	900	345	600	1160

(*Pres = Presbyterians; Ind = Independents; B = Baptists)

As can be seen in the years leading up to 1750 there was a considerable drop in the number of those worshipping at Dursley's Water Street Chapel – though one hundred families must have been a fair congregation if all attended any one service. This decline continued until by the early 1770s the chapel stood empty on a Sunday.[55] This dwindling of a Nonconformist cause was not unknown in the eighteenth century. Sometimes the vigour of its early days of freedom gave way, in an age of scientific discovery and rationalism, to dry withering theology. However, if this was the case in Dursley, one would expect a comparable effect in Cam since both were served by the same minister.

Clues to the real cause of the demise of the Water Street congregation came from the short ministry of Rev. William Billingsley of Cam Meeting (1772–5). A young man of weak constitution, he came to the area from Dr. Ashworth's Academy at Daventry, full of expectations and zeal. His pastorate was not a happy one however, and ended with his death, or the prospect of it, from tuberculosis.

While in Cam, Billingsley corresponded with the Rev. Job Orton of Shrewsbury, one time assistant to Dr. Doddridge, and Orton's replies were published in 1806[56] Relevant and interesting parts are as follows.

> March 1773 Dear Sir,
>
> *Yours of the 2nd instant I received with great pleasure and I heartily rejoice with you in your encouragement at Cam and the agreeable prospects you have of usefulness there. I have heard from Mr. H. of your great acceptance among the people. Though there is great fickelness among Dissenters, yet I hope your sermon preaching . . . will not be in vain in the Lord.* Preach in Dursley *especially as you have so convenient a place. Perhaps a lecture now and then on a weekday, especially at some holiday time . . .* Orton then goes on to suggest that proper benches be got for the gallery and says that if the people want Billingsley to preach they will pay for them.

Nov. 1773

Job Orton begins by commiserating with Billingsley over his difficulties and suggests that he airs his problems at an open meeting *It is most unreasonable for the collector of your salary to expect to be paid . . .*

Persons that came to us from the Church or from the Methodists are seldom prudent and steady. Ministers frequently have a good deal of trouble with them. It is best to wait some time to see what their temper and behaviour are before they are admitted to communion . . . Orton cautions about too strong a stand on this however, as denying communion could cause trouble.

Job Orton then goes on to hope Dursley will bring Billingsley success and encouragement and ends by commiserating again over his problems asking if there is no experienced minister he can confide in. It would appear that Cam's young minister feels that he is being slighted – *you cannot expect politeness and a great degree of good manners from low people and mechanics.*

Late 1774.

Letters here show that Billingsley is very despondent to the extent that he feels he is unwanted. Those about him are fond of new things, new doctrines, new methods of address. Orton advises him to make light of these things in public as it would suit some people to see him hurt. God has work for him in Cam.

The correspondence ends with Orton saying that he has recommended Billingsley as a supply preacher in Bristol so that he has a chance to take the waters – presumably at the then fashionable Hotwells Spa.

Billingsley probably attempted to continue the earlier practice of preaching a sermon in the evening at Dursley he had given earlier in the Sunday at Cam. The practice seems to have died with him as his successor John Thomas, on his arrival in 1776 began evening services at Cam. Water Street was not abandoned however as Thomas preached a lecture there once a month, but by 1821 even this had ceased and the building was used just for the charity school.[57]

It is obvious from Orton's letters that William Billingsley had a rough time in both Cam and Dursley. His troubles, and the desertion of the Water Street Chapel, stemmed from the impact in the town of George Whitefield and his brand of Methodism.

Part Two

The Evangelical Revival in Dursley and afterwards

Praise the Lord!
Sing a new song to the Lord;
praise him in the assembly of his faithful people!
Be glad, Israel, because of your creator;
rejoice, people of Zion, because of your king!
Praise his name with dancing;
play drums and harps in praise of him.
The Lord takes pleasure in his people;
he honours the humble with victory.
Let God's people rejoice in their triumph and
sing joyfully all night long

(Psalm 149)

3

Some Background — George Whitefield and the Calvanistic Methodists

In 1743, Philip Doddridge allowed George Whitefield to preach from the pulpit of his chapel, Castle Hill, Northampton. He gained the disapprobation of many of his fellow Independent or Congregational ministerial colleagues.

> I will take this occasion with great freedom to tell you my opinion of those people who are called Methodists. I have carefully inquired after them; was willing to think well of them; loth to censure them or hear others do so. And I think still there are serious people deluded by them. But after a candid attention to them, their proceedings appear not to be wise and good. Their devotion is unseasonable, irregular and injudicious. Their sermons are low and loose and not at all like what they seem to assume. Their spirits appear to me to be turbulent, unruly and censorious. They practise upon weak men and poor people. They call them up to pray and sing when they should be in their business or their beds. They disturb peace and order of families. What they pretend above their neighbours, appears to me mere enthusiasm. Their people are rather slothful, mopish and dejected or pragmatical, then sober, considerate, judicious, exemplary and regular Christians. And I have no expectation but that Methodism, like other enthusiasm, will promote infidelity and turn out to the damage of religion and the souls of men. Though I judge not their hearts, views and motives, which are secret things that belong to God, yet I thought it needful very lately to warn my hearers of these people's errors and advise them to avoid them.[1]

At the beginning of the eighteenth century it was obvious to most that the possibility of creating a national church which would encompass Anglicans and Nonconformists was dead. From the death of Queen Anne in 1714, Established Church and Dissenting Chapel went its own way, each with its particular style of worship and each with its own method of providing education. Denied entry to universities, Dissenters created their own

George Whitefield 1714–1770.

academies, such as that of Dr. Doddridge, and many achieved great fame. It was a time of reason and religious tolerance in England, a time when men's minds turned from thoughts of religion to the developing arts and sciences; the music of Handel and Italian Opera; the astronomical discoveries by Halley and others, made possible by advances in the technology of optics; the invention of the atmospheric pumping engine by Newcomen; and the discovery of how to use coke for smelting iron ore by Araham Darby; to world exploration and overseas trading on increasing scales; painting, engraving, drama, literature and the establishment of newspapers such as the *Gloucester Journal* — all opened and broadened men's minds.

The Signature
of a famous son of Gloucestershire,
" The Prince of Preachers " :

Yours most affectionately
in Xt Jesus
George Whitefield

It was unthinkable to return to the bitterness and rancour of inter-denominational disputes of earlier times but without 'fire in its belly', religious practice and theology stagnated in the background of national life. There were exceptions in both church and chapel. Isaac Watts (1674-1748) for example, developed from the psalms, first paraphrases and then purposely written hymns so that his congregations at Mark Lane Chapel, London, could have a greater diversity of material for congregational singing, but the age saw also the flowering of Deism or National Religion — the idea that God was no more than a 'First Cause', a force which created the world and the physical laws by which it operated, and then let it run without interference. In its theology man was not to be held responsible for his actions and, for those who rejected moral restraint, its tenets were very attractive. Many in public life professed openly their complete rejection of Christianity and its dogma while believing that the Church of England should be kept as a prop to support the monarchy and maintain the peace of the state. It was a time of increasing cruelty and callousness to the sufferings of man and beast. While the monied enjoyed their pleasures, the great poor suffered lives of deprivation and hopelessness, turning frequently to cheap gin for comfort, and the cruelties of cockfighting and badger baiting for amusement. Lawlessness was prevalent, particularly in large towns, and at one time 160 offences were punishable by death, reflecting both the low price put on human life and the desperation of the law makers in searching for a remedy to the situation.

In 1738 Archbishop Secker wrote

> In this we cannot be mistaken, that an open and professed disregard to religion is become, through a variety of unhappy courses, the distinguishing character of the present age. This evil has already brought in such dissolute-

> ness and contempt of principle in the higher part of the world, and such profligate intemperance and fearlessness of committing crimes in the lower, as must, if this torrent of impropriety stop not, become absolutely fatal.[2]

The 'variety of unhappy causes' included the characteristics of the churches. The National Church had become lethargic and barren. Some country parsons did a reasonable but uninspiring job in looking after their parishes. Some were outstanding, but in general the clergy were very worldly having more interest in being sportsmen, politicians, magistrates, merchants, lackeys of men of power and so on, than in men's souls. Many took incomes from several parishes — Dursley contributed in this way for much of the eighteenth century — and frequently their parishes were left in the hands of ill paid, ill educated curates.

Dissenting or Nonconformist causes declined in number after the rapid expansion at the beginning of the century. Austere, often dry in spiritual message, lacking force and enthusiasm, they lost most of their middle and upper class support which with financial prosperity, preferred to indulge growing interests in travel and fashion, to maintaining Puritan traditions.[3] Into this religious desert burst the leaders of the Evangelical Revival. Of its two greatest English principals only George Whitefield played a personal part in the history of Dursley and it is therefore on him we concentrate. John Wesley was often in Gloucestershire but his concern lay with the larger centres of population and there is no record of him ever having visited the town.

George Whitefield[4] was born at the Bell Inn, Southgate Street, Gloucester in December 1714. The inn was the foremost and largest in the city. It was the centre of much of the community's social life, with assemblies and balls and continual comings and goings of coach and foot travellers, and as such it attracted all classes of society from rich merchant to skulking foot pad. There can be no doubt that young George, brought up for sixteen years in the hurly burly of such a place, developed there the extrovert confidence, ready wit and ability to get on well with most degrees of men which were to characterize his adult life. He was no saint — a typical boy of the age, not above occasional petty stealing, swearing and 'reading romances' — a boy with considerable zest for life. One source of mischief concerned a nearby Dissenting meeting house whose members later built, and moved to, Southgate Street Chapel. Its minister was Thomas Cole, and it was occasionally young George's delight to run in and shout 'Old Cole, Old Cole, Old Cole' and sprint out before he was caught. He attended several schools including that of St. Mary de Crypt, and it was during his last year here that he sobered down and began attending Anglican festivals and daily services regularly.

When about eighteen he went to Oxford University as a 'servitor', a student receiving free tuition in return for being a servant to three or four more affluent students. It was a degrading position which cut him off from much of college life, but he endured all the humiliations for three years.

He continued his religious practices, but without companions, until in 1733 he caught the attention of Charles Wesley. Charles, his brother John, and some twenty others, were members of a religious society, — referred to by scoffers by such names as the Bible Moths, Bible Bigots, Godly or Holy Club, and Methodists, — and Whitefield, when introduced, quickly became accepted.

The Society was strict over religious observance and generous in work with the local poor and needy. Academically learned, it played a major part in Whitefield's life at Oxford, but brought little spiritual satisfaction. This came early in 1735 when, after some six months of mental wrestling with the problems of salvation, during which he became quite ill and neglected his studies, he became aware suddenly of the assurance of God's presence and became a new man. He wrote later :—

> O! with what joy — joy unspeakable — even joy that was full of and big with glory, was my soul filled, when the weight of sin went off, and an abiding sense of the pardoning love of God, and a full assurance of faith, broke in upon my disconsolate soul ! Surely it was the day of mine espousal — a day to be had in everlasting rememberance At first my joys were like a spring tide, and overflowed the banks!

— and anyone who has seen a good Severn Bore rolling in on the Spring tide to Gloucester, as he must have done, can easily understand his metaphor. Whitefield returned to Gloucester to recover his physical strength and while there in 1735 he records that 'God made me instrumental to awake several young persons who soon formed themselves into a little society and had the honour of being despised at Gloucester . . . . I likewise visited two other societies not my own'.

The group of 'several young persons' was the first Whitefield Methodist society formed and it seems to have met every weekday evening for prayer, singing psalms, Bible study and exhortation. The comment regarding 'two other societies not my own' is interesting. As has been said earlier in the chapter, religious life nationally was at a very low ebb at this time but parts of Gloucestershire seem to have been an exception as there is evidence of a religious revival pre-dating Whitefield and Wesley.

Diocesan records from 1724 onwards show a continuous flow of registrations of premises, mainly private houses, for public worship by Dissenters. Of the thirty-seven noted between that year and 1740, a high proportion (twenty-six) were registered by men who can be identified as being members of Southgate Independent Church, Gloucester, Thomas Cole's church. Blakeney and Mitcheldean in the Forest of Dean, Avening, Horsley, Painwick, Minchinhampton and Wotton-under-Edge in the Cotswolds, Cheltenham and Gloucester itself all had registrations effected by them.

Thomas Cole started his ministry at Abergavenny, in 1703, and moved to Gloucester in 1718.[5] It has been said of him that 'his manifest sincerity, allied to an eager evangelism, made him a force in the city (Gloucester) and impelled him to quit the conventional stiltedness of the pulpit style of the day'. It is easy to see that he would want to carry his enthusiasm out into the countryside and that this could give rise to a religious revival in the county. In this Joseph Twemlow of Cam possibly played a part as we have seen.

After George Whitefield's explosive religious experience in 1735 he and Thomas Cole — 'Old Cole' — became great friends, suggesting that they shared a common spiritual outlook. Cole called himself 'Whitefield's Curate' and frequently ministered to the societies formed locally under the greater man's influence.

It is interesting to speculate at this point on whether the two societies, not Whitefield's but visited by him in 1735, had come about through the activity of Cole and on whether they inspired Whitefield to form his own, his first. What does seem likely, however, is 'Old Cole', working in the limited field of mid-Gloucestershire was the harbinger of the great eighteenth century evangelical revival in England, in which case the old saying *As sure as God is in Gloucestershire* takes an extra meaning. Thomas Cole is recorded in later life as visiting Avening frequently, and on 5 August 1742 he died at Nympsfield after preaching in the village. One man who never forgot the power of that last sermon was Thomas Wilkins who, as a young lad of eleven, walked up from his home in Uley to hear Cole. Wilkins eventually entered the ministry himself, his sole pastorate being with the Congregational Church, Weymouth, where he died in 1800 aged sixty-nine.[6]

The Wilkins family was already acquainted with Thomas Cole for a Mrs. Wilkins, probably Thomas's mother, had opened her home for cottage meetings in Uley and was visited by Cole and other ministers.

Uley had a strong Nonconformist element in it, and later in the century it was nurtured by John Thomas of Cam Meeting and others. This resulted in the erection of the Whitecourt Union Chapel in 1790.

Whitefield returned to Oxford in March 1736, graduated, and in June, in Gloucester, was ordained deacon by Bishop Benson. On the Sunday following his ordination, aged twenty-two, and in St. Mary de Crypt, he preached his first sermon. It was planned to encourage the members of the society he had formed in Gloucester and its effect must have been greater than he could have hoped for.

> As I proceeded. I perceived the fire kindled, till at last, though so young and amidst a crowd of those who knew me in my infant, childish days, I trust I was enabled to speak with some degree of Gospel authority. Some few mocked, but most for the present seemed struck, and I have since heard that a complaint has been made to the Bishop that I drove fifteen mad at the first sermon. The worthy prelate, as I am informed, wished that the madness might not be forgotten before next Sunday.

It was the start of a long and remarkable career as a preacher which took him to most parts of Britain and to the American Colonies.

Early in 1739 he was ordained priest in Oxford.

Whitefield's style of preaching brought him fame and with it came adoration by some, and opposition by those who came to regard his enthusiasm as fanaticism. Anglican churches one by one closed their pulpits to him and he began to entertain the idea of open air preaching. It was not new and would have been known to Whitefield through correspondence with Howell Harris in Wales, who was already roaming the south of his country preaching to excited crowds in and out of doors, wherever occasion arose. On a bitterly cold Saturday, 17 February 1739, to a few hundred colliers and their families of the Kingswood coalfield, at Hanham Mount near Bristol, he preached for the first time under open skies. It is doubtful if those astonished miners, who worked in appalling conditions and whose lawlessness and ferocity were dreaded by the worthy citizens of the city of Bristol, realised the significance and momentousness of the occasion. It was the beginning of thirty-one years of intense crusading evangelism such as the country had not seen before, nor has seen since, and in this he was to be joined by John Wesley. Before seeing the effect of his activity on Dursley, we should look at the man and the societies he created.

Whitefield was a man of the people, who had an extraordinary affection for him, a man of tremendous enthusiasm who could brush away problems, and found such institutions as an orphanage in America and a school in Kingswood. At times brash and unrefined, of passionate temperament, uninhibited in speech, he was able to speak extempore for long periods, judging accurately the mood of his listeners so as to be able to hold the attention of nobleman or kitchen maid and able to talk directly to individuals or groups in a crowd. Often he propounded fundamental religious truths with exciting brilliance but sometimes produced little of worth. He was generous natured in his catholocity and ecumenism, and a splendid narrator of Bible stories, history and tales of distant lands, which held his listeners spellbound because of the paucity of travel in their own lives. He was a lover of humour and jokes, capable of mimicking his opponents, able to give dramatic representations of events, able to reduce his audience to tears, a man with a great ringing voice. Accounts of his open air preaching often mention the thousands who could hear him. American scientist Benjamin Franklin, once decided to test the accuracy of these reports. His result was astonishing for he says 'I computed that he might well be heard by more than thirty thousand'.[7]

And his themes? Like Wesley these were on the great Christian doctrines as developed by St. Paul and others. He preached the need for salvation, justification by faith and, but unlike Wesley, the Calvanistic doctrine of predestination. It was this Calvanistic attitude that made him acceptable to a broad spectrum of religious persuasion in the country and his friends were to be found among Anglican Evangelicals, orthodox Dissenters, Welsh Methodists and Scottish Presbyterians. It enabled him to revive in these who had lost it, the fervour and relevance of gospel preaching.

John Wesley came to believe in universal salvation and it was largely this difference that caused the separating of the ways of him and Whitefield. It also isolated Wesley from all but high church men, who would have little to do with him, and, coupled with the well developed organisation of the societies he founded, it made the formation of a new denomination almost inevitable — much against his personal desire. Whitefield's Calvanistic societies became in time, much less well organised on a national pattern and found it easy to move into the ranks of Congregational Dissent after his death, some even before.[8] Whitefield was not universally acclaimed. Throughout his preaching life he produced much virulent opposition and from the printing presses came a continuous flow of material deriding him and his followers. Sometimes he suffered actual physical assault, particularly from mobs whose antagonism was often fanned by hostile clergy and local gentry. In reading his story and those of his co-workers one can only marvel at the bravery and love they showed towards their persecutors — and the same can be said for Wesley and his followers.

Whitefield's detractors continued their work after his death and, with no denomination to defend him, his prestige has slowly declined so that mention today of the evangelical revival and Methodism will often invoke only the name of Wesley with perhaps Whitefield as an afterthought; whereas a case can be made out for Whitefield being as, or even more, important at the time.

Anglican, the Rev. John Newton could say 'I bless God that I have lived in his time; many were the winter mornings I have got up at four, to attend his Tabernacle discourses at five; and I have seen Moorfields (London) as full of lanterns at these times as I suppose the Haymarket is full of flambeaux on an opera night. As a preacher, if any man was to ask me who was the second I ever heard, I would be at some loss, but in regard to the first, Mr. Whitefield exceeded so far every other man of my time, that I should be at none'.[9] Newton's remark that he heard Whitefield preach at 5 a.m. ties in with the comment in the passage at the beginning of this chapter, that Whitefield's followers were called upon 'to pray and sing when they should be in their . . . beds.' Whitefield, like the Wesleys and Harris remained a firm believer in, and adherent to, the Church of England. His early societies were formed to complement the Established Church. They were composed of earnest Christians who came together to strengthen their spiritual lives with prayer, psalms, Bible exposition and exhortation. For this reason the gatherings were called 'societies' and not churches, their members met outside normal Anglican service times, their preachers were called 'exhorters', not ministers, and their enrolled members had to be communicants of a church or Dissenting meeting.[10] Slowly, however, through the indifference and even hostility of the clergy, coupled with the admission of members, who had no allegiance to the Anglican church, these societies assumed an independent existence, though they still looked to the Anglican church and did not consider themselves a new denomination.

An English Calvanistic Methodist Association was established in 1743 and its first meeting revealed that its preaching force was of six Anglican priests, two Non-conformist ministers and sixteen laymen. The latter were divided into three classes —

> Superintendents who had whole time oversight of large territories
> Public Exhorters who had oversight of 12-14 societies
> Private Exhorters who looked after 1 or 2 societies[11]

George Whitefield was not indifferent to organisation, but left this to others. Thus for seven years from 1744, Welshman Howell Harris took charge. At a Conference at Gloucester, on 12 November 1747, it was revealed that the English Association consisted of thirty-one societies and had, apart from these, twenty-seven established preaching stations. There were seventeen 'brethren that read and overlook as stewards',eleven 'publick preachers that go about continually' and eleven 'that are in places and only go about occasionally and assist as far as is consistent with their calling and places'.[12]

In 1751 Howell Harris[13] left the Calvanistic Association, and complete collapse of the English organisation was only prevented by the intervention of the Countess of Huntingdon. This good lady of Donnington Park, had been an early convert of George Whitefield. She had been widowed in 1746 and thereafter, until her death in 1791, she assiduously promoted the evangelical revival — mainly among the upper levels of society. Testimony to her activity remains with us today in the churches of the Countess of Huntingdon's Connection.[14]

Whitefield's Calvanistic Methodists societies were now only held together by local grouping arrangements, the most prominent of which seems to have been that based on the Gloucestershire village of Rodborough and which took the name of the Rodborough Connexion. George Whitefield resumed his position as leader of the English Societies in 1756 but a national structure was not revived. In 1770, while in America, George Whitefield died. There died also in the same year other leaders of the Calvanistic Methodists and it was left to local men to organise resources and continue the pattern of itinerant ministry which supported and held together the societies. One by one however, the societies invited ministers to settle permanently with them. They became Independent or Congregationl churches but frequently remained in close association, as happened in the Rodborough Connextion, until the early decades of the nineteenth century. Some of the ministers chosen, as at Rodborough in 1778, and Dursley in 1795, had been trained in the Countess of Huntingdon's own College, established in August 1768 at Trevecca, near Brecon, South Wales. It was formed when the supply of Anglican ministers for her chapels ceased and

Thomas Adams, 1718–1770, leader of the Rodborough Connexion of Calvanistic Methodist Societies. *(Minister and Elders of Rodborough Tabernacle)*

emphasised preaching the gospel with enthusiasm. In this it differed from traditional Dissenting academies which put emphasis on learning and literacy. In 1792 the college moved to Cheshunt, north of London, and is now within the United Reformed Church, with Westminster College, at Cambridge.[15]

Leader of the Rodborough Connexion was Thomas Adams,[16] an Anglican, who had been deeply affected by Whitefield when, during his first tour of Gloucestershire, in 1739, he preached on Minchinhampton Common from a burial mound still known as Whitefield's Tump. Filled with enthusiasm Adams felt it his duty to encourage his neighbours spiritually and is said to have licensed his house in Minchinhampton as a meeting place for the society he gathered together. He became an evangelist, or minister without episcopal ordination, and a great friend of George Whitefield. In his will, Whitefield calls Adams his 'only surviving first fellow labourer and beloved much in the Lord', and left him £50. In 1749 Adams built a chapel at nearby Rodborough — the first Rodborough Tabernacle. The money for this probably came from house societies at Frampton-on-Severn, Ebley, Stonehouse, Ruscombe, Rooksmoor and elsewhere and whose members probably then combined. Thomas Adams died in 1770. His funeral sermon was given by Torial Joss who lamented 'Oh, what must poor Rodberow feel? and what must Dursley, Castle Coom and Chippenham feel at the loss of so faithful and laborious a preacher?' The places mentioned were all in the association of societies over which he presided but records show him as travelling more widely and preaching in Bristol, London and elsewhere and taking part in the early national Calvanistic Methodist conferences. He travelled on horse back, his horse having huge saddle bags. His and Whitefield's preaching raised the fury of some local people as part of a letter written by Whitefield from Minchinhampton shows.

Hampton July 25th 1743

Dear ——

On Thursday I came here and expected to be attacked because I had heard that the mob which had been so outrageous towards you and others for so long time had now threatened that if ever I came there again they would have a piece of my black gown to make aprons with. No sooner had I entered the town (Minchinhampton) but I saw and heard signals such as blowing of horns and ringing of bells, for gathering the mob. My soul was kept quite easy. I preached in a grass plat from these words "and seeing the grace of God he exhorted them with full purpose of heart to cleave unto the Lord," and as it happened I finished my sermon and pronounced the blessing just as the ring leader broke in on us, which I perceived disappointed and grieved them much. One of them, as I was coming down from the table, called me a coward; but I told him they should hear from me another way. I then went into the house (of Thomas Adams?) and preached upon the staircase to a large number of serious souls; but these real troublers of 'Israel' soon came in to

> mock and mob us. But feeling what I have never felt before, as you know, I have very little natural courage, strength and power being given us from above, I leaped down the stairs and all ran away before me. However they continued making a noise about the house until midnight, abusing the poor people as they went home and we hear broke a young lady's arm in two places. Brother A — (Adams) they threw a second time into a pool, in which operation he received a deep wound in the leg. John C —s (Croome) life, that second Bunyan, was much threatened. Young W — H — (William Hogg) they wheeled in a barrow to the pool's side, lamed his brother and grieviously hurt several others.

Whitefield states that it was the second time that Adams had been thrown into a pool. On the first occasion he was exhorting in his house, when the mob burst in, carried him off and threw him into a tanning pit or 'skin pit full of noisesome things and stagnant water!' Undeterred he returned to his preaching, whereupon he was seized again and dragged to a stream one and a half miles away. After one of these two occasions he was lame for a fortnight. Whitefield appealed to the local clergy, constables and justices, but they retorted that his troubles were brought on by himself. He therefore took the ring leaders to court and, at the County Assize in March 1744 they were convicted but, on Whitefield's plea, let off with a warning — Gamaliel's warning 'Leave them alone! If what they have planned and done is of human origin it will disappear, but if it comes from God, you cannot possibly defeat them. You could find yourself fighting against God!' Such mob action was not uncommon as two other cases from Gloucestershire will indicate. In December 1744 John Cennick was at Wickwar. 'As soon as I began preaching the mobs came with sheepbells tied to a stick and they did ring them. They had also frying pans, horse rugles, salt box and a post horn. Some of the mob did put their mouths to the windows and made a noise like dogs; and they called me a false prophet and all manner of names they could think of; but Satan can go no further than his chains'.[17] James Relly was at Tewkesbury in December 1747. 'Yesterday many assembled to hear the word . . . but we were assaulted by such a furious mob that all turned to confusion. They flapped the tables, stamped on the floor, pushed the people, swore, cursed, laughed, pricked with dirt, threw handfuls of snuff and brickbats and dirt. I discoursed about an hour but the noise increasing I let off.'[18] Thomas Adams met similar trouble when preaching in Dursley in 1743 though how serious this was is not recorded.

Whitefield's letter quoted above gives the names of two of Thomas Adams' senior assistants, — William Hogg and John Croome; there was a third, William Vines. These four men for many years were the great roaming evangelists who served the needs of the Calvanistic Methodist societies of Gloucestershire's Rodborough Connexion.

John Croome was born in 1718 in Horsley to Quaker parents.[19] He became a wild youth, 'going with the multitude to do evil' but sometime after 1739 he was converted by Howell Harris on Hampton Common (Minchinhampton) after going to mock. He joined the Rodborough Connexion and became a preacher. He visited the Dursley Society from time to time, but his main concern became the three societies in Wiltshire — Castle Coombe, Chippenham and Christian Malford, often spending three weeks or a month between these, once he had given up his trade of weaving.

Six feet tall, morose by nature, seldom laughing, retaining the manners and language of the Quakers, often worshipping leaning on his staff, he must have been an awesome person. In 1761 he began a season in London. Here 'his appearance as a poor plain countryman with lank, undressed hair and mean attire at first created surprise; but the simplicity of his manner and style and the power of his preaching, soon removed all prejudice . . .'. This was Whitefield's 'second Bunyan'. He died at Christian Malford in 1780 and was buried at Rodborough, the society at which supported his widow until her death.

William Vines lived at Randwick and was foreman in a quarry belonging to a local farmer.[20] 'He was unassuming in character, homely in appearance and attire with very limited education. His simple and spiritual addresses were well received; he knew his bible and preached it; he knew the power of religion and proclaimed it'. 'In the itinerary that was established among neighbouring congregations, viz, Rodboro', Wotton-under-Edge, Dursley and Frampton, Mr. Vines always took his turn every sabbath day and continued to preach for many years, generally going and returning on foot the same day.' William Vines lived to a great age and continued his preaching even after going blind. Like the others, he sometimes travelled great distances. The Bristol Tabernacle cash book has an entry for 14 August 1787 'Mr. Vines given 10*s* 6*d* for walking thirty miles to Bristol and back.'

Perhaps the most colourful of the Rodborough men was William Hogg — Butcher Hogg.[21] He was born in Pitchcombe and, as a lad and young man, was the terror of the neighbourhood. He heard George Whitefield preach, was converted and became a highly respected member of his community, a man of integrity. He joined the Rodborough society of Thomas Adams, and in September 1742 registered his house in Pitchcombe for public worship. Later he became a preacher in the Rodborough Connexion and such was his standing that on the death of Whitefield and Adams in 1770 he assumed its leadership. He died in November 1800 above eighty years in age.

Many anecdotes survived William Hogg, who was a thick set muscular man, open handed and somewhat eccentric.

> In the early period of his ministry, he had been preaching at Rodborough, amidst the interruptions of a very considerable mob, which was not uncommon when the gospel was first introduced to that place, and not being satisfied with having caused a disturbance while he was in the pulpit, they

> followed him on his return home for nearly three miles, pelting him with stones. At length he turned suddenly upon them, put them to flight, and pursuing them closely, gave some of them to feel he was capable of self-defence. Driving one of them into a deep ditch, he kept him for some time in the mire, trembling through fear of severe castigation: but the Apostle's account of a Bishop, that he should be no striker, occurring to his mind, he desisted, and let the man go free, whilst he himself was deeply humbled that he had not suffered more patiently.
>
> It was his custom never to have his plate changed while at dinner, and never to partake of more joints than one, except sometimes a little pudding. But though so moderate respecting his own appetite; yet it was usual for him to purchase tarts, &c. and carry them with him, to present to any of his friends to whom they might be acceptable, or give them away to the poor.
>
> He never changed his linen more than once week; and being at one time subpoenaed to appear before the House of Commons, on an electioneering affair, the propriety of putting on clean linen was suggested to him; but he paid no regard to this and went just as he was, without being shaved, or making the least alteration in his dress. Perhaps no person ever discovered so little concern, or attention to etiquette on such an occasion.
>
> In a large circle of ministers, after having peremptorily refused to drink a glass of wine, one of them urged it by referring to Paul's advice to Timothy, to which Mr. H. replied, 'Timothy was a poor, weak, sickly creature, worn out with hard and constant preaching; had the Apostle given directions to a man so corpulent as you are, and who labor so little he would have advised him to drink water instead of wine.'
>
> The late Countess of Huntingdon once paid him a visit, and dined with him. When her Ladyship came into the parlour, he took her by the hand and placing her in a Bee-hive chair, said; 'This is the first time your Ladyship ever sat in a Hog-sty.'

Such were the men who lead the Rodborough Connexion for most of its existence, who had the oversight of the Dursley society for fifty years and whose names are to be found on its deeds for lands and buildings. One point worth recording is that all were about the same age.

When he first preached on Minchinhampton Common in 1739, sowing the seeds of the Rodborough Connexion, George Whitefield was twenty-four. Hogg, Adams and Croome were about twenty-one; Vines was probably in his twenties. Howell Harris, leader of the English Calvanistic Methodists for most of the formative 1740s, and a frequent visitor to Gloucestershire then, was twenty-five. Young, restless, with great spiritual and physical energy, these men were the founders and leaders of a remarkable itinerating brotherhood which enriched the religious lives of many in the south Cotswolds and beyond for over half a century. William Hogg, for example, even into his seventies, thought nothing of closing his butcher's shop at around midnight on a Saturday, snatching a few hours sleep then leaving Pitchcombe without breakfast at about 4 a.m. by horse,

The tomb of William Hogg in Painswick Churchyard. In part the inscription reads – 'To the memory of the late William Hogg who died at a very advanced age on the 8th of November 1800. He was for fifty years a much esteemed gratuitous Preacher of the Gospel in the Tabernacles of London, Bristol, Rodborough and various other places in this and the adjoining Counties. It is incredible the sums of money he expended in Charity . . .' It also records that Williams and his wife Betty had eight sons and four daughters 'whom they lived to see comfortably established in life'. *(Photo. David E. Evans)*

One of the preaching places in the Rodborough Connexion — Christian Malford, Wilts.

bound for some distant place. Here after a light meal he would preach 'with great animation' at say 7 a.m.; preach twice more during Sunday, stay the night but leave at 3 a.m. to be back to open his shop on time on Monday morning.

Their influence echoed on well into the following century and could be detected in a long continuing special relationship among the Congregational Churches — often called Tabernacles — into which their societies evolved. At least one of the societies kept a special room for the use of those travelling preachers. At Castle Combe this was over a weaver's workshop and was known as 'the Prophets' Chamber'.[22]

4

From Stancombe to Dursley; the Calvanistic Methodists arrive

George Whitefield toured Gloucestershire on many occasions, the first being in 1739 after he had preached for the first time in the open air to the Kingswood colliers. His influence on Thomas Adams of Minchinhampton has been recorded. By 1742 Adams had gathered a Methodist society at Stancombe under the shadow of Stinchcombe Hill and was visiting and nurturing it, for in November of that year he wrote to George Whitefield that he was 'going Sunday next below Dursley if the Lord permit . . .' It is to Thomas Adms and this society that Dursley Tabernacle United Reformed Church can trace its origin. The society flourished and it is likely that because of it George Whitefield included Dursley in his itinerary in 1743. The occasion was Sunday March 27th, probably a very cold day as on the previous Friday he had ridden to Minchinhampton from Gloucester 'the snow falling and freezing on us all the way'.

> 'On Sunday morning I preached at Dursley about seven miles from Hampton (Minchinhampton) where our dear brother A — (Thomas Adams) had been taken down the Sunday before; but no one was permitted to touch or molest us. The congregation consisted of some thousands; and the word came with a most gloriously convincing power. I came away rejoicing; and in the afternoon preached to almost ten thousand on Hampton Common; . . . preaching in Gloucestershire is now like preaching at the Tabernacle at London.[1]

Quite where Adams and Whitefield preached in Dursley is unknown, but the reference to thousands seems to rule out the market place. The market house, erected some five years before, would have been closely hemmed in by buildings. A more likely place was Woodmancote Green, the large open space at the junction of the present Uley Road and Woodmancote, which then was a grassy area. It contained at this time the usual manorial equipment for dealing out justice in Woodmancote Manor, stocks probably, a whipping post certainly, for it is recounted that in about 1790 the then owner of the Bull Inn, which fronted the green, had a man whipped at the post for stealing a bottle of wine from the inn cellar.[2]

Nine days after his visit to Dursley, George Whitefield was back again. He was on his way on horseback from Gloucester to Bristol and a letter he wrote when he reached his destination shows the activity which characterised his adult life.

> I preached and took leave of the Gloucester people, with mutual and great concern, on Sunday evening last. It was past one in the morning (of Monday) before I could lay my weary body down. At five I rose again, sick for want of rest, but I was enabled to get on horseback and ride to Mr. F — s, where I preached to a large congregation, who came there at seven in the morning. At ten I read prayers and preached, and afterwards adminstered the sacrament in Stonehouse Church. Then I rode to Stroud and preached to about 12000 in Mistress G — s field; and about six in the evening to a like number on Hampton Common. After this, went to Hampton and held a general love feast with the United Societies and went to bed about midnight very cheerful and very happy. The next morning (Tuesday) I went and preached near Dursley to some thousands with great convictions accompanying the word.[3]

It must have been on this occasion that he preached on Stinchcombe Hill, though whether he used the mounting block at the far end as a pulpit as tradition states, is doubtful as anyone who has tried to balance on it will understand! In travelling from Minchinhampton to Bristol, Whitefield could well have used the old highway across the hill to reach the Gloucester — Bristol road.

So far as is known Whitefield did not return to Dursley again until 1769, though he was often in Gloucestershire in intervening years. However, those 1743 visits must have been unforgettble, powerful sources of inspiration and encouragement to the Stancombe Society which under Thomas Adams's leadership grew increasingly strong. By 1744 the Society had a considerable following and held an important position in the network of preaching stations that covered mid-Gloucestershire and North Wiltshire and which were served by itinerant preachers.

Thomas Adams exhorted it in May 1744[4]; in July Edward Godwin reported to him:-

> Thursday (I) arose and went to a place called Stancombe near Dursley . . . where I was to preach that morning, as I did about six, to upwards of one hundred and fifty souls, with great freedom, the people seemed much affected and God I believe will bless the word. I spoke there at night . . .[5]

In October Isaac Cottell wrote:-

> When I came to Stancombe (from Hawkesbury) I met Brother Humphreys of Hampton and a young man, an exhorter in Gloucestershire. I desired Brother Humphreys to preach but could not prevail with him . . . I then desired the other would preach but he declined also . . .

> The house was full of people within and a pretty many without. The Lord stood by me there and I preached the everlasting love of Jesus Christ to poor sinners. I believe there were many filled with the love of God . . .
>
> They desired me to preach there the next day but I refused because Brother Adams was to be there the next night. I lay that night at a place called Fordkins Brook and the next day returned home into Wiltshire.[6]

A few days later several itinerants gathered at Adams's house.

> We spent the evening comfortably together with my dear wife and family and more friends . . . Brother Cross went next morning to Stancombe, Godwin to Burford and Pugh for Gloucester . . . .[7]

William Vines wrote to Thomas Adams in April the following year.

> Sunday last I went to Pitchcombe and heard Brother Lewis. And then, with some of the brethren, I went to Stancombe, though it rained all the way, so that we were very wet indeed, where we met with a very attentive congregation and the Lord opened my mouth to declare his righteousness and His only . . .[8]

Up to 1746 meetings must have been unofficial, but in that year the house of Mary Chiltenham in Stancombe was registered with the diocesan authorities and the position regularised. The registration was signed by John Higgins, William Williams, John Shipway, Matthew Hale and James Fisher.[9] Chiltenham is an unusual name and it is likely that Mary was of Quaker stock, the house of Elizabeth Chiltenham having been registered for Quaker meetings in Stancombe in 1706.[10]

In 1747 the English Calvanistic Methodist Association met at Gloucester and among the 'societies in connection together under the care of the Reverend Mr. Whitefield' were four in Gloucestershire — Gloucester, (Minchin) Hampton, the Roadway (identification uncertain) and Stancombe. At Stancombe, as one of the 'brethren that read and overlook as stewards' was 'Brother Huggins' easily confused with Higgins if reported verbally in a broad Gloucestershire accent to a stranger! Regular preaching stations where there were no established societies were to be found at Tewkesbury, Randwick, Stroud, Friggs Mill near Rooksmoor, Tockington and elsewhere.[11]

Stancombe was a tiny hamlet and many of those attending meetings must have come from Dursley. It was however remote from the town and attendance involved a long journey round or a stiff climb over Stinchcombe Hill. By 1755 the meeting place had moved into the town and a house registered.

> These are to certify your Lordship (the Bishop of Gloucester) that some of His Majesty's Protestant Dissenting Subjects do intend to hold a meeting for the Worship of God in the Dursley House of Nathaniel Parry in the parish of Dursley . . . and desire it may be registered in Your Court according to an Act made in that behalf in the First Year of the Reign of King William and Queen Mary.

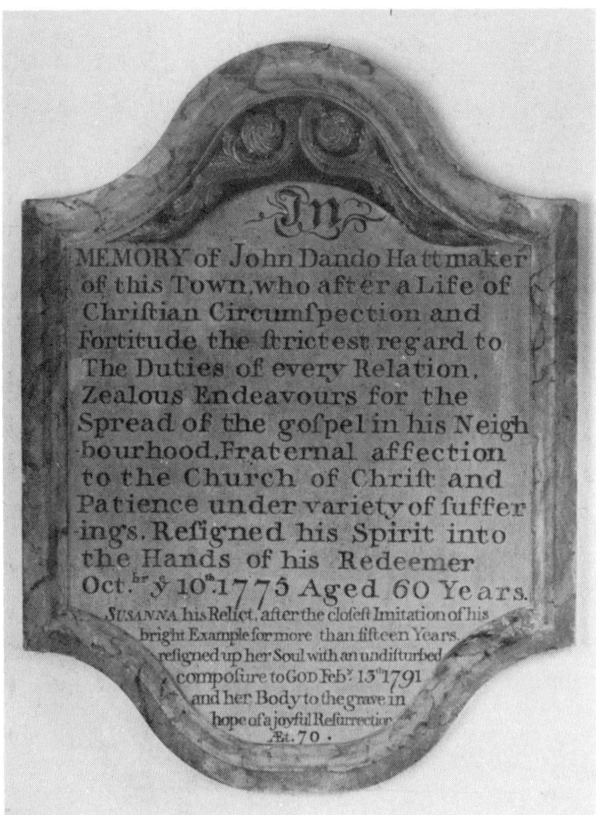

A plaque in Dursley Tabernacle to the memory of John Dando, a leading figure in the establishment of the religious society which gave rise to it. *(Photo. David Evans)*

This was dated 17 February 1755 and signed by

John Dando
John Shatford
Thomas Browning
John Higgins
John Shipway
Nathaniel Parry
James Derrett[12]

The present Dursley Tabernacle contains a plaque to John Dando 'Hattmaker' describing him as 'zealous . . . for the spread of the gospel in his neighbourhood' a statement substantiated in Diocesan records wherein he is found registering with others a house in North Nibley for public worship in February 1749.[13] In the Evangelical Magazine it is stated that it was John Dando 'who was the principle instrument in introducing the gospel' into Dursley so that it seems that it was he who initiated the move from Stancombe.[14]

John and his wife, Suzanna, had several children. John junior, the eldest, seems to have been a highly religious child but

> 'as he grew to manhood the propensities of his corrupt nature soon withered these early blossoms; and for some time, youthful folly prevailed above his better judgement; but God, by his special grace, would not permit this indifference to his best interests long to remain; for when he was about the age of eighteen, he was led from the motives of curiosity, to hear a Mr. Darby preach (in Dursley probably), who, at that time was a drummer in the army, but who afterwards settled as a preacher at Witney . . .'

In about 1768, John junior moved to Rodborough and on the death of Thomas Adams in 1770, he became a trustee of the Tabernacle there. Just before 1800 he moved to Bristol, joining Penn St. Tabernacle, and died in 1809 much mourned.[15]

Another son, Stephen, took over his father's hat making business in Dursley when he died. Later he moved to London, dying there in 1834.[16] One of Stephen's grandsons emigrated to New Zealand in 1866, settling as a farmer in the North Island near Raglan. His grandson, another John, visited England in 1980 and it was a great pleasure to meet a direct descendent of old John and Suzanna who had had 'the happiness of introducing the Gospel into Dursley' thereby laying the foundations for the present United Reformed Church.

Within five years of moving to Dursley, the society was able to erect a proper meeting house, the first Tabernacle, and this was registered on 17 September 1760 by

Thomas Mercer
William King
Christopher Brown
Samuel Griffin
John Dando
William Vines[17]

The name 'Tabernacle' was commonly used for the meeting houses erected by George Whitefield's societies. It stemmed from the early days of the movement when it was hoped that their use was to be temporary, ceasing when the societies could be accepted and absorbed into the National Church. It is almost certain that the drop in numbers attending the Water Street Presbyterian/Independent Chapel in Dursley was caused by change of allegiance to the enthusiastic Calvanistic Methodist society and increasing numbers made the erection of a chapel both desirable and necessary.

The first Tabernacle was built, probably between May and September 1760 on land opposite the present Tabernacle. The plot, forty-four feet by thirty-five feet had been part of an orchard belonging to the Danford family and from whom it was rented by Samuel Griffin, a Dursley baker. It fronted the present Kingshill Road and was separated from the 'Parsonage House' or Rectory, today 100, Kingshill Road, by a path leading towards Stinchcombe Hill, called Parsonage Lane, now non-existent.[18]

On 28 December 1764, the responsibility for the land and buildings was vested by Samuel Griffin, in the following Trustees.[19]

> Rev. George Whitefield, Chaplain to the Rt. Hon. Countess of Huntingdon, Clerk.
> Stanley Middleton, City of London, Preacher of the Gospel.
> Thomas Adams, Rodborough, Preacher of the Gospel) (all leaders
> William Hogg, Painswick, Butcher) of Rodborough
> John Croome, Rodborough, Broadweaver) Connexion)
> William Vines, Randwick, Yeoman)
> John Dando, Dursley, Hat maker
> John Shatford, Alkington, Berkeley, Yeoman
> Christopher Brown, Dursley, Cordwainer
> James Derrett, Stancombe, Broadweaver
> William King, Dursley, Cardmaker

Three of the trust conditions were

1. That the building should only be used for the word of God and by 'people who profess themselves to be of Calvanistic Principles in connection with the said George Whitefield according to the doctrines contained in the Articles of the Established Church and who are commonly called Methodists'
2. that before anything could be altered, the agreement of a majority of society members had to be obtained.
3. that the Trustees were not liable for costs. If the society did not pay all necessary expenses, the trustees were entitled to sell up and dispose of the money as they thought fit to public charity.

In November 1780 William Danford, Junior, Yeoman of Dursley, sold for £3 8*s* 0*d* the land on which the Old Tabernacle stood to the members of the Society who worshipped there — land that up to that point they had paid a rent of a pepper corn, if demanded.[20]

We are lucky to have an idea of what the old Tabernacle was like — at least in its later days — because of the initiative in 1864 of the then Church Secretary Alfred Bloodworth. Interested in the beginning of Sunday School work in the church he interviewed as many of the old church members as had memories of years before about 1820 and noted in detail much of what they told him. One described the Old Tabernacle as he remembered it in the late 1780s when he was a child.

> The building was rather lofty. The ceiling close to the roof all over. It would accommodate about 400. The galleries three sides of the square. Singing

> gallery over doorway, the main entrance fronting the road — there being but one other entrance which was to the end, almost, of the right side of the building by which the minister usually entered. The pulpit faced the singing gallery and on the railing to the stairs leading thereto, placed in a position that all the people might see, was the inscription 'He that hath ears to hear, let him hear' and on a board fitted to the gallery so that the preacher might see it was the following 'His blood will I require of the watchman's hand'. The main entrance was reached by means of a flight of steps. (Probably the steps that still exist, 1980, leading up to the old burial ground). There was no vestry — no room nor building of any kind attached to it.[21]

No other details of the building remain but for Chippenham Tabernacle there exist plans and a reconstruction of this meeting house is shown below. Admittedly Chippenham's Tabernacle was erected ten years later than Dursley's but the general appearance was possibly similar except for the door which in Dursley was in the long wall. As with Dursley, Messrs. Whitefield, Croom, Vines and Hogg were among its trustees.[22]

Portsea's Tabernacle built in 1754, six years before Dursley's, was not floored or plastered and had no ceiling whereas Chippenham had all three, the floor being 'square bricks.' Dursley Tabernacle had a ceiling but possibly no floor — no signs of flooring, brick or otherwise exist now. At

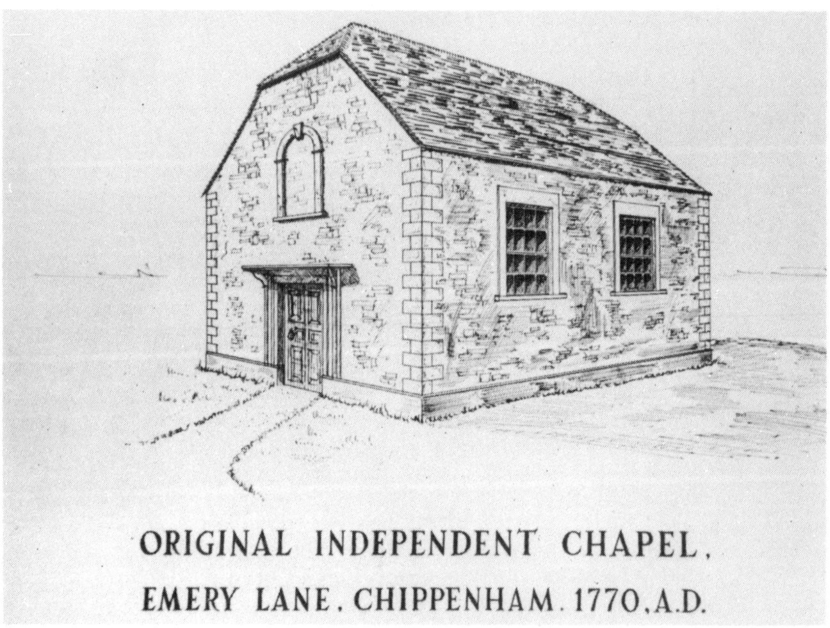

Chippenham's first Tabernacle reconstructed from its plans. Dursley's first Tabernacle probably had the same simple compact appearance, though with the door in the long wall.

(Artist Peter Freeman)

The site of the first Tabernacle in Dursley. It was very close to the Rectory, seen here top right, which until the mid nineteenth century extended down the right hand side of the site.
(Photo. David E. Evans)

least nine burials took place in the old Tabernacle, all between 1776 and 1790. Eighty-one year old bootmaker, George Hill, speaking in 1864 recollected the funeral

> 'of a good man who died at the bottom of Long Street. He was buried in the Old Tabernacle on a Sunday evening in winter — the procession guided by the light of (flaming) torches to the Tabernacle where the coffin was put in front of the pulpit and remained there during the service — after which buried . . .'[23]

Records of Bristol's Pen Street Tabernacle describe the lighting for services in winter evenings — tin candle holders hung on nails driven into pillars. The holders had tin backs for safety and held tallow candles called dips which guttered and had to be snuffed and perhaps relit while the service proceeded.[24] At Hanham Tabernacle it is recorded that it was not unusual to see old men in the congregation with their heads covered with handkerchiefs. These not only gave protection from draughts but also from falling candle grease.[25]

One curious point about Dursley's burials is that the earliest known (some tomb stones are blank) is of a person not of the town. This was William Mandrell, cardmaker of Chippenham who died 10 December 1776. Possibly he had settled recently in Dursley and had been a prominent member of the Chippenham Tabernacle — or maybe he was refused burial in St. James's Churchyard. In 1792 the members of the old Tabernacle leased land on the opposite of the road for a burial ground. This measured 'seventy-nine feet along the turnpike road' and is roughly half the present burial ground. The land was part of a field called eight acres and was leased from Robert Harris, Gentleman, for 1000 years at one shilling per year to be paid on the Feast of St. John the Baptist beginning in 1793.[26]

The list of those who signed the agreement on behalf of the Tabernacle Society makes interesting reading as it gives an idea of the sort of person who was prominent in the society at this time. The comments in brackets give additional information.

Rev. Rowland Hill (Wotton-under-Edge)
William Hogg } (Rodborough Connexion
William Vines } preachers)
William King, card maker, Dursley
James Derrett, broadweaver, Stancombe
Nathaniel Lloyd the elder, clothier, Uley, and his son, also Nathaniel (Owner of Upper Cam cloth mill, Angeston workshops and, later, Dauncey's cloth mill, Uley)
Stephen Dando, hat maker, Dursley, (son of John)
Thomas Parsons, yeoman, North Nibley
James Morgan, pig killer, Dursley
Thomas Gethen, card maker, Dursley
John Rugg, dyer, Wotton-under-Edge
Nathaniel Rudder, card maker, Dursley
Richard Trotman, baker, Dursley
Thomas Trotman, his son
Thomas Morgan, peruke (wig) maker, Dursley
George Harris, clothier, Uley (Related to Robert Harris, lessee, and his successor to extensive property in Dursley)
Orlando Harris, son of George
Edward Jackson the younger, clothier, Uley (Jacksons Mill)
John Cook, yeoman, North Nibley
Abraham Parsons, yeoman, Stinchcombe
Marmaduke Cox, broadweaver, Stinchcombe
Nicholas Underwood, blacksmith, Dursley
John Ford, kersey weaver, Dursley
William Marsh, yeoman, Lorridge Farm, Leonard Stanley
John Trotman, cardboard maker, Dursley
Adrian Newth, card maker, Dursley
Samuel Newth, cloth maker, Dursley
Charles Clark, peruke maker, Dursley

The old Tabernacle was pulled down in about 1810 and in this open space, more interments were made until the ground was closed in about 1855.[27]

Seating arrangements in the old building are unknown. However at Rodborough Tabernacle benches were used, men sitting on one side of the pulpit — as in Dursley opposite the main door — women on the other;[28] it was not until the 1790s that the Rodborough building was pewed. It was almost certainly the same in Dursley, the random pattern of stone burial slabs gives no indication of having to take into account fixed seats or pews. Even in the new Tabernacle, erected in 1808, ground floor seating was at first largely of benches. Of services and service times, again we have no direct information and can only surmise. It has been stated already that Methodist society meetings were not designed to be a counter attraction to Anglican services and it is likely that Dursley followed the pattern of Rodborough. For many years its Sunday gatherings were held at 8 a.m. and 5 p.m.[29] Many folk came to Dursley from considerable distances, Uley, North Nibley and Berkeley for example, and while walking or riding on horseback could have been very pleasant early on a Summer's morning, it must as today have been very different in Winter. Probably services in the newly erected old Tabernacle were based on the Anglican pattern as is known to have been the case in other of Whitefield's Calvanistic Methodist Chapels. Here the liturgy of the Church of England was read but hymns with a strong evangelical basis were substituted for psalms. Sermons were more dramatic than the Anglican equivalent and the congregation expected some extempore prayers and exhortations.[30]

One great problem was the administering of the sacraments. From time to time ordained Anglican ministers visited the Dursley society but so far as is known, not frequently. It was a problem which affected the Weslyan Methodists as well and it is known that many of their early societies after meeting together, went forth as a body to the Parish Church for morning prayer and holy communion — and nor is this surprising as they considered themselves part of that Church. At Bradford-on-Avon the practice continued until 1810.[31] Possibly many of Dursley's Calvanistic Methodists did the same at first, but the situation changed when the preachers that served it began to accept non-episcopal ordination. This seems to have become general policy in 1771. Howell Harris writing in December of that year said 'I find Mr. Whitefield's people have agreed on an Association among themselves and to get Independent Ordination with reading some of the church prayers with extempore. The door seems open for all to leave the Established Church and to form themselves into Independent Churches over the kingdom' — which is what eventually happened.[32]

It is significant that the baptismal register of Dursley Tabernacle dates as a careful record from this time. Before this there are only four entries — all, it would seem, entered in 1771 long after the events:-

5 August 1754	Suzanna, daughter of John and Suzanna Dando, baptised by Rev. Mr. Edwards
25June 1760	Stephen Dando, by Mr. Whitefield (sic)
22June 1761	Mary, daughter of James and Billa Griffin by Mr Whitefield

4 May 1767 Richard, son of Marmaduke and Mary Cox, by Mr. Shepperd

From May 1771 until March 1795, 222 baptisms are recorded as being performed by twenty different people, some of them identifiable as ministers of non-Anglican congregations at Rodborough, Wotton-under-Edge and Frampton-on-Severn. 1771 then was a watershed in the history of the Tabernacle. From its beginning and while George Whitefield was alive, its members were, at least nominally, members of the Established Church — baptisms, burials, Holy Communion, all performed by its clergy. John Dando's daughter Sarah was baptised in St. James' Church in 1748. A year after Whitefield's death in September 1770 the Tabernacle Society was free of that tie. A study of Tabernacle baptismal records show that from two performed in 1771 the number reached a peak of twenty-three in 1776, Anglican baptisms at St. James's Church showing an overall decline from fifty-six to thirty-five in the same years. It is not known whether this rise came about through a rapid increase in adherents or through increased confidence in non-Anglican baptism. Whichever it was, it is obvious that the Tabernacle was becoming a place of increasing standing in the community.

In the Spring of 1769, George Whitefield left London for Bath and, accompanied by the Countess of Huntingdon for much of the time, made an extended tour of the area — Bristol, Bradford-on-Avon, Frome, Chippenham, Castle Combe, Dursley, Rodborough, Gloucester, Cheltenham . . .

By now he was a very sick man, travelling by four wheeled carriage and at times barely able to preach. It was the last time he visited Dursley. Probably he preached in the old Tabernacle and out in the open air, using a Bible the Church has still. Of this tour he said 'Never were there places so endeared to me as at this last visit. Old friends, old gospel wine and the Great Governor ordering to fill to the brim'. In a letter to Torial Joss he wrote 'Ebeneezer! Ebeneezer! Through infinite mercy I just now arrived here (Rodborough, 11 May). Blessed seasons at Chippenham, Castle Combe and Dursley . . . It is good to go into the highways and hedges. Field preaching, field preaching for ever.'[33]

It is likely that the Countess of Huntingdon came with Whitefield to Dursley in this May and that this therefore was the time when she took tea with the wife of William King, best known for the Sunday School we will return to later.[34] The Countess had toured Gloucestershire on several occasions and took a continuing interest in Mr. Whitefield's Societies' after he died in 1770. In 1771 she sent John Hawksworth, one of her itinerant preachers, to visit some societies in the country and from that occasion two letters survive — both to the Countess.[35]

"Near Dursley Nov. 19 (1771)
Glo'shire

The chair and Bible believed to have been used by George Whitefield during his visit to Dursley in 1769

Dear and Much Honoured Madam,

The very great kindness received from your Lady'sp in getting me the happiness of dear Mr. Hawksworth's company into Glouctershire, I now gladly acknowledge with my many thanks for so great a favour. Blessed be our God that his journey has not been in vain. He tells me himself that his heart has been very much enlarged and all that have heard him bless God for the visit that he has made into these parts.

According to your Ladyships orders I have spoken to a Hatter who has sent his terms in letter by Mr. Hawksworth. I shall also this evening speak to a clothier who shall also write you his terms as I believe them both to be real Xtians. I hope there is no reason to doubt but you will have Xtian treatment from them both.

In less than three weeks time from hence our New Tabernacle in Gloucestershire is to be open'd (at Wotton under Edge) I think after that with your Ladyships permission to wait upon you once more into Wales and shall then be thankful to yr Ladyship for your further advice and assistance in my present domestic trials. O that all things may be conducted in such a manner as may fully end in the Glory of God. My many trials fill me with fears. O that I may be supported and directed for the best. I at present write in company with dear Mr. Hawksworth in a farm house. Have to ride some miles this eve and to preach so that I am in haste to conclude with assuring you that I am for your many favours yr Ladyships.

Rd, Hill

Dursley Nov 17th 1771

Most Excellent Lady,

At the request of dear Mr. Hill I have sent you the prises of Hatts both Retaile and wholesale a Hat we sell for 6 shillings Retale we sell for 5 wholesale and so on a half guinea Hat Retale we sell for 9 shillings wholesale, and sell as few wholesale as what we call a paper which is 3 so may have 3: 6: 9 or a dosen or Dosens of what sort you please. We dont in common Button and loop them in the wholesale way, but shall not stand with you as they are for such purposes. Shall think it my Duty and Intress to go on the Best and lowes Terms possable I can.

Mr. Hawksworth have been greatly Blest among us and have been much Intreated by our friends to come againe but he says he is not his own. Therefore we Intreat your Ladyship to let him now and then to take a Round amongst us. — here seems to be a great revival thousands flock after the Bread of life beside fresh places all Round our nabourhood that is set out for Zion with their faces thitherward — beside the great and wonderfull work at Wootenunderedge chiefly by the Blessd Instrumenttalety of dear Mr Hill must conclude your Ladyships unworthy servant

Jn̊ Dando

I am also Desired by our christian Frends in the late dear Mr Whitefields Connecttions in these partts to send you our kindest thanks for this visit which you was pleased to suffer Mr Hawksworth to make us praying all your

Ladyships undertakings for the Gospel may meet with many Blessings from our Lord.

If your Ladyship have any Orders please to Direct to John Dando Hattmaker In Dursley Gloucestershire."

John Dando's hat shop was halfway down Parsonage Street, close to the site of the old Bell and Castle. Quite obviously the Tabernacle in Dursley was flourishing when he wrote. Apart from the contagious enthusiasm of George Whitefield's spiritual heirs there is possibly one other reason why this was so. Because of the way the Tabernacle society, and the Rodborough Connexion as a whole, operated, men from all walks of life probably had a chance to take part in the total responsibility for the running of its affairs, and in so doing found themselves to be of great value to the community — which was likely to have been a revelation, at least to the humble working man. In this it would have differed from the Anglican church with its hierachial structure and diocesan framework. In later years, many an ordinary man gained high position following responsibilities undertaken in the local chapel.

The Revd Rowland Hill 1744–1833

Among the preachers serving Dursley Tabernacle at this time was the Revd. Rowland Hill.[36] A son of a Baronet, he was once called by the Countess of Huntingdon a 'second Whitefield'. When about twenty-two he met George Whitefield, was greatly influenced by him and became an itinerating preacher. In the summer of 1771 he found himself in Gloucestershire and preached at Stroud, Painswick, Rodborough, and on Sunday June 16th to a great crowd in Dursley. A few months later, in December, he opened his Tabernacle in Wotton-under-Edge.

In 1773 he was ordained deacon in the Anglican Church by the Bishop of Bath and Wells, but could go no further, being refused priest's ordination by no less than six bishops because of his religious enthusiasm. He set up house in Wotton and for many years spent the summer months in the town. The rest of the year he itinerated or preached in London. Like George Whitefield, he was an energetic man, travelling great distances, preaching continuously — he is said to have delivered 23,000 sermons — an average of 350 a year. There are many records of his visits to Dursley in his diary and in the Dursley Tabernacle baptismal registers. When in Dursley for any length of time — up to six weeks is recorded – he stayed with John Dando. John and his wife entertained many of the visiting ministers and it was said that 'this house was ever open — and might with all propriety be called the preachers home'. John died after 'patience under suffering' in 1775 aged sixty-six, his wife in 1791.

Hill's Sunday services at Wotton-under-Edge, and at Dursley, often closed in the following way:-

> Tomorrow evening meet Society . . . Anybody here from Nibley? (nod of assent) Tell them I shall preach there Tuesday, Wednesday preach here, Thursday Wickwar, Friday Uley, Saturday, must have some rest, Sunday here again — God willing.

Rest probably included gardening as he was a keen gardener growing flowers and fruits, including strawberries, at Wotton-under-Edge. Much he gave away to the sick and aged, some of whom lived in the almshouses he had built at the bottom of his garden. Sometime after the death of William Hogg in late 1800, Rowland Hill became superintendent of the Rodborough Connexion. By then nearly all of its constituent churches had settled ministers but they seemed to have remained in close fellowship. As late as 1825 Benjamin Rees of Chippenham Tabernacle made the fifty mile round trip in March weather over the top of the Cotswolds, to preach and baptize in Dursley during an inter-pastorate period. As superintendent, Hill had the job of recommending and approving ministers though his advice was not always heeded.[37]

Rowland Hill was strongly Calvanistic in outlook and Alfred Bloodworth in 1865 wrote of him that 'he used to preach at Nibley occasionally and there and elsewhere some people speak of the harsh language he used against Weslyanism — viz — Arminianism. . . . So there was at that time a certain "sound" here and in the neighbourhood.'

One passion, which developed from his friendship with Dr. Jenner of Berkeley, was vaccination against the scourge of small pox. From its acceptance as a method of prevention in 1804 he often announced after preaching 'I am ready to vaccinate tomorrow morning as many children as you choose and if you wish them to escape that horrible disease, the small pox, you will bring them'. He is credited with vaccinating 10,000 people — doubtless not a few in Dursley — and with practically wiping out the disease in the area of Wotton-under-Edge.

Assistant to Rowland Hill in Gloucestershire, and often heard in Dursley, was sea captain Torial Joss, dubbed by his detractors, 'Captain Crazy'. In 1772 Joss wrote

> 'I have been cruising in the latitude of Gloucestershire for fourteen days and have met with some pretty smart engagements at Wotton, Dursley, and Rodborough in particular. Last night at Frampton, we had one shot fired at us which struck Brother Glover between wind and water; he careened and stopped his leak, and we presently silenced the enemy. . . .'[38]

It is interesting to try to visualise the reactions of his country hearers — most of whom had probably never seen the sea, if he preached in this manner! As Joss shows, in the years following the 1740s opposition to Methodists had not ceased. Partly this came from some of the Anglican clergy who were witnessing, in the late eighteenth century, a great and unwelcome increase in dissenting places of worship under the continuing influence of the Evangelical Revival.

Joss's comments show that Dursley's Calvanistic Methodists were not leading an unruffled existence. More evidence for this came from George Hill, bootmaker, who, at the age of eighty-one in 1864, recounted a tale of persecution. His parents had been members of the old Tabernacle. His father, a singer, had told him of the tyranny of 'Madam Webster'. This happened it seems in the 1780s.[39] Madame Webster was the wife of Archdeacon Webster, rector of Dursley 1774-1804, and as such lived in the old Rectory, now 100 Kingshill Road, very close to the old Tabernacle. Her hostility to the members of the society that met there for worship was so great that she set about making life as difficult and unpleasant as possible. On one occasion she had a deep trench dug along one wall of the Tabernacle in order to weaken it but was forced to fill it in.

> 'She then planted trees to hide the Tabernacle and darken it — these however, died with one exception and that did but little harm. On one occasion she employed a farmer, Hunt, to break up a meeting held outside the Tabernacle by sending his noisy dogs through and through the crowd. . . , Madame Webster watching with high glee from a window of the rectory. . . .'

Possibly Mme. Webster was just exasperated by so much Sunday and week-night evangelical fervour within a few yards of her windows, but it is more likely that she had been influenced in her attitude by her uncle Bishop

Warburton, between whom and her husband 'there seems to have been much affectionate intercourse'.[40] William Warburton, Bishop of Gloucester 1760-1779 had a very low opinion of Methodists. Of George Whitefield he once wrote '. . . he appears to be as mad as ever George Fox the Quaker was. . .' while Wesley was ranked among 'overheated bigots' and 'idle fanatics'. He knew, and not surprisingly contended with, the Countess of Huntingdon.[41] Of immediate interest is Warburton's attitude to the Rev. John Andrews LL.B who became associated with the Countess and preached for her. Subject to ill health he had been given the living of Stinchcombe, before Warburton's preferment to the See of Gloucester, and here, because the income was small, £36 p.a., he was required to preach only once each Sunday. When itinerating for the Countess — generally a month at a time — she provided a curate to stand in for him.

John Andrews's enthusiasm annoyed his new bishop.

March 1763

Mr. Andrews,

I have received several complaints of you. . . . I shall insist upon your constant residence in your parish, not so much from the good you are likely to do there as to prevent the mischief you may do by rambling about in other places.

Your Bishop and (though your fanatic conduct has almost made me ashamed to own it). Your Patron

W. Gloucester[42]

The Countess interceded with the bishop on Andrews's behalf but received short shrift and eventually he transferred to Kent. Perhaps some of the bishop's anti-Methodist sentiment was passed on to Mme. Webster.

Stinchcombe at this time must have been a lively village. In 1767 the Rev. Henry Venn, an Anglican who also itinerated for the Countess, preached at Stinchcombe for John Andrews while on his way from Bath to Trevecca College.[43] In 1767 too John Brown, wire drawer, registered his house as a meeting place for dissenters. A Mrs. Brown, perhaps his wife 'used to exhort the people every Sunday evening in the Parsonage house and. . . with very great power'[44] Another source suggests she was the wife of a farmer who after her daily work in the dairy 'used to preach the cross under the brow of the hill. . . .'[45]

Rowland Hill in his letter of 1771, quoted earlier, stated that he was staying at a farm house near Dursley. This must have been Sheephouse Farm between Dursley and Uley. In the 1760s it was occupied by a family called Parsons, whose sons attended Uley Parish Church. They went to listen to George Whitefield when he preached in Dursley in 1769 and were electrified.

Confessing their faith and declaring themselves on the Lord's side, they became members of Dursley Tabernacle, and in a short time had the

Sheephouse Farm near Dursley, home at one time of the Parsons family. Uley and its parish Church are top left. *(Photo. David E. Evans)*

> happiness of bringing their aged father to a knowledge of the truth. Sheephouse Farm was now thrown open in hospitality to the preachers who travelled through the district; meetings for prayer and praise were held under its roof; and the valley often resounded with the psalms and hymns and spiritual songs of joyful believers.[46]

One venerable minister, Matthew Wilks later stated that sleeping at the farm 'made a great impression on his mind, because of the large quantity of apples with which the rooms were stored.'[47]

Another family of like godly character were living at the time at Holts Farm, in the parish of Berkeley. These were the Shatfords, who 'were accustomed to cross Stinchcombe Hill every Sunday to worship in Dursley Tabernacle and listen to the glorious gospel as preached by Captain Torial Joss, Sir Richard Hill (brother of Rowland) Butcher Hogg and others. There the Parsons met them and in their only daughter, Anna, Thomas Parsons, when nearly forty years of age, found a good wife (about 1790). They settled in the village of Nibley. . . at the end of the green, on the way to Wickwar.'[48]

Apart from showing that a Calvanistic Methodist meeting house could be a romantic place these passages again indicate the wide territorial influence of the Tabernacle in this period.

The story of the Parsons of North Nibley has an interesting outcome.

Thomas and Anna had eight children — the youngest Benjamin was born February 1797 and baptized in the old Tabernacle. His father died when he was six. Much later he recalled:-[49]

> My mother had been very much troubled about my want of education, and one morning she had risen very early, and spent a large portion of time in praying that God would produce for me in this respect, and before eight o'clock two young gentlemen came to the door — the one a lawyer's clerk at Mr. Vizard's of Dursley, the other a medical assistant of Dr. Fry's of the same town — and told her they should be happy to pay for my education at the Parsonage School.

This school was run by the then Tabernacle minister, the Rev. William Bennett.

Benjamin Parsons then went to Wotton-under-Edge where Rowland Hill 'introduced me to the Black School' — so called presumably because each pupil wore a 'black gown and trencher cap' — now Kathrine Lady Berkeley's School. Eventually he became an apprentice tailor in Frampton-on-Severn, and a Sunday School teacher in the Tabernacle there, moved to Stroud, joined Rodborough Tabernacle, was persuaded to enter Cheshunt College and became minister of the Countess of Huntingdon's Chapel at Ebley. There he became one of the most respected and influential ministers in the area. So much so that he became known as the 'brave bishop of Ebley.' His pastorate witnessed the collapse of the wool trade and the tremendous deprivation that this brought on the cloth workers in the 'hungry forties' and he was at the forefront in attempts to relieve this.

> We have heard it said that upon the occasion of the (1839 Chartist) riots under Frost, Williams and Jones in Monmouthshire, it was proposed by the leaders to sweep through the Stroud Valley and try to rouse the artisan and factory hands there. But it was said 'No! it was of no use; Parsons has educated them! If we do so, he is sure to come to out and speak to the people, and they'll follow him and not us.[50]

Two other Tabernacle men of the period became ministers of religion — Joseph Surman and Richard Stiff.

London born Joseph Surman at some time in early life moved to Gloucestershire and became a regular attender at Dursley Tabernacle. His earnestness was noticed by another of the Evangelical Revival's great men, Cornelius Winter, who often preached in Dursley in the 1770s.[51] Winter, having been influenced by George Whitefield, joined him and was at his death in America in 1770. He returned to England and in about 1776 took charge of the Rodborough Connexion's Wiltshire meeting houses at Castle Combe, Chippenham and Christian Malford. He was ordained in 1777 as a Non-conformist minister at the suggestion of the Rev. Rowland Hill. In 1778 he moved to Marlborough.

Winter, 'that celestial creature' (Bishop Jebb) was greatly concerned at the lack of village preachers and it is said that it was through meeting

Joseph Surman that he conceived the idea of starting his own academy to train such men. Surman, in 1782, was his first student. In 1788, Winter, his family and academy, which acquired a considerable reputation, moved to Painswick where he took charge of a long established Independent Church and where he died in 1808. Joseph Surman was ordained in 1786 and his sole pastorate, twenty-six years, was at Chesham, Buckinghamshire, where he was said to have been 'a very acceptable and useful minister.'[52]

Richard Stiff is believed to have been a nephew of Jacob Stiff, cardboard maker and builder of the house near Dursley Market Place which still bears the date 1751 and the initials of himself and his wife.[53] Richard seems to have attended Dursley Tabernacle. The trade he followed is unknown but early in life it took him across the River Severn.

> It was in the year 1783 that Mr Stiff came to reside in the neighbourhood of Blakeney. He found this part of the Forest in an awful state of moral darkness, and destitute of the Gospel.
> Moved with concern for the salvation of his fellow immortals, he did all he could to introduce the Gospel among them. At first having no place of worship within his reach where he could hear the Word of Life, he went on the Lord's Day with his family to some sequestered spot in the Forest, where they took their station under one of the trees for the purpose of reading the Word of God. This novel practice soon attracted some of his neighbours, whose curiosity led them to watch his movements most narrowly. At first they looked on at a distance, being afraid of approaching too near saying he was one of the false prophets.

This was a beginning and soon, Sunday by Sunday, Stiff was walking many miles through the forest, often preaching three times a day. Like fellow preachers he visited the Forest folk —

> Sometimes, perhaps he preached in a poor hut, with a stone to stand on and a three legged stool for (a) desk, surrounded with thirty or forty. . . smutty neighbours.

A man of lively, devotional talent he returned to Dursley after nearly thirty years in the Forest. He died in 1815, aged seventy-two and was buried in the Tabernacle burial ground.[54]

Thomas Adams should be honoured for founding the Society which gave rise to Dursley Tabernacle, and John Dando for bringing it into the town. William King's great contribution to the Society was wisdom and foresight in beginning Sunday School work. King's was not the first such school but it existed before the Sunday School movement got under way and it has the longest history of any in the town, over two hundred years.

William King was born in about 1830.[55] He joined Dursley's Calvanistic Methodists while a young man and quickly became a person of importance. He was still only about thirty in 1760 when he signed the document registering the newly erected Tabernacle. He was a card maker by trade — one who produced wire 'brushes' used in the wool trade and he

William King. (From 'Robert Raikes and his Work' J. Henry Harris c. 1890.)

employed a number of workers. His house and workshops were in Woodmancote — approximately where number twenty-one is now. He seems to have been a short man with a rather large head. His nose was prominent and because of a 'little prominence' on each side of it, he got the nickname of 'King with three noses'.

It has been said that in his day Dursley was a place where 'men, women and children rambled in the woods and fields' and where 'dog fighting, badger baiting, ball or marble games' and drunkeness filled Sunday for the ordinary person — at least for those not working for 'buying and selling were commonly practiced on the sabbath. . . . Ethical and religious teaching were equally conspicuous by their absence'.

William was kindly, caring, a man of great generosity of spirit.

> Mr. King was a prison philanthopist of the most zealous and genuine character. Poor creatures were condemned and hanged. . . for trifling offences. He visited the condemned prisoners in that horrible den the old Gloucester Castle. . . (He) was in the habit of leaving his house at great personal inconvenience and visiting the condemned. . . in their miserable holes, stopping with them during the last night of their earthly existence, affectionately exhorting them and reading and praying to them. . .

Probably he also visited the debtors in the same prison. John Howard reported in 1776 he had found that debtors half naked and near starvation had been helped by the benevolence of several gentlemen.[56] Maybe King was among these. Debtors had to fend for themselves over food and other items and the 'miserable wretches were sometimes starved to death, and all day long let down boxes and bowls from the grated windows and whined for 'pity on the poor debtors'.[57] To do this visiting King sometimes rode, but often walked the thirty miles from Dursley to Gloucester and back. Such was his work among prisoners that it has been suggested that he ranks with John Howard and Sir Onesiphorous Paul in the cause of prison reform and deserves the title of 'the Howard of Dursley'. Quite why he took up this arduous and time consuming interest is not known, though it is probable that it was brought about by his son William. This young man was 'a great grief' to his father. He was a poacher and drunkard, and 'old Lord Berkeley sent him to Gloucester Gaol thirteen times for poaching on Cam Peak.' It is reasonable to think that William, senior, went to see his erring son in prison and there was appalled by the callous, inhuman conditions endured by the inmates.

William King's visits to the condemned were made before the county goal was rebuilt by Sir Onesiphorous Paul in the early 1790s. Although from thirty years after this, an account of the public execution at the new prison in 1821 is of interest as it concerns two local people. Actually three were hanged, in front of 'an immense concourse of spectators' using 'the drop' over the gaol lodge. Joseph Ford, twenty-eight of Coaley (who had a wife and four children) and John Badcock, twenty-two, single, of Birmingham were convicted for two offences of horse stealing. John Baker sixteen, of Wotton-under-Edge, considered a hardened thief of over two years activity, was convicted of breaking into a house and stealing thirteen handkerchiefs, a shirt, and other wearing apparel.

On the way to the gallows Baker read a psalm.

> 'When they were tied up to the fatal beam, Baker made a short address to the populace exhorting them to avoid the evil ways which had brought him and his fellow sufferers to an untimely end. He then recited part of a psalm and a hymn after which he gave the signal by dropping a handkerchief and they were instantly turned off. After being suspended the usual time their bodies were cut down and delivered to their respective friends for interrment.'[58]

William King must have witnessed such scenes, and grieved. Robert Raikes was also a prison visitor and it is possible that the two men came to know each other in this way. Raikes and King became friends on Christian name terms and Raikes often visited his friend at his home in Dursley. William King's concern for the well being of young people led him to open a school in his house — a Sunday School. The manner of its founding is said to have been as follows.

William King and Rowland Hill were acquainted. On one occasion King visited Hill, presumably in Wotton-under-Edge, on a Sunday and on the way saw men playing football. That men could so waste the sabbath saddened King and on his return to Dursley he consulted his works manager, Adrian Newth, as to what could be done. They decided to invite all the workmen to the workrooms the following Sunday 'for the purpose of enjoying a dish of tea', which at that period was considered a great luxury. After tea he addressed them in these quaint words:-

> I invited you to come and take something good for your bodies and you are all here. Next Sabbath I want you to come and bring your children and I will give them something for their souls.

Quite when this happened is unknown but has been narrowed to the period 1775-8.

William King brought his school to the notice of Raikes in the course of conversation in the following way, according to one of William's daughters — Mrs. M. Oldland.

> My honoured father. . . , being in business at Painswick on a Saturday, was informed that two men were to suffer death at Gloucester and, instead of returning home to Dursley, his strong feelings for them led him to resolve to go to Gloucester to see if he could go and converse with them, intending to spend the night with them if permitted, but the keeper of the prison thought it not proper as they were desperate characters. He abode in Gloucester and on the sabbath hour called on Mr. Raikes and both walked together. . . to where were many boys at different sports. My father said, 'What a pity the sabbath should be so desecrated.' Mr. Raikes asked, 'How is it to be altered?' 'Sir, open a Sunday School; I have opened one at Dursley with the help of a faithful journeyman, but the multitude of business prevents me from taking so much time in it as I could wish as I feel I want rest'.

The date of the encounter was about March 1781 according to a writer in 1883 who claimed to have found in the Sherriffs' records of this date, a note of the execution of 2 desperate men, members of a gang who 'had long infested the country.' This double hanging was the only one in a long period of time.

Mrs. Oldland's account continued —

> 'Mr. Raikes replied "It will not do for Dissenters." Then my father answered, "Then why not the Church do it?" Mr. Raikes named this to a clergyman of the name of Stock who paid a person to teach a few.'

In the oft fought battles in the nineteenth century between Anglicans and Dissenters as to which party could claim the honour of 'inventing' Sunday

Schools, this passage and William King's name were frequently used to support the Dissenters' case. It is clear, however, that King's was not the first Sunday School, and it is unlikely that it was only from King's suggestion that Raikes developed the idea of the Sunday School movement. There were other schools in the county and as a newspaper proprietor it is more than conceivable that he knew of these. Be this as it may, this should not detract from King's achievement in establishing an isolated school before the Sunday School movement got under way nationally, a school that was to bear such fruit in Dursley. He once met the woman Raikes persuaded to begin a school in Gloucester and gave her a suitable lesson book.

The creation by King of the Sunday School was a subject which in later years he refused to discuss, even with his relatives, and it is for this reason that little definite is known of its early years. His reluctance to talk on the subject seems to have stemmed from concern that he might bring discredit on the school as he, himself suffered the disgrace of imprisonment in later life.

William was an open handed man and so honest that the expression 'As honest as William King' was a local saying. The story is told of how on one occasion he heard that a local farmer had lost corn and barn in a disastrous fire. He called to sympathize, was welcomed with refreshment and after he had left, the farmer's wife found several gold guineas under his plate. That he was admired and well thought of in the town is obvious from the fact that in 1778 he was elected Bailiff of Dursley by its prominent citizens — an honour in itself, the more so as he was a staunch member of a society which had separated itself from the Parish Church. The cloak and wig he wore for his year's term of office existed until at least 1880. William's granddaughter, writing in 1880, gave more evidence of the esteem in which he was held. On one occasion a 'mob drew Mr. Whitefield's carriage in the Broadwell at Dursley and took his horses out. . . . My grandfather hastened to read the Riot Act but had no occasion to take it out of his pocket for directly they saw him, the man that got him (Whitefield) in, went armpit deep into the water and drew him out, asking my grandfather's forgiveness.'

There may be exageration over the depth of water in the Broadwell (though a little further down Water Street there was at the time a considerable mill pond feeding Howard's Upper Mill, now owned by R.A. Lister & Co. Ltd.) and it was more likely to have been Rowland Hill or his brother Sir Richard Hill and not George Whitefield, but the point is made. By 'principal inhabitant' and working man, William King was highly regarded. His imprisonment seems to have come about through no fault, but through absolute integrity and caused great indignation in the town. Details are unknown except that a woman in Bristol was involved. How long he was in the Debtors' prison is also unknown, but after his release he retired from public life, broken in spirit and health. Even the new prison at Gloucester was a grim place. Although, constructed on lines

'The Boy' statue inscribed with William King's name. *(Essex Church, Kensington, Unitarian Congregation)*

suggested by John Howard, it must have been terrible, though far better than its predeccessor. Debtors still paid for their food, which was brought in for them by a messenger who was not always above being dishonest. Most had single cells, which were usually clean, but the debtors themselves were frequently described as dirty and untidy as were the day rooms where they had to prepare and cook in their own utensils over a cast iron ship's stove. Unless incapable, they had to work to keep themselves, retaining one third of the proceeds of their labours if they worked in the 'ward of industry.'[59] It is not hard to imagine the effect such a confinement would have on a sensitive mind like William's, even if for only a short time.

William King died on 8 December 1803 aged seventy-three and was buried in the old Tabernacle. His death was caused by infection of a wound or 'mortification' resulting from a splinter of wood running into his hand.

In 1880 a memorial to pioneers of Sunday school work was erected outside Essex Street Unitarian Chapel, London, and among the twelve names on it was that of William King. The monument, in white marble with a red granite pedestal, came to be known as 'The Boy' from the figure surmounting it. It was transferred to The Mall, Kensington, in 1887 where it stood until recently, when, in being moved to allow development, it disintegrated.

William, and Anna his wife, had a large family. Mrs. Oldland who began the first Sunday School in Tewkesbury, in Old Baptist Yard, and n'ere do well William, have been mentioned already. Another son was John — a steady lad and a good musician. One of John's delights was to go down to the water powered 'grice' or flour mill at the bottom of Long Street, to hear a journeyman miller play an organ. This musical instrument, which John was allowed to practice on, had an interesting history. William Hopkins, the journeyman, barely able to read or write, became interested in music

> 'and fancying himself capable of making a violin, he set about and soon finished one in a complete manner, without any assistance whatever; and when finished he quickly learned to play on it without help of any living instructor. Shortly afterwards he began and finished a bass viol without assistance, which instrument he soon learned to play on in the like manner. Elated by this success, he began to build a chamber organ in his master's mill and, wonderful to relate, after a long process, and wholly unassisted, he brought it to perfection; and by a most curious invention he so contrived that the great water wheel of the mill, whilst performing its ordinary function, should also work the bellows of the organ, and at the same time turn a spit with meat on it, roasting before the kitchen fire; and this too at the identical time that he (self taught) was playing sacred music on this his organ! To crown the whole he has recently built and completely finished an entire new organ in the Protestant Dissenters meeting house at Dursley, which is admired by the best judges for the fulness, purity and harmony of its tones — and which he began and finished without the least assistance from any person.'

The Gloucestershire historian Fosbrooke, writing this in 1807,[60] seems to have been expanding a newspaper article of October 1790 reprinted at some time in *The Antiquary*. That the mill[61] mentioned was on the Churnworks site was stated in 1864 by ninety-four year old Charles Champion, bootmaker and sadler of Upper Cam, who knew the King family well. Champion, John King and others often spent happy musical evenings at the mill and when the Tabernacle acquired its first organ, John was the organist. In thus having an organ by 1790, the Tabernacle society was well ahead of Nonconformist churches in general. The *Christian Witness* magazine for 1850 shows that only then, some sixty years later, did organs start to become common in such places of worship and even so there was much opposition to these 'popish monsters. Maybe the Tabernacle was reflecting its Anglican origin. Before the 'box of whistles' was installed, hymn singing would have been led by a singing leader.

Of the Sunday School began by William King only a little is known. Children were taken at an early age. Samuel Attwood, weaver, in 1862 stated that he first went to the school in about 1788 when he was aged four. He could remember William Trotman standing on a form to give out hymns. From one of the visiting ministers, Mr. May, he received an award, but whether for knowledge or attendance is not recorded.[62] This was a copy of *Janeways Token* or 'A token for children being an exact account of the conversion, holy and exemplary lives and joyful deaths of several young children, to which is now added prayers and graces, fitted for the use of little children' by James Janeway. By all accounts this was a morbid collection of stories of highly religious children who died young, but one which was read by children for some two hundred years after its appearance in the late seventeenth century. The same book was received by Jehoida Morgan, weaver, when a lad, also from Mr. May. He attended the school from the age of five in 1789 for seven years, and could remember another itinerant minister, Mr. Dunn, who was called the 'Little Apostle' because of his small stature.[63] Nathaniel Thurston, eighty-three, weaver and ex-clerk of the parish, stated in 1864 that he had come to Dursley from Uley when he was seven and could remember William King. With 'a Mr. Moore', King tried to establish schools in places outside Dursley.[64]

In the beginning King ran the school himself but, as has already been recorded, by about 1781 King's business commitments were preventing him from taking as active a part in the school as he wished. Eventually he had to give up being its superintendent and it was transferred to the house of his journeyman cardmaker, Adrian Newth. Here it existed for about a year before moving to the old Tabernacle premises in about 1783. Newth lived in Water Street, also called Back Street, two or three doors down from the Twemlow School.[65]

James Edmonds in 1864, eighty years old fly (carriage) proprietor, could remember going as a lad to a Christmas treat given by Adrian and his wife Sarah in their house.[66] Adrian Newth became another of Dursley's highly respected inhabitants. William King 'loved him as a son' and he was a great favourite with the family. He frequently took tea at his master's hospitable table. He was a highly intelligent man and, although self taught, he was well educated and accomplished in many directions. He taught his own children and one, Elisha, having come under the influence of the Rev. Rowland Hill, received ministerial training. As the Rev. Elisha Newth, for nearly thirty years he helped Hill with the oversight of Surrey Chapel, London, built near Blackfriars Bridge especially for Rowland and opened in 1783. The area then was one of the worst in the metropolis — 'the very paradise of devils'. Two of Elisha's sons, Adrian's grandsons, reached eminence.[67] Both were first educated by their father. Alfred became a lecturer at the Lancashire Independent College and taught there from 1857 until his death in 1875, eventually becoming its Professor of Philosophy, Hebrew and Church History. His brother Samuel became the first person to gain an M.A. degree in mathematics at London University. Later he entered the Congregational ministry. In 1872, having been Professor of Mathematics and Ecclesiastical History at New College, London, since 1855, he became the college's Principal. From 1870 to 1880 he was one of 'a number of learned and illustrious men' who undertook the revision of the New Testament. In 1880 he was Chairman of the Congregational Union of England and Wales and died in 1898 aged seventy-seven.

Another of Adrian's sons, Elijah, had a short leg and had to wear an iron. He was at one time Tabernacle choir master. An ancestor was Thomas Garrett who was burned at the stake at Smithfield, London, in July 1541, for circulating copies of the banned New Testament in English of William Tyndale.

One anecdote of the esteem in which Adrian Newth was held survives. Newth 'was loved alike by rich and poor, Churchman and Nonconformist. (Once) a rich man named Harris, being afflicted with a dangerous malady, his medical advisors gave him timely warning of his critical position. His friends repeated their desire to send for the parish clergyman and although the sick gentleman was a staunch churchman, yet he replied to their entreaties "No, I do not want the clergyman; send for Adrian Newth"'. Newth went and was 'unremitting in attention, reading and praying with him to his spiritual comfort and consolation.' Harris can be identified as either Robert or George Harris, of Oaklands, now Rednock, already mentioned as being a wealthy landowner and clothier. He got well and never forgot Newth's ministrations. It is likely that this is the reason why in years to come the Tabernacle was able to obtain lands on the east side of Kingshill Road, part of the Harris estate, on such advantageous terms.

Adrian died in 1820 aged sixty; Sarah, for many years chapel cleaner, died in 1843 aged ninety-one. Jehoida Morgan, who knew Adrian said in 1864

> 'For years before his death he attended weekly church meetings held in the old vestry (built on the other side of the road to the old Tabernacle in 1808).

> These meetings were very precious; were for conversation etc., anyone feeling so inclined stating his or her spiritual experience which often tended much to the edification of the rest; they were for singing and prayer also. When about to separate, Adrian would often give out with energy a hymn beginning with —
>
> Come on my friends, let's mend our pace,
> For glory, glory, glory,
> And you shall see him face to face,
> In glory, glory, glory.

Adrian's brother, Samuel, was a teacher in the Sunday School. During the week he worked as a cloth shearer 'at Mr. Lloyd's factory at Cam. His employer lived at Angeston House near Uley near which he had some factories too.' The 'factory at Cam' was Cam Upper Mill which stood where now (1981) are the lower main gates to R.A. Lister & Co. Ltd.

For many years Adrian was a Deacon of the Tabernacle and its Clerk, from which, Alfred Bloodworth in 1864, deduced he had the important post of announcer of hymns. This meant that he read the hymns line by line for the benefit of those in the congregation who were unable to read. Apart from Adrian Newth's brother, the only other names of teachers that have survived are:-

Thomas Denley, corn miller at Danford's Mill
Joseph Dainton, Card maker for Richard Williams in Long Street
William Trotman, who later became superintendent of the Wesleyan Sunday School before moving on to the Parish Church where he was sexton for many years. At one period in his life he was Town Crier and Beadle.
Margaret Trotman and her sister, name unrecorded, probably daughters of that 'eminent saint of God' Richard Trotman, baker, an exhorter in the old Tabernacle.[68]

Instruction was mainly religious but probably included the teaching of reading, if not writing, and the teachers were not paid, unusual for the period it seems. Alfred Bloodworth, in 1864 thought that in its heyday the old Sunday School had upwards of a hundred pupils, boys and girls in roughly equal numbers. Many of those interviewed by Bloodworth could remember the ministers who visited the old Tabernacle and played an important role in its school. For these was provided a copy of the third edition of Cruden's *Concordance* published in 1769 which was inscribed 'Dursley Tabernacle Society's Concordance for the use of the Minister, 1793'. Some, like May and Dunn were itinerants, continuing the pattern set by George Whitefield and the Countess of Huntingdon; others like Mr. Lewis of Wotton-under-Edge, were settled ministers of neighbouring churches. In 1795 Dursley Tabernacle joined these by calling its first settled pastor, David Ralph.

5

Into the Nineteenth Century 1795 - 1825

The Rev. David Ralph trained for the ministry at the Countess of Huntingdon's College at Treveca, a few miles east of Brecon, sometime before 1792.[1] His movements after he left the college are unknown, but as it was there to produce itinerant ministers, it is likely that he moved around constantly, preaching, until invited by the Calvanistic Methodists of Dursley Tabernacle to settle with them. Quite why he was called at this particular time is conjectural. There are a number of possible reasons.

Although itinerant work was continuing unabated in villages and towns where Nonconformist causes were not established, it was becoming the rule that once established, societies took settled ministers. Among the churches of the Rodborough Connection, most had already their own pastor. The increasing number of settlements being made by evangelical ministers may have brought about a decline in the general quality of those remaining or made it more difficult to ensure a constant supply of preachers Sunday by Sunday. With the gradual loosening of the bonds which held the Rodborough Connection together, the society at Dursley Tabernacle may have felt a general lack of direction and guidance in its affairs. Rowland Hill still visited frequently when he was at Wotton-under-Edge, but his pattern of life took him away from the county for much of the year.

The society at Dursley Tabernacle, which was a strong one in terms of numbers of adherents and of sphere of influence in the surrounding countryside, may have felt the need for a permanent leader to forward its evangelical work. This was the time when the London Missionary Society came into being (1795) and it is said that representatives from Dursley Tabernacle were present at the meeting in 1794, in Bristol, held to discuss its formation. The L.M.S. grew quickly into a great ecumenical organisation for missionary work overseas and remained so until the end of the first decades of the nineteenth century when the rise of denominational missionary societies turned it into a purely Congregational Church organisation. The roots it and the Commonwealth Missionary Society put down internationally, have become independent churches in the Congregational and Reformed tradition. Today they are linked by the Council for World Missions (C.W.M.) in which the United Reformed Church in England and Wales plays its part.

The Revd David Ralph, first settled minister at Dursley Tabernacle, 1795–1802. (*Original in Evangelical Magazine for 1814.*)

It was a time when Nonconformist ministers were forming county associations to allow for exchange views and ideas and to co-ordinate village preaching. Some ministers in Wiltshire in 1804 for example, created 'The North Wiltshire Religious Society for preaching the Gospel on the borders of Wilts. and Berks. by Distributing Tracts and Preaching'.[2] By 1798 the Bishop of Salisbury was worried by the evangelism in the 'dark places' of his diocese and preached against it. It is perhaps a matter of interest that it was a minister of a church in the Rodborough Connection and a former student of Cornelius Winter, Samuel Clift of Chippenham Tabernacle, who leapt to the defence by publishing a spirited reply to his Lordship.[3]

There was a general air of enthusiasm for missionary work at home and abroad and Dursley Tabernacle's members may well have felt the need for a leader in their own projects and, David Ralph, with his training, must have seemed well qualified. At the time of his settlement 'the ministers of Gloucestershire formed themselves into an associated body and a county Missionary Society'. Among its fifteen members in 1798 was Ralph, as well as John Thomas of Cam Meeting, Cornelius Winter of Painswick and Rowland Hill. Possibly the arrival of David Ralph came about by an

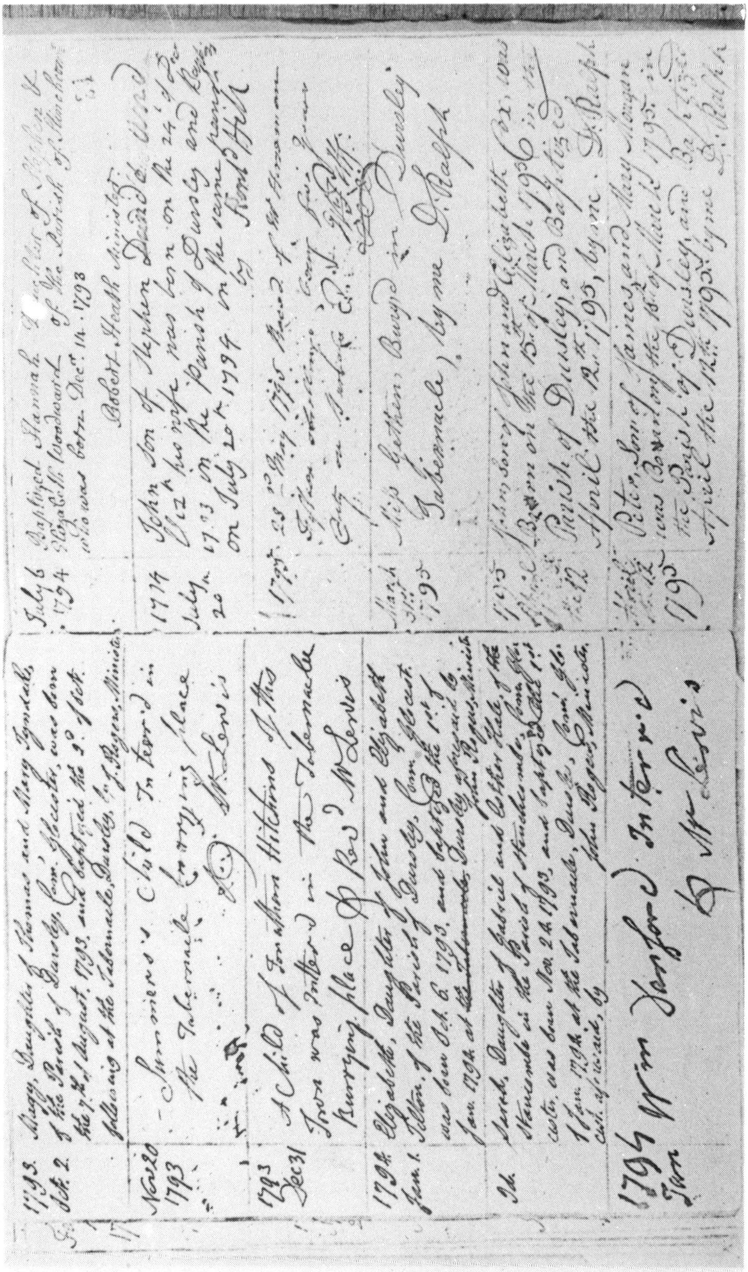

Two pages from the first Dursley Tabernacle register — mainly of baptisms with an occasional burial — illustrating the dependence of the church on visiting ministers until the Revd David Ralph arrived in 1795. One entry seen here refers to the payment of 'fifteen shillings being five years duty on burials'. This is almost certainly the Government tax of 3d on every burial levied to help pay for the war against America. Although the tax was repealed in 1794 doubtless monies still owed were zealously pursued.

amalgam of all of the above. For their pastor, the Dursley people rented a house from Richard Hopkins, owner of the Bell and Apple Tree public house.[4] It was near that inn, at the bottom of Water Street, close to Yellow Hundred. Considered by its valuation for the purposes of a poor relief rate it was no mean dwelling, though not as big as the present Parsonage.

At first, judging by baptismal records, Ralph's pastorate was successful, though seemingly he quoted too much scripture in his sermons to please some of his hearers.[5] The success however was short lived and by about 1800 religious life seems to have dropped to a low ebb. By this time the Tabernacle had been partly pewed. A pew renting system was instituted but only three or four were so let. The Sunday School faltered and perhaps even ceased for a while. The evidence is inconclusive.[6] Financially, backing was still considerable. In 1801 the Gloucester Infirmary, supported by public subscriptions, made one of its periodic appeals for money and the *Gloucester Journal* listed donations. Among these was one from 'Mr. Ralph's Tabernacle, Dursley', of £9 9*s* 0*d*, well above the average of about £6.[7]

In early 1802 David Ralph resigned. After two more pastorates, at Tisbury, Wilts, 1802-4 and Wimbourne, Dorset 1804-11, he settled at Pill on the outskirts of Bristol, where he disappears from records.[8]

A large measure of Ralph's decline in success must be attributed to the arrival in Dursley of Wesleyan Methodism. Dursley was a growing town. The wool trade was, in general, buoyant, largely because of the cloth being supplied to the British Army in its wars with France, and it is likely that among the influx of cloth workers were Wesleyan Methodists. With characteristic ardour they would have gathered in house meetings for worship. It is said that the first organised society was formed in Woodmancote.[9] Their view of universal salvation would have contrasted strongly with the Calvanistic view of salvation as being limited only to those whom God had predestined it, as preached at the Tabernacle, and we know that at least one man, William Trotman, switched from being a staunch member of the Tabernacle to become eventually Wesleyan Sunday School Superintendent.[10] It is unlikely that he was the only person to jump the barrier between the old Calvanist and the new Wesleyan fields in Dursley.

By 1799, the Wesleyans were strong enough to think of having their own place of worship in the town. Premises, on the site still used, were acquired in August for a peppercorn rent, from William Vizard, a victualler.[11] Earlier they had been used for brewing and pig keeping by John Ball, inn keeper of 'The Sign of the Boot' at that time roughly where Wilkes' drapery shop now stands.[12] Evidence suggests that at first the premises were just adapted and that three years later, in 1802, substantial alterations, even rebuilding took place.[13] Be this as it may, by October 1799, work was sufficiently advanced for John Sansum, Samuel King and others to licence the premises for public worship with the diocesan authorities and presumably the congregation moved in soon after this. The lane that led up from the Town hall was then known as Market Street.[14]

Lower Cam Methodist Church, built 1825. On the left is Henry Mabbett, organist, whose workshop for dressing mill stones was nearby *(Miss V. Taylor)*

The Revd William Bennett, minister 1804–23, through whose exertions the present Tabernacle was built. *(original in Evangelical Magazine for 1808)*

It is probably about this time that Wesleyan Methodism came to Cam. For some while the preaching room there was an attic in a cottage in the High Street, on the Cam Pitch side of The Berkeley Arms Inn. The chapel was built in 1825, largely it seems through the initiative of one Samuel Holloway, a man prominent in village affairs and builder and keeper of a large shop at Sandpits which sold 'groceries, drugs and spirituous liquors'.[15]

During the two and a half years following David Ralph's departure, the Tabernacle was served by a variety of preachers including Rowland Hill. On several occasions David Ralph returned, and as his name also occurs in the baptismal registers in following years, it is obvious that he did not depart under a cloud.

The Tabernacle Society called to be its next pastor the Revd. Edward A. Dunn from Hoxton College, London, but though he may have spent a little time in the town he declined the invitation[16] and it was not until December 1804 that the second settled minister arrived. This was William Bennett. With him came a quickening of the religious pulse and a great era of prosperity. The Revd. Bennett, like his predecessor, was a product of the Countess of Huntingdon's College, though in its new situation at Cheshunt, north of London.[17] He finished his ministerial training in the late 1780s. He was a highly intelligent, literate, dynamic man and in his career published a number of items.

Adrian Newth, Son of Charles and Elizabeth Thornhill of Dursley was born Nov. 2d 1820 and baptized Jan. 7th 1821. By me W Bennett.

One publication was *The Guide of Youth, a sermon* preached to Young People at Sion Chapel, White Chapel, London, *on Sunday December 21st 1806 and published by request.*[18] Although couched in the somewhat melodramic, even lurid style of the period, it shows that some of today's problems are not new.

> Why are some young people averse to God, and his ways ? Why do they voluntarily prefer the play-house to the sanctuary of the Lord ? novels, romances, jests and story books, to the bible — the book of books — the BOOK OF GOD ? — ludicrous and idle songs, to psalms, hymns and the praises of the Lord ? — the company of vain and trifling men, to those who

THE

GUIDE OF YOUTH:

A

SERMON

PREACHED TO

YOUNG PEOPLE,

AT

SION CHAPEL, WHITECHAPEL,

On Sunday, December 21, 1806;

AND

PUBLISHED BY REQUEST.

To which is added,

A PETITIONARY HYMN FOR YOUTH.

BY WM. BENNETT, *Dursley.*

" Grace leads the *right* way, if you choose the wrong,
" Take it and perish.—— COWPER.

" Forsake the foolish, and live; and go in the way of understanding."
PROV. ix. 6.

—— Τὰς δὲ νεωτερικὰς ἐπιθυμίας φεῦγε.—— 2 TIM. ii. 22.

LONDON:

PRINTED BY H. TEAPE, TOWER-HILL;
AND SOLD BY
WILLIAMS and SMITH, Stationers-Court; BAGSTER, 81, Strand;
and HIGHAM, 6, Chiswell-Street.

1807.

> are pious, serious and wise ? They can sit with pleasure, hour after hour, in the house of variety — in reading books of folly — and in social intercourse with the sons of earth. But, for the house of God — the word of truth — the praises of Jehovah — and the Society of the saints, they have no relish. In these they have no delight. This is obvious ; for when decency, and custom demand their attendance upon them, how soon do they complain, saying 'What a weariness', how dull, lifeless and insipid ! When will the tedious time elapse !' Such complaints are seldom heard at the play — the opera or any other places of flesh-pleasing amusement. . . .

On his arrival in Dursley in 1804 he found the Tabernacle in a depressed state, but his enthusiasm galvanised it into action. His residence, at first, was the house in Water Street[19] used by David Ralph, but it was at a distance from his meeting house and he persuaded the society to build a manse much closer to hand. To this end, in July 1807, land was acquired from George Harris, gentleman clothier of Oaklands. It was opposite the old Tabernacle and next to the new burial ground and was gained for £50 down and a rent of 1*d* per year for 1000 years payable on the feast of St. John the Baptist. On it was to be erected 'a dwelling house with convenient offices for the constant residence and occupation of the minister or preacher for the time being of and belonging to the Tabernacle or Meeting House of a certain Society of People of Calvanistic Principles'.[20] The building now called The Parsonage included among its convenient offices, a vestry. Curiously this was upstairs where now is the schoolroom, but was smaller in both height and floor area. It was used by William Bennett for many years for a private day school — a 'Classical and Commercial Academy'.[21] A Mr. Parker, an usher or assistant teacher to Mr. Bennett, later started his own school in North Nibley.[22]

His accommodation now reorganised, William Bennett set about the Tabernacle itself. The old building was becoming dangerous for, under too heavy a roof, the walls were cracking. Thus in August 1808, a second agreement for land was reached with George Harris, this time for £82 19*s* 0*d* down and an annual rent of one shilling. By the time the deeds were signed work had already begun on the new Tabernacle for it included the phrase 'whereof a Tabernacle or Meeting House is now erecting and building'.[23]

The agreement was signed by

Rowland Hill
Daniel Lloyd of Ashcroft, Newington Bagpath, gentleman
William Long, Wotton-under-Edge, clothier
William Smith, clothier of New Mills (now Kinver Grange)
Thomas Trotman, baker and maltster
Stephen Dando, hat maker
Joseph Packer, butcher
John Packer, currier
Thomas Tyndall the elder

Thomas Tyndall the younger pig butchers
John Harding, grocer
John Trotman, cardboard maker
William Harris, plumber and glazier
Thomas Trotman, framework knitter
James Taylor, baker and innkeeper
John Olpin, Cam, fellmonger (i.e. trade of preparing skins for a tanner)
Robert Buckley, North Nibley, yeoman

It is not hard to imagine the interest provoked in the town by the great new building rising on its outskirts. Neither is it difficult to visualize the bustle of workmen on rope lashed wooden scaffolding, using simple block and tackle to lift into place the stones brought down carefully from the Granny's Tump Quarry[24] at the top of Union Street, nor the activity of the quarry-men themselves. The architect is unknown but it has features in common with Whitecourt Chapel, Uley, (1790) and may have been designed by the same man. Within a year, all was finished and on 22 August 1809 the New Tabernacle was opened. In the morning, Rowland Hill, who had laid the foundation stone, preached from 1 Peter II 5 'come as living stones and let yourselves be used. . . .' Sermons in the afternoon and evening were based on Psalm 32, 13 'The Lord has chosen Zion . . .' and Hebrews 13, 17 'Obey your leaders and follow their orders . . .' and present were people from London, Gloucester and Bristol as well as more local places. The building overflowed and hundreds were unable to get in. It was a great day.[25]

The present (1981) seating capacity is 600. Whether it was more or less at its opening is unknown, for we have little information on its internal layout. What we see now is the result of a massive refurbishing project later in the century. The main door was in a long wall facing the old building. The pulpit and galleries, one a singing gallery, were probably in the same position as they are now. Pews existed only under the galleries and perhaps in them, the ground floor centre space was taken up with forms for the children of the Sunday and night schools, of which more later.[26] After the great opening came the bills. The cost of the building programme was £1,600[27] a considerable sum at the time and it is not clear if it included the cost of building the Parsonage. To take it on was an act of great faith and it is reported that within a short while all debts were paid, mainly through the efforts of William Bennett himself who did most of the collecting outside the town.[28] It was customary at this period for country congregations to appeal to their London brethren for financial assistance when chapel building and William Bennett's visit to Sion Chapel in 1806 may well have been a money gathering exercise.

Soon after the new meeting house opened, the old was demolished — much against the wishes of Adrian Newth who wished to use it for the Sunday school.[29] The ground left open was used for a while for more

The present Parsonage and Tabernacle as they were built. The original water colour was painted by Wm Bennett's daughter, Mary, in 1850.

A highly enlarged fragment of an old photograph showing the present Tabernacle as built on the edge of the estate of clothier George Harris. *(Gloucestershire Gazette archives)*

The Crescent and Tabernacle, Dursley, c. 1900. The first Tabernacle stood at the far end of the Crescent, the last house of which overlaps its site.

Woodmancote Green c. 1905. On the left is the Bull Inn. The site of William King's house and workshops is further along the terrace, roughly above the head of the third child from the right.

burials, and sometime before 1860, pieces at each end were sold. Part went to the owners of the old rectory and part to Edward West, a builder who lived a little further down. On his piece, and adjacent land he built the present row of Georgian houses called 'The Crescent'.[30]

In 1968 a little more land was sold in order to allow vehicular access to the back of the premises of insurance brokers E.H. Morgan & Son Ltd. Amid some secrecy the side of the graveyard was carved away, revealing just one grave with five skeletons. With time these had slumped into roughly sitting positions one above another. No stone marked their presence or their family name and they were quietly reinterred nearby.

Another problem to which the Rev. Bennett turned his attentions, when he settled in 1804, was the Sunday School.[31] In James Taylor, baker and keeper of the Bull Inn, Woodmancote Green, he found the man he wanted to revitalise it. At one service, probably in 1805, it was announced that the reorganised school would open for admissions on the following Monday at the inn. The Green that evening presented a busy spectacle as mothers took their children in to be registered by James Taylor sitting at his dining room table. First name was that of Sarah Attwood, later wife of rope maker George Harding, and at the time she would have been in her late teens. For a long time the school catered for such young adults in its top or sixth class. Instruction was both religious and secular, reading, writing and arithmetic. For many of the young people who enrolled, the school, on their only day free from work, must have given them their only real education in these subjects. Religious work filled morning and early afternoon, the secular the rest of the post noon period. The latter however 'met with some opposition from several . . . who thought it too worldly and that if writing was done, there should be nothing written but texts of scripture'. Secular instruction, then, on a Sunday was abandoned and a night school opened and this thrived for many years. Religious instruction was based on the Assembly of Divines' Catechism of 1648 and remained so until at least the 1860s. new copies of the catechisms were given to the scholars soon after the school re-opened, it would appear, by Rowland Hill.

The revived school was held in the old Tabernacle to begin with, and at the end of each session the desks and forms had to be cleared out of the way to make room for the evening congregation. When the vestry was built they were stored there. The new building gave increased space for the school and it burgeoned, children coming in from Cam, Stinchcombe, North Nibley, Coaley, Uley and even as far as Cat's Castle beyond Gossington. In 1818 it had over 400 scholars and in the thirteen years to the beginning of that year a total of 1536 had attended at some time, roughly half and half girls and boys and mostly in their middle teens.

The school was very orderly and at times was so quiet that 'a penny might be heard to drop' according to one teacher of the time. There were printed Rules, now lost, which were read over quarterly. Teachers who were late were fined and the proceeds were used to fund teachers' tea

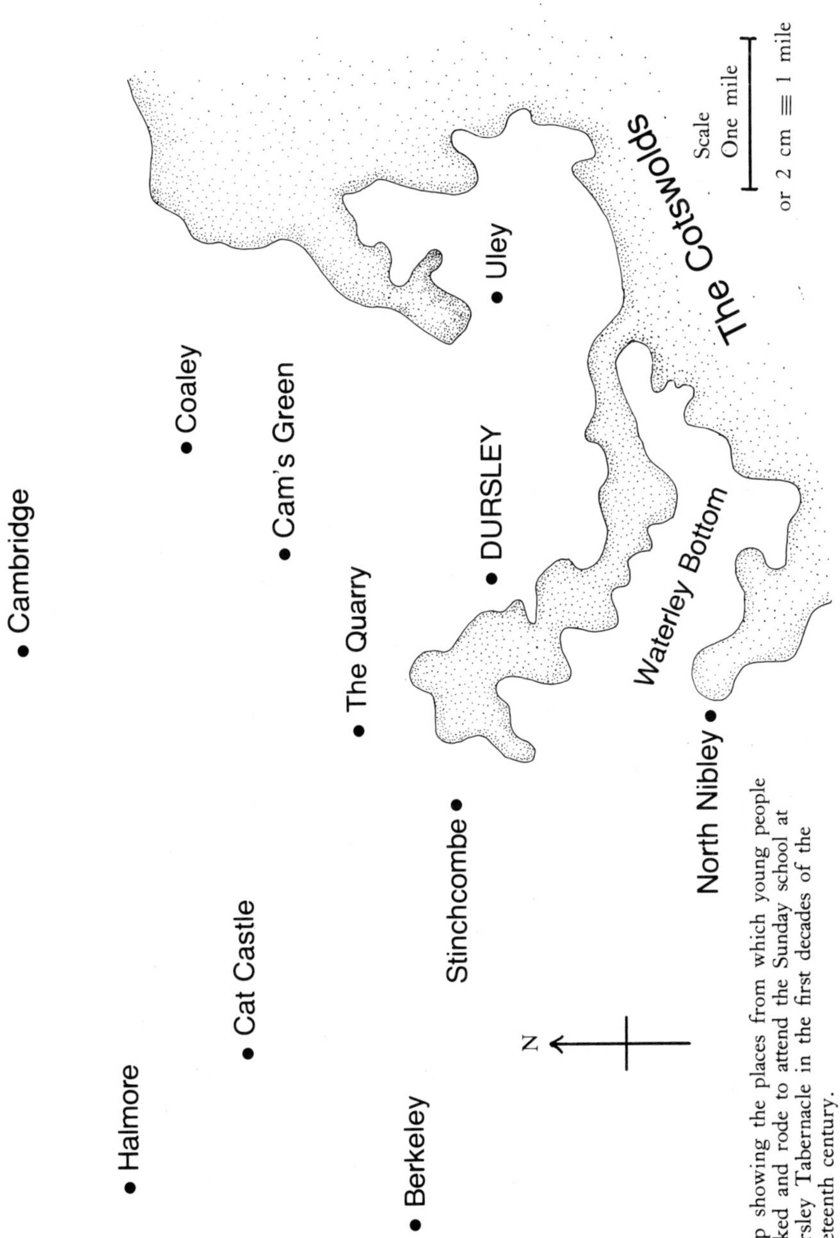

Map showing the places from which young people walked and rode to attend the Sunday school at Dursley Tabernacle in the first decades of the nineteenth century.

meetings. If a scholar was absent for four successive sessions a person specially appointed for the task, visited the home to make enquiries. Contact with other Sunday Schools, particularly the Wesleyan was friendly and combined treats for some 700 children of the two churches — tea, cake and games in one of the fields of Castle Farm, now the recreation ground — were not uncommon.

In 1813 the Tabernacle, Wesleyan, Cam Meeting and Uley Chapel Schools formed a local Union affiliated to the National Sunday School Union which had itself been created in 1803. The local organisation was commended in *The Teachers' Magazine*. It commented first on the inaugural meeting —

> The Teachers assembled together to present their united supplications to the throne of grace, to improve their methods of instruction and animate each other in increased activity. They were addressed on this occasion by the Rev. T. Flint (Uley) and after a very pleasant and encouraging interview, they separated with animated feelings, resolving to labour more abundantly in the work of the Lord. Other schools are now desirous of joining the Union ; it is in agitation to assist in the formation : and we trust this humble commencement will lead to the most beneficial consequence.[32]

So far as the Tabernacle was concerned, it was certainly keen to establish new schools and sent teachers out to Berkeley, Halmore, North Nibley, Cambridge and other places and was successful.

North Nibley had had, from earliest days, followers of Calvanistic Methodism. For some fifty years these folk walked or rode over Stinchcombe Hill to Dursley Tabernacle Sunday by Sunday. In 1810 a house was licensed in the village for preaching and then in 1815 a small chapel was built for these people, still known at that date as Calvanistic Methodists. Thus came into being North Nibley Tabernacle. William Bennett's name appears on the property deeds[33] and he seems to have been its overseeing minister until he left Dursley in 1823, for Dursley Tabernacle registers continue to include frequent North Nibley baptismal entries until that date.

Lest it should be thought that at this time only the two Chapels having Methodist origins had Sunday schools, the Wesleyan's beginning in 1804 under the direction of the Rev. W. Williams, we ought to look at the others. One was run independently by William Harding,[34] a wire drawer in one of the Holywell Cottages, Woodmancote, for some 30 years until about 1830. At first,Harding was a member of Cam Meeting but later changed allegiance to the Tabernacle, where he was a Deacon for about twenty years, but finally returned to Cam Meeting. He died in 1849 aged seventy-seven. The Parish Church also had a school.[35] This was begun in about 1788 by William Watkins and William Vizard, both wool cloth press men of Mr. Lloyd's factory in Uley. They were concerned at the activities of children in the Boulton Lane area and opened a school in what was then The Brewer's Arms. This was then a thatched cottage next to 'The Cross

Keys' Inn on the Poole Cottages side.[36] It grew and under the direction of the rector's wife Mme. Webster, moved to the Town Hall. While here, for some years, the children on Christmas Day received a treat of roast beef and Christmas pudding. Tabernacle children were regaled in a similar way. Later, the Church School moved into the Church then in turn to Twemlow's Water Street School; a cottage opposite the Bull Inn, Woodmancote; back to the Parish Church and the Town Hall; eventually settling in the buildings of the National Schools when these were erected behind St. James' Church in 1833.

Not surprisingly, in view of its frequent moves, it was not always strong in the first decades of the century. Glimpses of it exist. While in Water Street the master of the day school supervised. He, however, only opened and closed proceedings ; the actual teaching was left to one William Nicholls who heard the small number of children who attended recite their letters. Later in life William Bruton, a blacking and ink maker who was one of these children, described the exercises as being 'uncommonly dull'. By about 1816, the school had shifted to Woodmancote. A typical lesson here was later recounted by Thomas Brothers, a carpenter. The room used was long and low and down the centre was a table covered in sand. As the young monitor in charge called out letters, the twenty or so children drew them in the sand. The superintendent was Edward Wallington, but he was frequently absent and on those occasions often left six pennyworth of humbugs, or the like, with the monitor to reward the children who did well. Once letters were over, the church catechism and collects were chanted by rote. Thomas Brothers, who was the monitor, later joined the Tabernacle school as a senior scholar.

Church children were expected to attend morning service in St. James and for them, forms were provided in the aisles. Adult users of the church became irritated by the inconvenience of the cluttered ways and in 1814 it was agreed to build a special gallery for the children across the back of the church. In this the girls sat at the south end, the boys at the north.[37] Through the munificence of Henry Vizard, the church authorities were able to build National Schools and one can imagine the thankfulness of the Rector in finding, at last, a permanent home for Sunday's pupils as well. It is probable that it is from this time, 1833, that the following church rules come :—[38]

I. Every child to be in the school room with clean hands and face, and hair combed, exactly at half past eight o'clock in the morning.

II. The children's names to be called over exactly at a quarter before nine o'clock.

III. The duties of the schools to commence at nine o'clock by the children singing the morning hymn after which a short prayer to be read by the master, mistress or one of the visitors.

IV. The collect of the day to be repeated — reading and spelling till ten o'clock, when the whole of the children standing round the room, the master, mistress or one of the visitors shall hear them repeat with a loud and distinct voice the church catechisms 'till twenty five minutes past ten o'clock.

V. The children to be taken by the master and mistress orderly and quietly in the church and every one who can read to be supplied with a prayer book.

VI. The children to assemble in their respective school rooms exactly at half past one o'clock in the evening and read and spell 'till ten minutes before three o'clock, and then proceed to the church in the same order as they did in the morning and after service return orderly to the school rooms to be dismissed, after singing the evening hymn.

VII. The books of the school to be placed under the immediate care of the master and mistress who will be accountable for all that may be lost.

VIII. No prayer to be used or books introduced into school, excepting such as are sanctioned by the Society for Promoting Christian Knowledge and regularly entered in their catalogue.

IX. The children regularly attending the Sunday schools to be instructed in writing every Wednesday evening. (By 1845 arithmetic had been added to this.)

X. Every child conforming to the first fourth and fifth rules to be entitled to a weekly ticket, but should the visitors from their observations or from the complaints of the master or mistress, think proper to withhold the ticket they are to use a discretionary power. (So many tickets entitled children to certain treats.)

In the old Tabernacle grave yard is a tombstone inscribed 'Here lie the remains of the Rev. John Packer of Brighton, late of this town, who departed this life in the Hope of a Glorious Resurrection Oct 2nd 1837 aged 66 years.' John was a national figure in 1811-2.

To understand the reason we must go back some 150 years to the restoration of the monarchy after the Cromwellian Commonwealth period. As has been recounted those who dissented from the Established Church received harsh treatment. The 'Glorious Revolution' which followed, placing William and Mary on the throne, eased their lot with the Toleration Act. This did not repeal the repressive acts passed in the reigns of the Stuarts and Tudors but gave Dissenting preachers and teachers immunity from many of their provisions, providing each took an oath of allegiance to the crown, acknowledged its supremecy and subscribed to a declaration against popery, all before a Justice of the Peace at Quarter Sessions. Dissenters were still banned from the universities and most civic offices but the act did give them considerable licenced freedom and had worked fairly well for over a century.

The flowering of missionary work by Dissenters at home and abroad at the end of the eighteenth century and the alarm over this felt by the Anglican Church, as voiced by the Bishop of Salisbury, has been commented on earlier. This anxiety increased in the first decade of the next century and in 1811 Lord Sidmouth introduced a Bill in Parliament to tighten up the Toleration Act in such a way that it would have put most evangelising Dissenters outside its protection and so liable to the pains and penalties of the old Stuart acts such as the Conventicle and Five Mile Acts. All was to be done for the good of Dissenters said the 'noble Viscount' for the existing act 'had been abused and very improper persons had intruded themselves into the ministry such as blacksmiths, chimney sweepers, pig drovers, peddlars, cobblers etc. . .'[39] With this concurred the Archbishop of Canterbury who expressed great regard for the Toleration Act.

Dissenters however were not so sure that they wished to have 'good' done for them and swiftly all denominations rallied together and forced rejection of the bill. One outcome was the formation of the 'Protestant Society for the Protection of Religious Freedom' commonly just called 'The Protestant Society'.[40] Defeat of Lord Sidmouth's bill did not end the problem however — 'the agitation of the oceans will be perpetuated after the tempest has subsided' — and in the same year magistrates in Denbighshire decided to tighten up the Toleration Act in their own way, by refusing to permit a preacher to take the requisite oaths because he ministered to several Dissenting congregations and not just one as they now interpreted the Act.[40] The case went to the Court of Kings Bench which upheld the magistrates and immediately a spate of magisterial refusals was reported from all parts of the country. Most affected were Methodist preachers — both Wesleyan and Calvanistic.

In Gloucestershire, a Uley man whose name is unknown, was rebuffed by magistrates — as was Dursley's John Packer.[41] The Protestant Society entered the lists and took up three situations as test cases of national importance — those of John Packer, 'a respectable layman who itinerated to various congregations'; Mr. Brittan of Bristol, a student who needed to itinerate in his training; and a baptist minister in Mildenhall, Suffolk from whom magistrates had demanded a certificate from his congregation stating that he was their settled pastor. These cases were heard at the Court of Kings Bench. The third was won decisively — magistrates had no right to demand certificates. The other two were also won by the Protestant Society, but only nominally, and for each a mandamus was issued to local justices directing them to administer the Toleration Act oaths. Victory was, however, overshadowed by the pronouncement of the court that the Act was unclear on the point at issue — did it cover itinerant preaching? This left at risk Sunday school teachers, ministerial students and ministers itinerating or on probation in new pastorates. It was estimated that if all these fell foul of the law, fines totalling £25,000,000 could be extracted from them. Both the Wesleyan and Tabernacle societies in Dursley would have been hit severely.

The Protestant Society therefore approached members of both Houses of Parliament with a view to clarifying the issue. Among those favourably inclined to Dissenters was the Prime Minister, Spencer Perceval, and a meeting was held with him only two hours before he was assasinated as he entered the House of Commons. Eventually, in 1812, legislation was passed by Parliament, repealing the Conventicle and Five Mile Acts and amending other provisions of the Toleration Act in ways favourable to Dissenters.[42] The Nonconformist press hailed the events as great victories for religious freedom and it should be a source of some pride that John Packer of Dursley played an important part in them, even though mainly off stage. Of John himself, little is known. He was almost certainly the husband of Ann who bore five children. Sometime after the birth of the last, Edward Gardiner Packer in 1811, and, able now to become legally an itinerant preacher, he left for Brighton. Later he returned to Dursley and in the year of his death he was a trustee of The Tabernacle.[43]

In the family grave near John rests Joseph, affectionately known as 'Butcher Packer'. Joseph came to be a prominent figure in the Tabernacle after the schism which lay ahead. Some of his sayings were remembered in later days and have come down to us. In about 1816, the organ, which must have been transferred from the old meeting house, was replaced by a much larger version built in Hammersmith by the brother of James Taylor of the Bull Inn. Packer obviously disliked the organ music in chapel and roundly declared that 'the old one ought to be put in the big one and (the two) burnt together! He was a great believer in the doctrines of grace and would say, if he thought he saw signs of wavering on the part of his fellows 'May God grant that Ichabod may be never written on this Church!'[44] He died in 1844 aged eighty-two.

A topic which excited much comment in the Nonconformist national press in 1813 was missionary work in India, or rather its absence.[45] The East India Company, under a charter from the British Government controlled the sub-continent and consistently refused to allow Christian evangelism. In 1813 the charter came up for renewal and 'British Christians' put great pressure on the authorities to enforce a change of policy on the part of the company. Numerous petitions descended on the Houses of Parliament, beginning with those from Societies such as the L.M.S. and Protestant Society and culminating in a cascade of some 900 signed by ordinary people of towns and villages from Abingdon to Youlgreave, and among them was one from Dursley. It probably included all the villages of the valley and people of most religious persuasions. The Government took note and the new East India Company charter allowed the entry of accredited missionaries into India.

Collections for the L.M.S. seem to have been a regular feature of Tabernacle life:-

1812 The Rev. Mr Bennett and Friends, Dursley, including 14s 8d from Friends at Coaley £14 1s 2d

1814 Rev. W. Bennett and Congregation £10 10s 0d.[46]

Mary Ann Bennett

FAREWEL,

OR

VERSES

Expressive of Affectionate Regard

TO THE

CHURCH AND CONGREGATION,

WORSHIPPING IN

The Tabernacle

AND OF

HEARTY GOOD WISHES

FOR

THE HAPPINESS AND SALVATION

Of the Inhabitants of DURSLEY *and its* VICINITY.

By W. BENNETT.

"Finally, brethren, farewel. Be perfect, be of good comfort, be of one mind, live in peace, and the God of love and peace shall be with you. 2 Cor. 13 chap. 11 verse."

PRINTED BY W. RICKARDS, DURSLEY.
1823.

10

Farewel, Ye faithful Servants of the Lord!
My Brethren dear! in Christ, " Preach ye, the word."
In all your meetings;—may your Master meet,
His presence 'tis makes your assemblies sweet.

Farewel, My scholars! and My servants! too,
With heart sincere, God knows, I've pray'd for you;
By precept and example to you giv'n,
You know, I've shewn you Christ, the way to Heav'n.

Farewel, My kindred and relations dear!
May Christ to you, in life and death be near;
A kinsman, he, whose friendship never fails,
He for his own, with God, pleads and prevails.

Farewel, Ye neighbours! may you live in love,
Farewel, My Townsmen! may we meet above;
Immortals souls you have, O! for them care,
Should *they* be lost, not *well*, but *ill*, you'll fare.

No hazard run,—no danger risk,—I pray,
Your *souls*,—Your *all's* at stake;—make no delay;
Do time, health, wealth, the world, deserve *all thought*?
Your souls, and *things eternal*, are *they naught?*

Could you the *world*, and *all its riches* gain,
Then " into Hell be turn'd;"—What bitter pain!!!
Despair! despair! for ever reigns in Hell,
" Flee from the wrath to come!" Farewel! Farewel.

Farewel! Farewel! Thou art unknown, above!
Where all is peace and universal love;
Where Christian Friends of kindred mind and heart,
At home, shall meet,—No more,—No more, to part.

O! *Dursley*! *Dursley*! may thy children all,
'Scape for their lives, e'er storms of wrath shall fall;
Be found *secure*, when God his veng'ance hurls,
'Midst ruin'd nature, and the crush of worlds.

Part of William Bennett's farewell to Dursley.

The Bristol Branch of the L.M.S. was founded in 1812 and for three days in that October, meetings were held in the City in the main churches — St. Mary Redcliffe, Castle Green Independent, Pen Street Tabernacle and others. In the Tabernacle on the last day 1400 communicants with sixty ministers, among them William Bennett and Mr. Flint of Uley, took part in an impressive ecumenical service.[47]

In 1823 William Bennett resigned from the pastorate at Dursley Tabernacle and returned to his old college at Chesthunt to become classical tutor.[48] To mark the occasion he published a long poem of farewell to his congregation and to the town.[49] He was not away for long. It would seem that his physical constitution, apparently not strong but subordinated to his restless mental activity, finally gave way in 1828 and he returned to Dursley, a sick man. For a while he acted as school master in the Water Street School[50] but on 24 January 1830, aged fifty-four, he died after two years of 'paralytic Affliction' — a 'stroke'? Greatly mourned he was buried in front of the pulpit of the church he was instrumental in getting built and to his memory and that of his wife, Rebecca, who died in 1864 aged eighty-five, a tablet was placed close to the place where he had stood for so many years faithfully preaching Christ crucified.

One man who had good reason to be thankful for the life of William Bennett was Absolam Jones, born in North Nibley in 1800. For many years he attended Tabernacle services and in the year Bennett left he entered Hackney College, London. After ministerial training he held pastorates at Harting, Sussex, Portsmouth and Buckland where he died in 1870.[51]

Much of William Bennett's early ministry in Dursley took place against the background of the Napoleonic Wars. That the town had many men serving in the armies and navy of the period is testified by parish records which show concern at the plight of wives left without regular support.

In 1804, the Rev. James Webster of St. James paid £10 to Benjamin Williams, the third such payment, made by order of the 'Committee at Lloyds Coffee House in consideration of the loss of his son, Charles Williams, who was killed on board the *Majestic* in the glorious victory obtained off the mouth of the Nile on 1st August 1798.[52]

William Clark,[53] soldier, was luckier and survived the conflicts. Born in 1774, apprenticed as a shoemaker, he later served under the Duke of Wellington, of whom he had a high opinion — calm, dignified and courageous. He took part in most of Wellington's Battles, starting with Corunna in 1809 and ending with Waterloo in 1815. The final blow to Napoleon's activities was celebrated everywhere in the country with great enthusiasm, not least in Dursley 'Some members of the choir at the Tabernacle, as well as others, gave vent to their joy. . . by taking a good many drops too much on Stinchcombe Hill.'[54] Mr. Taylor of the Bull Inn was not amused. In one of his addresses he condemned the lapse — 'There will be no singing in Hell!' and this attitude offended some people. Taylor had a very strict conscience over drink and he would 'never draw more than two pints at a time for any man, and at the proper time would turn some out. Many used to go to (The Bull Inn) because they would never get drunk'.[55] However, back to William Clark. Just before his death in 1864 aged ninety he dictated some of his memories to his son Samuel.

> I enlisted Jan. 17th 1794, in the 52nd Light Infantry. At that time I was about twenty years old.
>
> I was away twenty-two years and six months; during that time I was engaged in nearly thirty battles and skirmishes.
>
> I got wounded in the leg at the Battle of Waterloo. When driving the French out of Spain, I put up a prayer to God (while engaged very warm) that if it was His will, He would defend me in the day of battle, and preserve me from being disabled, as I had two boys to labour for.
>
> The Lord answered my prayer word for word.
>
> I had not much concern about my soul, before I enlisted.
>
> When young I had no instruction, I was like a wild colt in a forest. Although convinced I was a sinner, when young, my convictions wore away. While I was in action, I had no fear when going into the battle, sometimes my pals would say "Thou wilt catch it now, Bill". I told them I should not, but that I should go home and die in my bed; I had **that** confidence.
>
> Not many in our regiment feared God; it was out of date then. After I came home, I began to feel more concerned about my soul, although for a time I acted very foolishly. I had a good wife, she earned ten or twelve shillings a week.
>
> I joined the church at the Dursley Tabernacle, when the Rev. Mr. Neeton first came there (about forty years ago).
>
> Before I joined this church, the power of sin worked upon me mightily. I could see I was going the downward road, I was always partial to reading.
>
> When under convictions of sin, I took more to reading the Bible than any other book.
>
> When I went to bed, I was afraid to go to sleep, lest I should wake up in hell. Some nights it was not quite so bad. My convictions lasted more than two years. One day I was in great distress, much cast down. I was brought to look to Christ, as the Saviour of sinners. I felt, like Paul, that I could glory in the cross — not the wood.
>
> I then found relief, but not satisfaction. Nearly five or six weeks after, as I was standing in the yard by the old house, my convictions came so powerfully upon me, that I was afraid to step, lest the ground should open, and swallow me up in hell.
>
> That was a queer state to be in.
>
> I felt as though I was nailed to the ground. At last I crept indoors, but did not know what to do.
>
> My convictions became heavier towards the last. I could not sleep. One night, after having a bit of a doze, this passage came to my mind "Come unto me, all ye that labour etc." It came very powerfully, and was repeated several times, I kept crying out "Come unto me" I tried to think of other passages, but could not. At this time I had not the notion to come in the right way, although the spirit of God was leading me. I longed to be in the house of God.

> When the services were ended on Sunday, I did vex that there would be no more service until Wednesday evening.
>
> While hearing the Rev. G. Neeton preaching from the thirteenth of Jeremiah and the last clause of the last verse "Wilt thou not be made clean?" "When shall it once be"? I was brought into the banqueting and his banner over me was Love, I could not help singing for joy. What a day that was! I had my heart and my soul full. When the words "When shall it once be?" were spoken, I cried — 'Now—Now—Now'. I was so light. What a glorious time that was. I had such a view of Christ's power to save, I had hard work to pacify myself.
>
> After service I walked home with my wife. She told me not to walk so fast. I told her I was so light, I could not help it. A short time after this, I said to my wife "I am going to establish a new concern in my house. I am going, by God's help, to establish a family altar." I did so and by the Lords help, continued it; and I often felt great liberty in speaking to my children upon the Word of God.

William Clark seems to have been a cheerful companionable man, not given to swearing but fond of his cups when he had money in his pockets. After discharge from the army he received a regular quarterly pension and this was just as regularly disposed of through a week's or a fortnight's bout of drinking. It was after one of these sessions that he had the experience which profoundly altered his life. 'He fell asleep in Jesus in the ninetieth year of his age' in 1863.

In his memoirs, soldier Clark stated that he joined Dursley Tabernacle when the Rev. Neeton became its minister. This was in 1825. Trained at Cheshunt College and called to Dursley from the Countess of Huntingdon's Chapel, Runcorn,[56] George Neeton arrived to find that his call had led to schism.

It is appropriate to pause here to consider the denominational position of The Tabernacle for it was changing from Calvanistic Methodist to Independent or Congregational. In 1810 the Evangelical Magazine published *a concise view of the present state of Evangelical Religion. . .* and what it reported probably gives a picture of the state of affairs at the Tabernacle — some points are certainly true.

> The Calvanistic Methodist are altogether perhaps a body little less numerous or little less active than their brethren (the Wesleyan Methodists); but broken into a greater number of distinct congregations and, not so united under any head or general government, they commonly adopt the mode of the Independents. . . . Numerous schools are taught by them; and much of the power of religion is manifested in their several congregations — none being admitted at their communion whose exemplary conduct and Christian knowledge does not assure, as far as charity must judge the truth of their profession, as unfeignedly faithful to the great Head of the church Jesus Christ. These are, I believe, seldom Dissenters by choice, or by conscientious objection to the Articles or worship of the established church; and often embrace the opportunity of hearing the gospel and uniting in communion

> with the evangelical ministers in their vicinity but as these are comparatively few, they choose a minister of their own sentiments, erect places of worship and multiply astonishingly through the nation.
>
> (They) are more lax in their terms of Communion (than those of 'old Dissent' such as Cam Meeting, whose roots went back to the 16th and 17th centuries) and maintain a more enlarged intercourse in their ministrations with the Calvanistic brethren of all denominations; can wear a gown and sometimes join in worship without revolting against a surplice.

(For additional information on the parish church at this time see addendum 'William Havergal')

6

Divisions and Reunions 1825-1840

The reason for the split in the congregation of the Tabernacle, which caused some of its most influential members to leave, is not known. In the two year inter-pastorate period that had just ended, the pulpit had been filled frequently by James Taylor of the Bull Inn. Possibly he and others felt that the status quo was satisfactory and that no outsider was needed, but had been over ruled by the majority. Another possibility is that George Neeton may have been too much of a moderate to suit the more dedicated Calvanists, such as the seceders were known to be. The fact that Rowland Hill supported the breakaway group supports either idea. In following years Hill gave great help to the secessionists and frequently preached for them at their meetings which at first were held in Hill Road Chapel. This place of worship came into being in 1821[1] as the meeting house of a group of Independent or 'Tent' Methodists,[2] who had originated in Bristol the previous year, under the leadership of George Pocock, John Pyer and others. Both Pocock and Pyer were Methodist Ministers in the city — the former was grandfather to W.G. Grace, the famous cricketer.[3] He was also a great traveller and inventor as well as preacher. In 1820 the villagers of Hanham had been startled to see him arrive in a horseless carriage pulled by an enormous wind driven kite flying over head.[4] Whether he made his entry into Dursley in a similar flamboyant manner is not recorded, but come he did, with John Pyer, and set up a tent mission. This must have been in one of the fields on the edge of, what was then, a very small town. At first he seems to have worked with the leaders of the established Wesleyans though their minister apparently was not too keen, but it appears that they demanded too much control over the work of the mission and a rift developed.

Large crowds flocked to the tent mission and eventually Hill Road Chapel was built to accommodate them. A Sunday School was started and it was not long before the Independent Methodists had a larger following than the Wesleyans — much to the chagrin of the latter who were still battling with the financial problems of paying off the outstanding £500 of the 1802 building costs, as well as an extra £300 spent more recently on buttressing up the building.

An enlargement of part of an old print of Dursley. On the left can be seen the gabled original Wesleyan Methodist Chapel. To the right of centre is St. James's Church before it was altered. The right hand lane is Boulton Lane. At its far end is a brewery, now Bymacks, and on its left is Boulton Lane Chapel. The other roadway is one of several which formerly ran from Parsonage St. to the Slade. This one seems to be that of which the remnant emerges now under the archway by Moon's green grocers shop in Silver Street.

The Independent Methodist cause collapsed as rapidly as it had arisen and in 1826 their chapel was taken over by the Tabernacle seceders. They were not to stay long, however, as they decided to build their own meeting house. This was erected halfway up Boulton Lane on the right and the cost was borne solely, it is said, by the leading figures of its congregation. It opened in about 1828. The Hill Road Chapel was sold by the trustees and subsequently became a warehouse and a garage. Two of the leaders of the 'Boultonians', as the separated brethren came to be known, were James Taylor and John Glanville.

Taylor, baker, inn keeper and Sunday School worker we have met already. He had been educated, first in the Water Street School, then Charles Whittard's School, Cam, 'where pupils of the better class were educated, among which were many county squires'.[5] This was a big house, now demolished, just below Cam Meeting and later it was occupied by the miller of Upper Cam Corn Mill.[6] As a young man 'he was very hostile to religion and hated, so he has been heard to say, God's People, and particularly Richard Trotman[7] an eminent saint, for when about to meet him he would pass by on the other side of the street or go another way. . . .

A view from the top of Boulton Lane up Union Street c. 1916. A bread cart of A.T. Walters can be seen on the right. The building on the left was Trull's shop.

(Maurice Owen)

But. . . The Lord caused a change to come over him and he could not help it. . . . He joined the Tabernacle, became a leading figure and 'an acceptable occasional labourer (preacher) in the towns and villages of that vicinity, as well as other parts of Gloucestershire. . . . From natural talents, acquirements and eminent piety (he) was particularly adapted for such a situation.' After four or five years with the Boultonians he left for Bristol to become, it is said, an agent for the Home Missionary Society. In 1835 he was ordained first pastor of Anvil Street Independent Chapel in the city and here he ministered with great effect. His retirement in 1864 was marked by a great tea meeting chaired by H.O. Wills, Esq., Congregationalist, philanthropist and tobacco baron. He died in 1871 aged eighty-five.

James Taylor retained a deep affection for Dursley all his life and at the Tabernacle his name was for long revered. Parents spoke of him to their children with something approaching adoration. In 1864 he was invited to return to Dursley to preach at the Sunday School anniversary, being a link with the great days of the school. He refused fearing that at the last moment he would breakdown under memories of past companions and associations.

John Glanville was born at Frampton-on-Severn in 1802 and, as a young man, was a clerk in 'Mr. Vizard's Bank' in Dursley. This was not to his liking and he left to begin a school in Uley Road which later he moved to Tilsdown House. In the 1830s he lived at Stanthill.

When James Taylor retired from the position of Tabernacle Sunday School Superintendent in about 1818, Glanville took on the position and, in spite of his extreme youth, he was an extremely able administrator of the 400 or so strong school. In 1828, after three years with the seceders he was persuaded to preach for the first time, at nearby Cambridge. From this beginning he was led to enter Homerton College, London, and received ordination as an 'evangelist' in Dursley on Monday 17 September 1832.[8] Presumably because it was bigger than the Boulton Lane Meeting House, the service was held in the Wesleyan Chapel. It was attended by many local ministers, (but seemingly not George Neeton,) and Rowland Hill, now aged eighty-eight and within seven months of the end of his life, preached in the evening to a 'crowded and very attentive congregation.'

The Evangelical Magazine for May 1836 records the opening of the Union Chapel, Berkeley which was attended by thirty ministers of several denominations from Dursley and elsewhere. Previous to the opening, on land given by him, Lord Segrave (later Fitzhardinge) of Berkeley Castle had granted use of the Town Hall for the 'preaching of the gospel by respectable Dissenting ministers'. It would appear that John Glanville was one of these and that he was prominent in getting the Union Chapel built. At least one of the building committee's meetings was held in Dursley.

John Glanville remained pastor of the Boultonians until, in 1835, he was called unanimously by the congregation of Kingswood Tabernacle near Bristol. The challenge of this historic church, founded by George Whitefield in 1739, suited him and his congregation outgrew its chapel and

The Revd John Glanville. *(Minister and Elders, Kingswood Tabernacle, Bristol)*

several extensions, such was the power and attraction of his preaching and the love and esteem he gained through his work to improve the lot of the ordinary person. He was its first settled minister.[9] In 1851 'a spacious and stately' new Tabernacle was opened near the older Whitefield Rooms. It was capable of seating 1250 people, which must have made it one of the biggest Nonconformist chapels in the Bristol area and it contained an organ. Previously hymns had been accompanied by a cello and maybe other instruments. H.O. Wills[10] laid the foundation stone and Lord Fitzhardinge of Berkeley Castle and Granville Berkeley were among those who gave generously to the building fund.[11]

The church at Kingswood built for John Glanville in 1851. The earlier meeting house, several times enlarged, is on the right. *(Minister and Elders, Kingswood Tabernacle)*

The interior of Kingswood Tabernacle. When built for John Glanville it seated 1250 people. Originally the choir seats were much higher. It is seen here as restored after damage sustained in the last war. *(Photo. Arthur G. Hancock, Kingswood)*

Its style, externally at least, was copied on a smaller scale when Rowland Hill's Tabernacle was rebuilt the following year in Wotton-under-Edge.

In 1855 John Glanville moved to Wotton-under-Edge and again his ministry was a great success but, while here, he and his wife received a great blow. His wife, a descendant of William Tyndale,[12] translator of the Bible into English, had borne him two sons. They were named after people he admired, Rowland Hill and Edward Gardner.[13] Both boys died in 1857,[14] Rowland, 21, while a student at Springhill College, one month before Edward, 27, then an assistant minister in Warwick. The double tragedy rocked John, but though his faith stood firm his health began to decline and he died early in 1866. His funeral was attended by a great concourse of ministers and people and, at the Tabernacle in Dursley, the breach of 1825 by then well healed, the Rev. Thomas Wallace discoursed on his death, preaching from Acts 8,v2 'to a numerous and deeply interested audience.'[15] His wife Sarah, and his daughter, returned to Dursley and became members of the Tabernacle.

In the early 1970s Rowland Hill's Tabernacle, Wotton-under-Edge, was sold to Woodward Brothers, builders, following the union of its congregation with that of the neighbouring Methodist Church. It is now being used to house a reconstruction of the famous Woodchester Roman Pavement. A condition of the sale was that all religious wall plaques were to

The Revd George Neeton, Minister 1825–34. (His name is sometimes spelt Neaton.)

be removed, except that to Rowland Hill himself. This was done and the tablets were placed in the adjoining graveyard. In 1979 a plaque to the memory of John Glanville was discovered there by the author and with the interest and cooperation of all people concerned and the technical skill of Mr. Barry Woodcock of Upper Cam, it has found a new home in Dursley Tabernacle, the nurturing church of his youth. One final point about John Glanville. H.O. Wills II named his first son Henry Overton III; his second, born in 1841, became Whitefield Glanville Wills — surely called after George Whitefield and John Glanville — and what greater tribute can one man pay another?

The exodus of many leading members from Dursley Tabernacle in 1825 left it much weakened. It also provided a source of local comment for 'some facetious play bills were published and posted about the town in September.' Our curiosity as to what these said must remain but that they were both interesting and scandalous is known because nearly sixty years later, in 1882, copies could be bought, privately, at two pence each, from Whitmore's Steam Printing Office in the town.[16]

In this time of need, men like Butcher Packer came forward to fill the void in Tabernacle leadership, also William Smith, clothier, of New Mills (Ferney) who at his death bequeathed £150 in 3% stock, and John Trotman, cardboard maker. With these men and Revd. George Neeton 'a good plain, sound preacher' the setback was checked and growth followed. Account books were begun. The first entry reveals that in 1825, income for the three months up to Christmas resulted from the quarterly collection of £6 8*s* 11*d* contributed by the whole congregation and £29 12*s* 6*d* paid as pew rents by just six people, all Deacons. Of the total sum of £36 1*s* 5*d*. Mr Neeton received £27 10*s* 0*d*, and Sarah Newth £6 for cleaning the Tabernacle. Seven shillings went on candles.

Three years later the accounts show that the Tabernacle was still instructing children in the basics of secular education, as well as the religion, as 2*s* 3*d* was spent on pens and ink and £1 5*s* 0*d* on copy books. In the same year, in August, a Sunday School sermon raised £15 for the school. Three months later, 'A Juvenile Society for the purpose of relieving sick scholars' was instituted with 130 members and in December 1828 came a similar scheme for teachers, twenty-three men and sixteen women. Similar arrangements operated at the Boulton Lane Chapel.

For teachers a monthly Sunday morning prayer meeting at eight o'clock was begun and in 1831, the school supervision was taken over by Samuel Stockwell, Keeper of Dursley Turnpike Gate (now the Pike House Cafe). It was in this year too that Mr. Brothers spent 6*s* 6*d*. on repairs to school chairs and benches in the Tabernacle, 18*s* 8*d* was spent on 'reward books and 6*s* 8*d* on beer and cider for the singers and children. It was also the year when, in September, Wesleyan, Tabernacle and Boultonian children joined forces to celebrate the jubilee of the Sunday School movement by processing through the streets singing hymns before attending a joint

RULES AND ORDERS

TO BE OBSERVED BY THE TEACHERS

OF THE

Tabernacle Sunday School.

DURSLEY,

INSTITUTED THE NINTH DAY OF DECEMBER, 1828,

FOR THE PURPOSE OF RELIEVING THE SICK TEACHERS

BELONGING TO THE SUNDAY SCHOOL.

REV. G. NEATON,	*PRESIDENT.*
MR. W. HARRIS,	*TREASURER.*
MR. T. WHITTARD,	*SECRETARY*

ARTICLE I.

EVERY Teacher shall pay for the use of the fund the sum of one penny per week, to be collected by the superintendant every Sabbath morning. No Teacher shall become a member until he or she have paid into the fund for the space of three months. After the expiration of such time, if it shall please God to visit any member with sickness, notice is to be given to the Superintendant who shall visit them, and he finding them sick, shall report it to the Secretary, who shall pay, or cause to be paid, the sum of two shillings and sixpence per week during such sickness.

II.

No Teacher shall have any benefit from the fund who has not duly paid four succeeding weeks prior to such sickness; but, should the nature of their vocation render them unable to attend, or should they reside at a distance from Dursley, that in such case three months shall be allowed to clear up their arrears.

III.

That if any member shall through neglect of pay be suspended, such member shall not be re-admitted until they have paid up all arrears.

IV.

It is agreed that there shall be a Treasurer and Secretary appointed, who shall keep a regular account of the sums received and paid; and that a quarterly meeting of the members be held in the Vestry on the second Tuesday in January—April—July and October, at six o'clock in the evening, to take into consideration the state of the fund, when any further improvement for the benefit of the society may be proposed.

V.

That a further subscription of sixpence per member be collected at the death of a member, to be added to the fund; and that when it shall please God to terminate the life of any member, the Managers of the fund shall pay or cause to be paid to the friends of the deceased, the sum of two pounds ten shillings, towards defraying the expense of the funeral.

VI.

That if the fund of this society should through sickness or deaths be reduced as low as five pounds, then, and as often as the same shall happen, there shall be a further subscription of threepence collected from each member.

VII.

That if any disputes arise respecting the administration of money, they shall be decided by a majority of the Society.

VIII.

That any young persons not Teachers in the school, but who may have left in consequence of age or being called out to service, (provided they reside within two miles of the Tabernacle) shall be eligible to become members of this Society upon subscribing to the foregoing rules; and that such persons shall be proposed by a Teacher at least three weeks previous to a quarterly meeting, and that the admission of such persons be determined by ballot.

IX.

That a number of these Articles be printed, and that each member pay twopence for a copy; and that on the admission of any members the said members receive a copy, for which they shall pay twopence.

The rules of the sick club for Sunday School teachers begun by George Neeton in 1828.

service at the Tabernacle. After this they departed to their own chapels to be 'supplied with buns'.

Among the usual recurring items which appear in the account books — candles, books and magazines from London, pens and ink, and the occasional beer, cider and cakes — two stand out. One is the annual payment of about 4*s* to Elijah Newth 'for instructing the children in singing' — no other teachers seem to have been so recompensed. The other took the form of 'to John Stiff for posting up bills 2*s* 6*d*'. The bills were hand bills and as Dursley was such a small town at the time, it is safe to assume that John Stiff and others toured the surrounding villages before big events with advertising material.

In the Spring of 1834 George Neeton left Dursley for Woolwich. Later he moved[17] to Norwich Tabernacle, then Tunbridge Wells, Canterbury and, after a further spell in London he returned to Dursley in 1867 to complete his retirement. He and his wife, Mary, lived in 'The Crescent' opposite the Tabernacle.[18] He died in 1872, a year after Mary, and both are buried in the Tabernacle grave yard.

One and a half years elapsed before the Rev. Eliakin Lloyd Shadrack took up the pastorate. Born at Talybont, Cardiganshire, 1805, trained for the ministry at Neuaddlwyd and Rotherham Academies, he began his life's work as co-pastor with his father in Aberystwth.[19] After his arrival in Dursley in 1835, he quickly became a popular preacher, his Welsh elequence filling the Tabernacle Sunday by Sunday.

The school continued; 'gas light in area to give sufficient light when instructing the children in singing' was installed in 1836 at a cost of 12*s*. In the same year the large sum of 17*s* 10*d* was paid for washing the Tabernacle and 32*s* 5*d* for emptying and mending the privy.

The Coronation of 'Victoria the 1st' came in 1838 and £1 7*s* 6*d* was expended on copies of the National Anthem, medals and ribbons. Children from all Sunday schools, some 700 in total, joined in the celebrations, chief of which was a great feast in June.[20] After the ritual of parading the town in best clothes and medals, accompanied by 'many of the most respectable inhabitants' of the town, a band and numerous floral garlands held aloft on poles, they swelled the crowds in the market place to create over 1500 diners. They fed on mutton and beef and plum pudding and beer. Among the several 'reverends' on the committee which organised the gargantuan meal were Eliakim Shadrach — and Mr. Clapp.

Jerome Clapp came to Dursley to be pastor to the Boulton Lane Chapel congregation after the departure of John Glanville in 1835, coming from Cirencester. There is evidence to suggest that he may have been the founder of the Independent Meeting which is now Cirencester United Reformed Church. It is known that he opened a chapel in the town in 1833.[21] It is said that he was the father of Jerome K. Jerome the author. Be this as it may, Clapp was a man of clever, lively temperament, 'a thorough Nonconformist, what some would call a "political Dissenting Parson". One challenge he took up in Dursley was the question of church rates. This was at a time when there was considerable agitation nationally against the centuries old custom of levying a rate on all families in a community for the support of its parish church. This was particularly irksome to those who dissented from that church. In Dursley, in March 1840, the church wardens proposed a *3d* in the pound rate to put the churchyard in order and repair. The customary vestry meeting of rate payers was called to approve it but the motion was lost — a most unusual state of affairs. It was decided to hold immediately a town poll and this approved the rate, 105 for, thirty against. Maybe this was the occasion when Jerome Clapp is known to have led the opposition to church rates in Dursley. Rallying behind him opponents filled the vestry so full that the meeting had to be moved into the church itself. Mr. Clapp spoke against the imposition of the rate and demanded that the church accounts for the preceding year be read. This was done, 'the items about washing surplices and wine etc. . . causing amusement and disgust.'[22]

If Jerome Clapp's action sounds petty it must be remembered that the question of church rates was a burning issue in this era. Many Dissenters were incensed that as well as supporting their own chapel and minister they were forced to pay also, by way of a parish rate on everyone, for the upkeep of the parish church from which they had separated themselves — its fabric including often substantial restoration work, its administration and its clergy. It was an injustice felt all the more keenly for it was not unknown for the parish clergy to behave arrogantly and high handedly towards Dissenters, for example refusing them burial in the parish graveyard.

All through the nineteenth century Dissenters battled for, and slowly gained by acts of Parliament, rights and privileges on a par with those enjoyed by members of the state church in such fields as local government and education, freedom from degrading legislation on the registration of chapels, births, deaths and marriages, burial in municipal cemetries and so on, and for freedom from the tyranny of church courts which in the first part of the century still had powers to imprison. The continual struggle accounts for much of the bitterness between Conformist and Nonconformist seen in that century.

The secessionists in Boulton Lane seem never to have been very numerous and Jerome Clapp decided eventually, that as the cause was unlikely to strengthen, it would be best if a reunion was made with the Tabernacle. This he recommended to his congregation. It was accepted and took place in the Spring of 1840 amid great rejoicing. To accommodate the increased numbers, the centre ground floor of the Tabernacle was pewed for the first time. Clapp preached in the Tabernacle several times after the reunion and then left the town for Appledore in Devon where he spent seven years. His movements after that are uncertain but evidence suggests he moved to Walsall.

We have information about the state of the town's Sunday Schools just before the Boulton Lane Chapel closed.[23]

	Boys	Girls	Total	Children working:-		Children at day school	
				Wire Work	Other work such as shoemaking	No.	%
St. James	130	69	199	140	39	20	10
Weslyan	61	84	145	36	69	40	27
Tabernacle	70	90	160	40	70	52	32
Boulton Lane	62	115	177	60	94	23	13

The schools were a matter of pride to their churches, too much so in the eyes of George Pryce, a day school master, who lamented over the 'sectarian zeal' and the 'contending factions.'[24]

One example of the zeal, though not necessarily sectarian, was shown by the Howard family who owned three wool cloth mills in the town — two small ones in Water Street and a third where now stands the churn works of R.A. Lister & Co. Some of them at least were members of the Tabernacle and it was said of the 'principal partner' that he required his men to attend religious worship and that he took an interest in the 'sabbath education' of their children. He demanded to see the tickets issued to the children when they attended Sunday school and, if it appeared that they did not attend regularly, the men were dismissed from his employment.[29] It is not known if he insisted that the Sunday school was to be one in particular.

It is interesting to note that while thirty-two percent of Tabernacle children and twenty-seven per cent of Wesleyan children received weekday schooling, percentages for the Anglican and Boulton Lane Churches were much lower. Probably this reflects the social standing of their supporters. For the former these seem to have been largely craftsmen and shopkeepers and drawn from a large geographical area around the town which stretched well outside parish boundaries. St. James's Church and the Boultonians must have taken most of their children from families living in the poor, crowded 'wretched and destitute'[26] dwellings immediately around them. Wealthy adherents of St. James's almost certainly sent their children to private schools.

One more event should be recorded before the end of this chapter. The date — Tuesday 30 July 1839;[27] the place — Stinchcombe Hill; the occasion — celebrations to mark the centenary of the first field preaching by George Whitefield and his first open air evangelising tour of Gloucestershire. The fact that Stinchcombe Hill was chosen out of the many places where Whitefield drew great, eager, crowds on his tours, though not until 1743, suggests that Eliakim Shadrack and his congregation were very conscious of the origin of the Tabernacle and at least inspired and perhaps even organised the occasion.

The morning of the great day broke under lowering skies but the threat of rain did not prevent great crowds flocking to the hill. Estimates of those present ranged from five to fifteen thousand, with the *Gloucester Journal*, which gave it extensive coverage, stating 10,000, — 'the great majority. . . remarkably well dressed'. With tents for the preachers, booths for refreshments where lunch could be had for a shilling and tea for sixpence, facilities where 'care will be taken for the comfort of the ladies' and all the foot, horse and carriage traffic associated with big gatherings of people, the hill top must have presented a lively, colourful spectacle. For the religious services two large platforms had been erected fifty yards apart, one for the hundred or so ministers of many denominations present and the other for important visitors. Presumably the mass of the people sat on the grass or stood.

The morning service began at 'half past ten o'clock' with the Rev. Shadrack announcing the first hymn. The Rev. East of Birmingham preached, Dr. Ross of Kidderminster spoke on the life of George Whitefield, 'the apostle of the English Empire', and John Glanville of Kingswood concluded with prayer. During the lunch break some people returned to Dursley but 'numbers also retired in little gipsy parties to the precincts of the adjoining picturesque wood where green turf served for tables and seats and provisions that had been brought to the hill for the occasion were produced and partaken in truly Sylvan fashion. The various groups profusely scattered in all directions, the tents, the booths on the brow of the hill, the miscellaneous vehicles drawn round the spot and the almost numberless horses released from their burdens and occupied in the same satisfactory employment as their masters, together furnished a scene of a most novel and interesting description.'

In the afternoon heavy rain began, and continued for the rest of the day, but in spite of this, thousands remained to take part in the two o'clock service and 'continued to brave the pelting of the pitiless storms for hours, apparently regardless of the fury of the elements and completely engrossed with the appeals made to them by ministers preaching from tent doorways. The evening service planned on the hill was abandoned in favour of acts of worship in the churches of the town below and so the crowds retired. 'The perseverance of the thousands of spectators in remaining for hours on the hill exposed to incessant rain was most astonishing and the appearance of the party, particularly the females, on descending the hill was grotesque in the extreme. Bonnets, silk gowns, ribbons etc. which in the morning added gaiety and splendour to the beauty of the wearers, were battered into the most unfortunate and ludicrous shapes by the heavy rain, and the high wind, which accompanied it, completed the delapidation of the feminine adornment. At every step, patterns, clogs, shoes and boots of the fair wearers became fastened in the moistened earth and numberless were the kind offices required from their male attendants who, whether beau or benedict, presented anything but a spruce and captivating appearance. Still in the midst of these disagreeable incidents the utmost decorum and pleasant feeling was evinced. . . .'

The chapels of Dursley were filled for the evening services, the Tabernacle for one being 'crowded to excess.' Here 'powerful sermons' were preached by Revd. Dr. Redford of Worcester and the Revd. Hinton of London. In spite of the weather, the day was a great success, one of tremendous enthusiasm and vitality. The organising committee met in its wake and decided to erect a 'monumental column' to the memory of George Whitefield. It was never built but in a way his memorial was there already — in the stones of the meeting houses like the Tabernacles at Rodborough, North Nibley and Dursley and in the continuing interest in the spiritual life which he and John Wesley had done so much to revive many years before.

7

Boulton Lane Hall

The return of the Tabernacle seceders left the Boulton Lane Chapel empty and thereafter it had a variety of uses. In 1842 it was opened by Benjamin Parsons of Ebley as a Temperance Hall[1] but it seems to have been used as such for only a short time, as in the same year it is recorded that a British School opened there — unless of course the building had dual usage.

The British and Foreign Schools Societies began in 1808 to promote education for the ordinary child based on non-sectarian Christianity. At first it drew support from some Anglicans[2] as well as Nonconformists, but in 1811 'The National Society for the Education of the Poor in the Principles of the Established Church' came into being and that support disappeared. Dursley, Cam and most of the surrounding villages had National Schools; Cambridge and Wotton-under-Edge had British Schools. Of Dursley's British School we know almost nothing. Tabernacle records refer only once to it — in 1848, *18 4s 6d* was received in cash on account. *Slater's Directory* for 1852 — 3 states that the master and mistress were Isaac and Elizabeth Briginshaw. It seems to have closed around 1856.

In June 1851, it was registered by Joseph Bloodworth as a place of worship — probably for the members of a Methodist splinter group, the Wesleyan Reform Church, which began to meet there at about this time. They were followed by another such group some six years later, the Wesleyan New Connection. Both Societies had Sunday Schools.

The structure of the Wesleyan Chapel near the Market House was by the early 1860s giving cause for considerable concern and a survey revealed that it was in a very poor condition, damp and without drainage, walls cracked and subsiding. The decision was made to demolish the building and rebuild and, while this was in progress, the congregation rented the Boulton Lane Chapel. This was used for a year until the new chapel was opened in the Summer of 1864. Builders of the new chapel were Edmund Bloodworth, and Charles his son, of Woodmancote[3] and the ends of the beams were carved by the Long Street cabinet maker James Newth.[4] The challenge of the rebuilding programme infused the Wesleyans with a new spirit and one result was the opening by them, on 10 January 1865, of a new day school under the care of schoolmaster Bennett Williams. It was

The Wesleyan Methodist Chapel c. 1900 in what was then The Knapp. *(Mrs E. Talboys)*

'intended that the school (should) be conducted on the most liberal basis and open to children of all denominations' — on payment of three pence per week.[5] The school was in the Boulton Lane Chapel and, as in later years, it was occasionally referred to as the 'British School' it may have been associated with the Society. It was a continuation of the concern Dursley Methodists felt for education, as before 1865 a day school had been run on chapel premises.[6]

The new Boulton Lane School seems to have been vigorous from the start and by 1868 had 200 children. An annual tea meeting had been instituted by then and in that year it was held on January 25th. The children ate first, at four o'clock, and then at five o'clock served tea to 200 mothers and friends. The assembled company was addressed by the Rev. Thomas Wallace and Mr. Lang of the Tabernacle, which gave strong support to the school, and then by the Wesleyan Reverends Blake and Anderson. The occasion finished with songs by the children and music played by the school drum and fife band.[7]

In the 1890s pressure came from Government sources to improve conditions. Several meetings were called to discuss the problems until it was suggested that a new school be erected, to commemorate the Diamond Jubilee of Queen Victoria. This was agreed and the Victoria Schools (now Dursley Technical College) opened next to the Methodist Chapel, and under its control, in May 1898. The children, all 125 of them 'with nice clean faces and tidily brushed hair' moved in, in June.[8] Management of the

An artist's impression of the Victoria Day Schools when they opened in 1898.

The Victoria Day Schools c. 1916. On the right is part of Castle Farm, the fields of which were used frequently for town celebrations.

Infants and babies at the Victoria Schools 1913. Judging by expressions, taking a photograph was a very serious event *(Mrs A.E. Hill)*

school was vested in the ministers of the Wesleyan and Tabernacle churches and six members each from their congregations. In 1914 the buildings were rented to the County Council which took over the running of the school and this situation lasted until the end of World War II when the premises were purchased by the county.[9]

Another school connected with the Methodists, though a private one, was at the south end of Prospect Place — the school of Mr. A.G. Hunt. It was founded in 1813, possibly by Methodist Richard Goodrich who was certainly proprietor in 1839. It lasted until at least World War I and Mr. Hunt, who has been mentioned already in connection with the closure of the Water Street School, used to take his boarders to the Wesleyan chapel every Sunday. His daughter was headmistress at the Boulton Lane school in its last days and infants' mistress when the Victoria schools opened.[10]

The vacated Boulton Lane Hall was bought by public subscription in 1898 and given to the Dursley Volunteer Rifle Brigade as a drill hall. It remained in volunteer soldier hands for many years before becoming a public hall. In about 1959 it was demolished by the Rural District Council for redevelopment purposes, much against the wishes of the Parish Council. The scheme has not materialised and the site stands open and derelict.

A mystery picture of about 1900. It is obviously a chapel converted to secular use and is probably Boulton Lane Chapel. *(Mrs M. Talboys)*

In 1858 Alfred Bloodworth became a member of the Tabernacle, and such were his talents that by 1864, when he was but twenty-four, he was Church Secretary. It is interesting to note how the Tabernacle then trusted the judgement of its young people. The erection of the Parsonage and the present Tabernacle came about when the Revd William Bennett was in his early thirties; the heydays of the Sunday school were when James Taylor and John Glanville were successive superintendents, each being only in his late teens when taking on the position. Of Alfred we know little except that he was the son and elder brother of the Edmund and Charles Bloodworth who built the present Methodist Church. He had a second brother, Sydney, youngest of the three, who became a builder himself and who was the last man to be elected Bailiff of Dursley. According to Alfred, all the Bloodworths in the area at the time were descents of one, a Welshman, who came to the county in 1744. One passion of Alfred was the history of his church and much of what has been written in this book so far has been based on the information he discovered, often from interviews from old people, and carefully recorded in small cramped writing in notebooks in preparation for a lecture in 1865. Without his searching, inquiring mind much of the detailed history of the Tabernacle from about 1770 to 1865 would not have survived to today.

Alfred's career as Church Secretary was short, for in August 1865 he vanishes from the scene. No record of a farewell gift exists and since his departure coincides with the arrival of the Rev. Thomas Wallace it is reasonable to assume that he disagreed with the new minister's appointment and shook the dust of the Tabernacle from his feet.

Alfred Bloodworth also recorded the material he uncovered about the parish and Wesleyan Schools, and this too has been used, and he included references to other groups. 'The Irvingites headed by Mr. John Vizard, now attorney here and churchwarden etc., carried on in a room in the Mill Tails near Long Street (probably roughly where now, 1981, is Lister's canteen) upwards of thirty years ago for a short time, and the Mormonites — that nasty religion — commenced in a room behind T. Hall's, Parsonage Street, and lasted about a year. . . . There are some Baptists and some having the views of the (Plymouth) Brethren. Will popery ever be re-introduced here? This may suggest the enquiry — is it not here already? Are there not some who take the name 'Protestant' who are sowing the seeds of that. . . system in this place? Oh, it is more than probable that that which has been a rumour hitherto may become reality and a building reared in which popery shall be avowedly taught'. His comments, which should be read against the background of revived interest in catholicism in the Anglican Church nationally, show that Roman Catholicism, absent from Dursley from the time of the Reformation, was returning. Today it is well established with a suite of buildings on the outskirts of the town built some forty years ago. The church, named St. Dominics after the Dominican monks of Woodchester, was opened by the Bishop of Clifton. Contacts between its adherents and these of the other main Christian denominations in the town are generally cordial, particularly at the social level, but a hundred years ago this was far from the case. Alfred Bloodworth, a moderate man in so many of his views was virulently anti Roman Catholic. He was, perhaps, a typical Victorian Nonconformist in this and his attitude would have been echoed by many, if not all, of his fellow Congregationalists at the Tabernacle.

Before St. Dominics was built Roman Catholics used the Y.M.C.A. hall in Long St. for a while. Evelyn Waugh, author, who lived at Piers Court, Stinchcombe 1937–54, wrote in his diary for 1937 of his disgust at having to worship among the cigarette stubs left from the previous nights usage.

8

Dursley in Decline

Quite when the members of Dursley Tabernacle considered it to be an Independent church is unknown. By calling a minister, David Ralph, in 1795, they had taken a step in that direction and the Revd. Ralph did join the Gloucestershire Association of Independent Ministers. It was, however, still in the Rodborough Connection, though by that time this seems to have been purely a friendly association of churches with Calvanist and evangelical roots. By 1825 it had deacons to advise and administer, part of the structure of an Independent church. Probably the change to conventional Independency came slowly, almost imperceptibly bringing with it relaxation of strict Calvanistic theology. The descriptions 'Independent' and 'Congregational' are difficult to distinguish and were often used interchangeably up to the time being considered. After the formation of the Congregational Union of England and Wales in 1831, the former term became less common in England though it survived in such names as The Independent Press.

In 1842 *The Church and State Gazette* published an article 'Dissenting Statistics.' Though written with a strong Anglican bias, it provides an interesting comment on the change which The Tabernacle Society had undergone —

> We perceive that the Whitefieldites, or Calvanistic Methodists, and Lady Huntingdonites or followers of her ladyship, are gradually violating the original trusts of the chapels founded by George Whitefield and by her ladyship and are enlisting under the banner of the Moorgate Union (i.e. the Congregational Union.) This ought not to be. Mr. Whitefield and Lady Huntingdon had views of a very different character with reference to the Church of England, from those held by the conductors of the 'Patriot' and the 'Nonconformist' and were, indeed, irregular at the Church of England. But can this be said of 'the Congregational Board'? By no means. It is time that the system of overthrowing all the trusts and intentions of the founders of charities and institutions, whether Dissenting or Methodist, should be put a stop to and Dissenters who respect themselves should not lend themselves to such frauds of the wills of testators.

It stated that Gloucestershire had fifty-seven Congregational meeting houses and continued that while Congregationalism in Essex showed 'generally, low vulgar cunning, in the latter (i.e. Glos.) it is less prosperous but much more quiet and conscientious.' Gloucestershire chapels had, on average, 400 seats of which no more than thirty or forty were free.

> 'Among dissenters, even poor servant girls, with their country wages of £4, £5 and £6 per annum are expected to pay for a seat in the gallery, costing them *6s* per annum; to contribute to the quarterly collections for 'defraying the expenses incidental to carrying on the worship of God' etc; to subscribe to the Missionary Society one penny per week; and thus, with ragged shoes and stockings and torn gowns, to part with twenty to twenty-five per cent of their hardly earned stipend. In Dissenting places of worship 'the gentry' are those who pay: and whose who do not, must stand, not sit, in the aisles.'

Just how much of this applied to The Tabernacle is unknown, but it is an interesting insight into what happened in some Dissenting chapels.

The early 1840s were politically active for Dursley's Nonconformists. In 1815 Parliament had put a new 'corn law' on the statute book. The reasoning behind this has been variously interpreted, one idea being that it was designed to hold the price of corn at a level which made it a viable crop for British farmers. Whatever the motives, in the general depressions of following decades, it put the price of bread almost beyond the reach of the low earning, ordinary worker. Richard Cobden, M.P., in 1841 stated that the average working family in the kingdom, earning ten shillings a week, had to spent five on bread. Forty per cent of this, or two shillings, was Corn Law tax. In the wool cloth areas of Gloucestershire, handloom weavers might only receive seven shillings a week.

The abject poverty of many working people, accentuated by the Corn Laws, led to the establishment of a vociferous Anti Corn Law League. In 1841 it called in Manchester a 'Conference of Ministers of all Denominations' at which, it claimed, 650 ministers and representatives, from Quakers to Roman Catholics, attended.[2] Among them were ministers from Slimbridge, Berkeley, Wickwar, Falfield, Wotton-under-Edge and Stroud. The Rev. E.L. Shadrack of Dursley Tabernacle was also there, and it was probably Eliakim who spoke of the town:-

> The working classes from Dursley and the villages of Cam and Uley never had so little employment (after the collapse of the wool trade) as at present. Many of them with their wives and families are prolonging their existence by means of potatoes and salt only, rather than enter the union workhouse; but they must enter ere long if they have no work or starve. . . . The labouring classes are prevented from attending religious places of worship because they have been obliged to pledge their wearing apparel to buy food. . . .[3]

Jerome Clapp was also present, as was Benjamin Parsons 'at Hebley' who stated that in his neighbourhood 'a great number of persons. . . were destitute of clothes. They contrived to wrap themselves up and came to the chapel at night, but were absent in the morning'. He spoke of beds at pawnbrokers, empty houses and of being able to stand on many a grave brought about by the operation of the Corn Laws.

The Laws were repealed in 1846.

1843 saw an attempt by Parliament to legislate in such a way as to remove some of the worst abuses of women and child labour in factories. It was a subject which roused great emotions for and against. Only fifteen years before, in Chippenham, replying to chiding by the town's M.P. on the working conditions of his child employees, a wool cloth owner proudly stated that he knew something about children 'having been an extensive manufacturer for more than thirty years in Wiltshire, Gloucestershire and Yorkshire. It was a well known fact that they imbibed nourishment from the oily quality of the wool and, as to the number of hours they were at work, experience, which was the best guide, had proved that they did not suffer from such a length of time —[4] six in the morning to eight at night — in fact it kept them out of mischief!

One of the clauses of the prospective legislation was that children should be freed from work, either mornings or afternoons, to attend grant aided schools. Dissenters opposed this vigorously, seeing it as placing the education of the young in the hands of the Established Church. Petitions poured in from all over the country, the Hon. Grantley Berkeley, local M.P., handling those from Wotton-under-Edge, Uley, Berkeley, North Nibley, Cam and elsewhere. There was also one from Dursley, probably a joint Wesleyan — Tabernacle affair.[5]

Caught between the opposing pressures of Anglicans and Dissenters, the Government withdrew the education clauses and the bill was passed in 1844. By then another proposed act had some Dissenters up in arms and this too brought a wave of protesting petitions upon the Government including, again, one from Dursley, presented by Grantley Berkeley.[6] The proposed legislation was the 'The Dissenters' Chapels Act'. Many English Presbyterian Churches had by the 1800s become Unitarian. The act was designed to protect their properties from claims made by Trinitarians and, despite the opposition of the latter, it became law.

In the light of the intense feeling the proposed law created locally it is interesting to remember that 'The Father of Unitarianism', John Biddle, came from Wotton-under-Edge. His views in the seventeenth century roused so much hostility, even clamours for his death, that Oliver Cromwell used his authority to protect him by banishing him to the Scilly Isles. After the Restoration Biddle was brought back to die in a fetid London prison in 1662.[7]

It is difficult for us, today, to appreciate the intensity of feeling that matters, like those just referred to, generated. Politically and religiously Nonconformists were assuming great power and, with confident righteousness, they were not afraid to express their views.

In Eliakim Shadrack, the Tabernacle had a great minister willing to lead

The Revd Eliakim L. Shadrack, minister 1835–56, from a painting by an itinerant artist.

his congregation spiritually and temporally, and there developed a deep bond of affection between him and his people. Between him and the Rector, there seems to have been at least mutual respect, for they were able to cooperate in such matters as promoting the British and Foreign Bible Society in the town. Thus in 1854 he and the Rev. Cornwall both spoke at a Bible Society meeting in the Town Hall when £7 was raised.[8] The Revd. Shadrack's has been the longest pastorate, so far, in the history of the church, over twenty years, and it covered perhaps the most desperate times the town has ever experienced. Its main industry, the wool cloth trade collapsed soon after his arrival and the hungry forties followed with their endless days of extreme privation for working folk. The Boulton Lane Chapel, witnessing the destitution around it, set up a clothing club for its Sunday school scholars. After reunion, this was taken up by the Tabernacle and enabled children to save up for clothes. Its details, in its original form, are not clear but it was reorgnised in later years and will be considered then.

The population of the town dropped by twenty per cent between the beginning and the end of Shadrack's pastorate. Many people left, some to emigrate to the colonies of North America or Australia, some to find other work as in the Great Western Cotton Factory in Bristol. Houses stood empty. This must have affected all three churches, numerically and financially. One reason for the founding of St. Mark's Church in Woodmancote was the general poverty of the town. The non-resident rector of the time revised the system of pew charges at St. James's, and as the poor would have been unable to afford these and, therefore, excluded, Henry Vizard conceived the idea of erecting a chapel where no such charges would be made. He provided the ground for it and a burial yard, most of the finance needed to build it and an endowment which brings in an income of £500 p.a.[9] St. Mark's was consecrated on the 16 April 1844 by the Bishop of Gloucester 'assisted . . . by thirty-two priests and two deacons who followed the Bishop in procession from an adjoining house. The appearance of so large a body of clergy, all clothed in surplices, in so retired a town and at the consecration of so small a chapel, produced a very striking and solemn effect'.[10]

For many years Eliakim Shadrack received an income of £100 p.a., this coming mainly from pew rents paid by a very few, and a quarterly collection made among the many. In 1844, five families only paid pew rents for the quarter ending April 6th:-

J.H. Howard, clother £16 *5s 9d* for pews in the gallery and below.

Joseph Gazard, farmer of Sheephouse Farm *10s* for a table pew.

Benjamin Weaver, brewer, of Uley Road, pews under the gallery £11 *6s 3d.*

George Harding, rope maker and Mr. Organ, pews in gallery £2 *8s 0d.*

The quarterly collection brought in £4 *10s 8d.*

Thus for the quarter, eighty-five per cent of the income was provided by five people, the balance by the hundreds who made up the general congregation.

A financial crisis hit the Tabernacle in 1854. What happened can best be seen by comparing the incomes over several years. To equate with todays values multiply by roughly fifty.

	1852	1853	1854	1855
From Pew rents:-				
Howard	£ 55-8-6	£ 60-7-0	£ 9-12-6	Nil
Gazard	£ 2-7-0	£ 2-7-0	£43-12-7	£40-10-6
Weaver	£ 38-0-0	£ 31-9-6	£19-5-6	£26-12-0
Harding	£ 10-3-6	£ 7-1-6	£ 7-5-6	£ 5-17-6
	£103-19-0	£101-5-0	£79-16-1	£73-0-0
From Quarterly collections:-	£ 17-3-3	£ 17-18-3½	£10-7-9½	£10-9-6
Total	£121-2-3	£119-3-3½	£90-3-10½	£83-9-6

From Burial fees:- Various small amounts.

The figures show that in 1852 and 1853 there were only four families renting pews and of these, James Hamnet Howard's provided nearly fifty per cent of the church income — in 1853 perhaps roughly £3000 in todays terms. Howard was owner of Townsend Wool Cloth Mill. He lived at The Priory and in 1851 employed eighty-five hands.[11] In March 1854 his mill was sold to Edward Gazard[12] who used it thereafter as a saw mill for his timber, carpentry and building business. A memorial to J.H. Howard's parents exists in the Tabernacle, his father dying in 1842. He had a brother John who had mills in Water Street and a son Charles who emigrated to the U.S.A. By 1856 both James Hamnet and John Howard had left Dursley, probably as a result of declining returns in the wool trade. Their departure must have left the Tabernacle almost panic stricken. Farmer Joseph Gazard stepped into the breach, taking over some of the Howard pews but his contributions did not match the Howards. Income from the other two families of seat holders dropped also as did the total of quarterly collections. In both cases maybe the drop can be related to the going of J.H. Howard. The Weavers and Hardings were traders and if by the departure of the Howards some eighty-five families lost their sources of income, both would have been affected too. So far as the drop in quarterly collection is concerned, can we see here the defection of some of Howard's former employees, present Sunday by Sunday till then through fear of losing their jobs — or simply that they lost them anyway? As we do not know how many hands Edward Gazard kept on when he took over, this can only be a point of conjecture.

LINES PENNED ON THE DECEASE OF THE

Rev. E. L. Shadrach,

The late beloved Minister of the Congregational Church, Pembroke Dock, and 22 Years Pastor of the Tabernacle, Dursley.

"*He, being dead, yet speaketh.*"—HEBREWS XI. 4.

FAREWELL, farewell, thou man of God,
Thy soul has passed away!
When gazing on thy earthly form,
We only look on clay;—
Thy spirit is with Jesus now,—
Its rest, the home of love,—
All cares, and pains, and sorrows here,
Are swallowed up above.

A Soldier of the Saviour's cross,
Endowed with courage true,
Firm in the battle thou didst stand,
Resolved to dare and do;—
Many a conflict stern and fierce,
For Jesus thou didst fight;
Now, faithful through the whole campaign,
The crown thou hast is bright.

A Teacher of the Church thou wert,
Christ's words of love to speak,
Devout and holy souls rejoiced,—
The humble, poor, and meek:
The Gospel thou didst e'er proclaim,
With plainness and with zeal,
And always was it thy desire,
That Gospel men might feel.

A faithful Messenger in thee
The sinner ever found,
In pointed, practical appeals,
Thy sermons did abound;
A wise Advisor numbers had,
In times of gloom or doubt,
And those who came to seek advice,
The clue from thee found out.

A Friend to all, the people had
In penury or woe,
None wanting aid didst thou contemn,
While sojourning here below.
And when thine eyes were sealed in death,
How many dropped the tear,
Fit tribute to thy memory,
From numbers far and near.

Farewell, farewell, dear man of God,
Thou wilt not be forgot,
Though thousands unremembered are,—
For 'tis the common lot!
The fragrance of thy character
Will fresh and precious be,
Until thy flock meet thee above,
The Saviour's face to see!

Dursley, April 12th, 1869. REV. T. WALLACE.

WHITMORE, PRINTER, DURSLEY.

In February 1855 the Rev. Shadrack received only £14 *5s 6d* instead of £25. Over the whole year his income dropped by a third to £66 *5s 7½d.* One can imagine the heart searching of minister and church leaders and the sad decision that pastor and congregation must part. Early in 1856 Eliakim Shadrack left for Pembroke Dock Tabernacle where he ministered until he died, aged sixty-four, in April 1869, 'universally respected and lamented'. The news of his death grieved his former congregation in Dursley and it was 'improved' upon by its then minister Thomas Wallace. Wallace was moved to compose a poem as a tribute and this was printed and widely distributed in Dursley and Pembroke Dock.

The problems of E.L. Shadrack in 1854-5 shows the absolute dependence many a Congregational minister had in Victorian times on just a few members of his congregation. In Dursley only four families committed themselves deeply financially. The rest of the members, some fifty families, and the adherents, numbers unknown but probably hundreds, were unable or unprepared to do likewise. It was a situation which continued at The Tabernacle until the early 1900s, though by this time other sources of income had altered the balance a little.

Before leaving the period of Mr. Shadrack's ministry there are three more events worthy of mention.

Richard Williams[13] was a son of Rice Williams, sometime baker and maltster, by 1844 keeper of the Bull Inn, Woodmancote, and probably a Tabernacle adherent. Richard in his youth attended the school of John Glanville in Dursley before the secession of the Boultonians and it is likely that he was also a member of the Tabernacle Sunday School. He qualified as a doctor, settled in Burslem, became an ardent Wesleyan Methodist and preached in cottages and the local army barracks. In 1850 he volunteered to join the third missionary expedition of a Captain Allen Gardiner, 'a christian officer of the British Navy and a member of the Established Church,' to Patagonia. He was accepted, and, with Gardiner, was landed on Tierra de Fuego, 'land of fire,' in December, to be a catechist to the natives. These however were hostile and the story of their ten month stay is one of great hardship and heroism — constant harrassment by the 'savages', loss of their boats, consumption of all powder so that game could not be shot, scarcity of fish and the failing of other provisions, 'comfortless

The Quarry Chapel c. 1900.

The interior of the Quarry Chapel as it was until recently. The plaque is in memory of Samuel Workman *(Elders of the Quarry Chapel)*

lodgings and inclement weather,' sickness and the onset of the terrible Fuegian winter. When a relief ship called in October 1851 all were dead, killed by the natives. Their bodies were buried on the spot 'the funeral service read, an inscription placed on the rocks, three volleys of musketing were fired, the ships colours were struck half mast high, and having fulfilled her mournful commission, the *Dido* went her way.'

In 1852 a little chapel was opened on the edge of the then isolated little hamlet of The Quarry. Sometime after 1840 Independent or Congregational worship had begun in private houses in the area, supported by enthusiastic members of Cam Meeting. In 1851 land was sold to the Rev. Andrew Gazard and thereafter local men worked in their spare time to quarry stone and build the chapel. It held one hundred people and remains largely unaltered today except for the addition recently of a modern kitchen and toilet facilities. The Quarry Chapel continues to flourish and, now within the United Reformed Church, it is linked with the Tabernacle.

In 1854, a Government order of November 27th closed all the Anglican, Wesleyan and Congregational burial places in the town except the newest at St. Marks and the Tabernacle. The three churches protested to the Queen that this would mean that vaults each had below the buildings could not be used and sought permission to continue their use. The request was refused in a letter from Lord Palmerston.[14]

By early 1858, the Tabernacle had mustered its resources sufficiently to call a new minister. This was done by encouraging increased quarterly collections and was helped by the decision of Mr. J. Hurndall, linen draper of the Market Place, to rent a pew for about £14 p.a. Apart from covering the minister's stipend, there were incidental expenses and a number of taxes to pay land tax, highway tax, lamp rate and poor rate. Then there was insurance to pay and also the organ blower who in 1862 received one shilling per quarter; in 1870 the organist was paid £4 for the year and 'the boy' *5s*.

The new minister was Richard Bentley. Educated at the Independent Academy and Trinity College, both of Dublin, he began his ministry in Cork in 1844.[15] Thereafter he moved several times, including to Cincinnati, U.S.A., and eventually to Dursley. He was a man of considerable administrative ability and it was from his pastorate that we have the first minute books to throw light on the way the church functioned.

One interesting point revealed is that Bentley conducted baptisms privately, sometimes in the church but frequently in homes, the Parsonage or the vestry and often on weekday evenings. With the invitation to Mr. Bentley to accept the pastorate, signed by seat holders and friends, went a memorandum with which he was asked to agree:-

I Sunday Services — morning and evening
Weekday Services — Preaching Wednesday evenings
— Prayer meeting Friday evenings

II A Meeting of the Church Members to be held monthly

III A Church book, list of members to be kept and a register of Baptisms, Burials and Marriages at the Tabernacle.

IV The salary to be £120 per annum payable quarterly and to be increased as soon as the financial ability of the church improves.

V The Doctrines required by the Trust Deed to be held by the Minister are those contained in the Articles of the Church of England as held by Independents.

The letters to and fro show that great care was taken by both sides over the settlement and he eventually arrived in April.

Equal care was taken over admissions of people to membership of the church. Every application, which frequently gave details of his or her conversion, was considered at a church meeting. Two deacons — usually at this time, the two senior of the four, Joseph Gazard and Benjamin Weaver — were dispatched to visit the applicant. If they were satisfied, and they were not always, 'the brethren' as the church members were often called, usually took their advice and accepted the applicant. Members were also accepted by letter of commendation from other churches.

The Revd Richard Bentley, minister 1858–63 *(Minister and Elders, Kingswood Tabernacle)*

Occasionally, very rarely, members were expelled, as for example Joseph and Ann Nicolls. Formerly farmers in a small way, they joined the Tabernacle as members in 1858. Two years later, a solemn church meeting considered their membership in the light of the fact that they had been found guilty and fined for using light weights and scales in their butcher's shop in the Uley Road, thereby bringing discredit on the name of the church. Joseph was present but could give no satisfactory explanation and so he and his wife were dismissed from membership, the meeting grieving and hoping that the couple would repent and apply to rejoin later. This must have been a humiliating experience for the couple but they survived it and were re-admitted in 1866 — which says much for them and the caring atmosphere which must have pervaded the membership in general.

The membership roll on the 1st April 1858 stood at seventy-seven persons, twenty-nine men, forty-eight women. From those listed it is possible to identify some trades. They included auctioneer, linen draper, shoemaker, maltster, rope maker, hair dresser, plasterer, farmer, weaver and cheese factor. Mary Bennett, daughter of the late Revd. William Bennett kept a small boarding school for ladies in Woodmancote. Elizabeth Box, mother of Frances, who became the wife of Mr. R.A. Lister, had for a while a milliners shop in Long Street. She became an ardent temperance worker in the town and The Elizabeth Box Memorial Lodge of Good Templars, a temperance organisation, was named after her.[16]

Another area where great care was exercised was over who should be allowed to take part in Holy Communion. Apparently it was not necessary to be a member, but application for permission had to be made and each was considered seriously it appears.

Late in 1858 the Bristol and Gloucestershire Congregational Union descended on Dursley for its Autumn Meeting. It began with an evening service in the Tabernacle on Tuesday October 12th. Twenty-two members and friends from a distance were housed for the night by church members and on the following day a business session filled the morning. At Two o'clock a hot dinner for seventy-four was served at The Bull Inn, Woodmancote, costing 3*s* a head. Two bottles of wine were also served, which seems frugal among seventy-four, but it is likely that most present were abstainers as the temperance movement was strong in these decades.

Public worship with the Lord's Supper was held in the evening when the Revd. Joseph Stratford of Cirencester was one of the preachers.

In the following year the fiftieth anniversary of the opening of the new Tabernacle was celebrated in August. Events began with a special prayer meeting on Wednesday the 10th and on the following Sunday sermons were preached by Revds. John Burder of Stroud and E. Hartland of Brunswick Chapel, Bristol. The big event though was on the next Tuesday, when a 'tea meeting was celebrated under a spacious tent, well decorated with evergreens and flowers, in an adjoining field. The weather was peculiarly favourable and about 950 persons sat down to tea, being the largest tea meeting for religious purposes ever held in the county.' After tea a public meeting was held in the Tabernacle which was 'crowded to excess, hundreds being unable to gain admittance.' H.O. Wills of Bristol chaired the meeting and present were many ministers of neighbouring chapels including the Revd. Davies from the Wesleyans.

One of the meeting's acts was to pass a resolution of appreciation to the late William Bennett and a copy was given to his widow Rebecca. Another was to make the decision to undertake a scheme to build 'school and lecture rooms'. Nearly £70 was collected immediately and to this was added £42 1*s* 3½*d* profit on the tea made by the ladies.

Collecting cards were printed by Richard Bentley and one was sent, with a request for a donation, to Henry Vizard of Ferney Hill, one of the most influential figures in the town. Henry, a staunch Anglican, declined to subscribe to the building fund, but offered to do as he did for the Wesleyans and that was to give an annual payment of a £1 for the support of the school. This was accepted and continued until he died in 1866, greatly mourned by the whole community. Under the provisions of his will, the Tabernacle received £49 for the Sunday School.

The new hall, called the Jubilee School Room, was opened in September, 1861, at a cost of £282 10*s* 0*d*. Of this, only about half had been raised and so, as has so often happened, the ladies of the church came to the rescue. On the following Tuesday they held an afternoon bazaar and, at an evening tea meeting, catered for 500 people. In one day they raised £121 15*s* 6*d* — in todays terms equivalent perhaps to a staggering £5000. Thus the builder, Richard Godwin of Prospect Place, received £250 then and there, but had to wait until 1863 before being fully recompensed.

Before the new building could be erected, the vestry built by William Bennett had to be demolished and so church meetings were suspended for a while. It appears that they were usually held on a Sunday after one of the services, but were not well attended.

The effort to pay for the schoolroom may have been the cause of the default on payment of Richard Bentley's stipend in 1861. In 1859 he had received his increase, taking all that the pew rents brought in over £120, but two years later he didn't receive even the minimum. Again the ladies:- 'It was proposed that with a view to the better management of the church's affairs in support of the Pastor, a Ladies Committee be appointed to cooperate with the officers of the church'. It was passed unanimously — and, one imagines, to the great relief of those officers.

Another matter which occupied Richard Bentley and the deacons was the graveyard. Its crowded condition was being 'painfully felt.' Thus in 1860 Mr. Bentley and Joseph Gazard were dispatched to Birmingham to seek an interview with the owners of the land adjoining, who were descendants by marriage of George Harris. The negotiations were not easy but eventually agreement was reached for the purchase of a strip of land on the east side of the burial ground, 84½ft by 16½ft, for £38 5*s*. The expense was covered

A view of Tabernacle buildings across the burial ground, 1981. Left to right: the chapel built 1808; a hall, 1861; classrooms, 1899; a second hall and more rooms, 1913. The chimneys are on the Parsonage, 1807. *(Photo. David E. Evans)*

One of a number of graceful Georgian head stones in the Tabernacle burial ground. This one is to John Baker, cardmaker. *(Photo. David E. Evans)*

The Victorian fondness for cast iron is seen here. The stone records the deaths of four people in the early man- and woman-hood in the years 1863–7, all children of John Davis, branch manager of the County of Gloucester Bank, and his wife Anne. *(Photo. David E. Evans)*

by selling grave lots at prices ranging from £1 to £5. The ground was extended again when another strip, 134½ft by 25ft, was acquired from George Harris's heirs in 1890.

A third matter attended to by Richard Bentley was the pattern of church worship itself. One custom he had found on his arrival and abolished, was the practice of the congregation of standing and turning their backs on the pulpit when prayers were being said. Its origin is uncertain, but probably it was a relict of the first days of the Tabernacle. A hundred years before, services based on the Anglican style were almost certainly the order of the day and in the old Tabernacle, standing backs to pulpit would have faced the congregation eastwards. Transferred to the New Tabernacle, its significance forgotten, they faced south!

Then there was the question of hymn books. Four were in use:-

Watts Psalms and Hymns
Rowland Hill's Selections
The Countess of Huntingdon's Selection (introduced by Rev. George Neeton in 1825)
The Congregational Hymn Book

In 1860, at his suggestion, all of these were replaced by the *New Congregational Hymn Book*. The old practice of having a clerk — always a senior, well respected person — to announce the hymns continued.

The old hymn books seem, on the surface, to have been a respectable collection and, with the organ, the Tabernacle may have avoided the poor music complained of in Gloucestershire (and doubtless elsewhere).

> Repeating, ranting tunes, many of them mere adaptations of the lowest songs, were commonly in use amongst all denominations. Those few melodies which were free from the taint of questionable associations were, for the most part, so tame and uninteresting as to offer no counteraction whatever to the pernicious influence of their contemporaries. Not only the tunes, however, but the whole mode of conducting the service of song was at this time very objectionable in many particulars. A number of instruments such as violins, bass viols, flutes, clarionets and even trombones and brass instruments were to be heard in many places up and down the land. And where these could not be found their place was supplied by a race of men known as clerks or leaders, who in some cases (to their praise be it spoken) did their utmost to amend the ignorance and bad taste by which they were encompassed; but who, in other circumstances were the sole hindrances to the growth of a better condition.[17]

The Revd. John Burder, Congregational minister in Stroud at this time, 'had long bewailed the evils connected with this part of public worship (ie the singing) and had repeatedly declared that during more than forty years' observation he had seen more contentions originated in congregations by the "singing gallery" than by any other cause'.[18] Did the Dursley churches escape entirely all these problems?

Alfred Bloodworth, Church Secretary, referred to in the last chapter, wrote in detail about the Sunday school in the period 1862-4. In 1862 there were six men and nine women teachers and the average attendance each Sunday was:-

Mornings	men	6	women	4
Afternoons	men	5	women	6

It improved in 1863, each teacher attending on average, sixty-one sessions but arriving late on fourteen of these.

At the beginning of 1862 there were fifty-seven boys and sixty-eight girls; at the end, fifty-six boys and seventy-three girls. In between twenty-three boys had left and twenty-two had been admitted; for girls the figures were fifteen and twenty. Some were enticed by the other schools in the town. In fact the children seem to have realized that they had 'market value'. Very few in the town did not belong to one or other of the schools and one could only grow at the expense of the others. Treats and rewards all played their part in the competition for allegiance.

Average attendance for the school was:-

mornings	23	boys	24	girls
afternoons	32	boys	34	girls

The children were not always good. In 1859 the boys were made to sit in the gallery during 'Divine Service Sabbath mornings' and a little later six were suspended for three months for bad behaviour.

There was a Sunday school library, begun in 1822, of 125 books. Fifty of these had been bought by Richard Bentley from the Religious Tract Society for £1. 10*s*. In 1863, books had to be returned on the last Sunday of a month — penalty 1*d* — and could only be borrowed during school hours. In 1864 the idea was considered of opening the library to the public but this doesn't seem to have been acted on.

A night school for secular instruction had operated from 1806 until about the time the British School opened in Boulton Lane. It was revived at the Tabernacle for the winter of 1858-9 and staffed by Sunday School teachers. Girls attended on Tuesdays, boys on Thursdays, and instruction, limited to reading and writing, lasted from 7 to 8.30 p.m. The school re-opened for the following winter when a curious entry appears in the school accounts: 'the sexton to receive 10*s* for his additional labours in connection with the night school' — It appears again for the winter of 1860-1. Probably the sexton was he who in later years became, in turn, chapel keeper and caretaker.

The Parish Church too had a night school; in 1869 the average attendance was forty-nine.[19] It also had a sick club, benefit society and library. This charged scholars 1*d* per month for loans; outsiders could join for 6*d* and borrow for 2*d* per month.[20]

Sunday School stock at the Tabernacle consisted of hymn books, registers, question books, catechisms, Bibles and Testaments, and magazines relating to Sunday school work. Finance came mainly from annual anniversary services. Expenses included cleaning the school room and church, coal, ink, postage, books, including reward books, and in 1862, a new school clock. Between 1828 and 1864 Anniversary Sundays brought in amounts ranging from £8 9*s* 0*d* in 1834, to £18 8*s* 2*d* when William Jay of Bath preached. The average was £11 2*s* 2¾*d*. In 1862 John Glanville had preached; in 1864 Handel Cossham, Esq., M.P. for Bristol East, coal mine owner and philanthropist, whose name is commemorated in Thornbury's Cossham Hall. On that occasion, from congregations of some 600 in the morning and 750 in the evening, £12 12*s* 0*d* was collected or roughly 2¼*d* per head. So highly regarded was Mr. Cossham that the Church Secretary and the School Superintendent travelled down to wait on him when the invitation was made instead of sending it by letter.

From 1860 onwards, the children raised £6 a year for 'John and Mary Dursley'. These two were 'Hindoo' children in Bangalore, India, real names Wanna and Ada Dasi, but re-named by the Dursley scholars. In March 1864 a juvenile missionary meeting was held to give the children information on the children. Chairman was the Revd. George Neeton, but it was not well attended 'owing to weather not being favourable, being very wet and cold, and partly due to the destructive fire at Rivers Mill, property of Mr. Geo. Lister, which was injurious to some connected with the school (and) which took place on March 7th between 6 and 7 p.m. Damages estimated at £10,000.' Collections for the two Indian children seemed to have ceased in 1873 when no information was forthcoming from the L.M.S. on what had happened to the children.

Apart from the general fund and a 'treat fund' there were two other accounts connected with the Sunday school. They were the 'Scholars Sick Club' and 'The Dorcas Club' funds. Initially in 1828 two sick clubs had been set up at the Tabernacle, one for scholars and one for teachers. The latter however had been disbanded in 1842 though dwindling membership, probably parallelling a fall in the number of people who acted as teachers. From the original forty-three, membership dropped to twelve, not a viable number, and so the assets of £33 were divided out, except for £5 which was set aside for a teachers' tea meeting. While in operation, teachers had paid one penny per week and had received for illness, thirty pence, and for the funeral expenses, £2 10*s* 0*d*. The scholars sick club was retained and, between 1844 and 1864, the number of calls on it annually varied from fourteen in 1845, to forty-three in 1856. Funeral allowances for the period ranged from £1 5*s* 0*d* to £2 0*s* 0*d*. In 1868 Drs. Leonard (who lived opposite the Tabernacle at the north end of the Crescent) and Baines were paid £5 for the year for attending sick scholars. The rules were revised in 1854. Rules six read '. . . if any member shall defame in any way the character of any member or Teacher, without just cause (he or she) shall. . . be excommunicated'. Rule eight read '. . . any member who incurs an accident in the act of breaking the Sabbath, or who may be sick through any immoral conduct, shall lose all benefit.' Rule twelve provided members 'with Cake and Tea annually on Easter Tuesday'.

The Dorcas (see Acts 9 v. 36 & 39) or clothing club, begun by the Boultonians some time before 1840, received revised rules in about 1860. These provided that children could pay in at the rate of one penny per week. Missed weeks could not be paid afterwards unless there was a very good reason. The organising committee was to meet quarterly at 'half past five' to consider cases, to arrange orders with the various tradesmen and to receive subscriptions from sympathetic adults. For every twelve pence paid in by a child, it received sixteen pence benefit. After the departure of Richard Bentley in 1863 the club, which had a membership of about thirty, drifted without proper management. Subscriptions were not collected and it had run up a big debt by 1865. A report from April that year stated:- 'Some (people) think the allowance (i.e. 4*d* on every 12*d*) too much and the necessity which existed once. . . for such a club does not now exist, the money being squandered on finery instead of necessary things.' The club wasn't closed however, though the rules may have been altered, as it continued to operate well into the twentieth century.

One should not get the impression from the report that Dursley had got over the recession caused by the collapse of the wool trade and was back to being a thriving town. Obviously conditions had improved but Alfred Bloodworth could still lament in 1865 that most of the former cloth mills remained closed.

> This trade has revived of late at Cam — Hunt and Winterbotham's — but even there it is not what it was formerly; but it is not likely it will be revived here for the 'gentry' seem to discourage it — they seem to desire to see this a 'gentleman's' and not a trading town so discouraged it, although the fortunes they have inherited were built up by the clothing trade — for even the little trade that is done here is distasteful to them. The wire drawing and card making done in the neighbourhood almost, if not entirely, confined to that which is done at River's Mill (now Mawdsley's) — the property of Geo. Lister. Poor Dursley! — it may now be called also Little, Quiet Dursley — little as regards population and trade. . . .

From the foregoing it must be obvious that there was considerable financial activity at The Tabernacle in the 1860s but it was not all directed at its own building and adherents. For example in 1862 Richard Bentley preached sermons on the distress in Lancashire, and The Ladies Committee over several months solicited subscriptions so that a total of £28 7*s* 2*d* was raised and sent via the County of Gloucester Bank to the Central Relief Fund in Manchester.

In October 1863 the Rev. Bentley announced that he had received, and had accepted, 'a cordial and unanimous invitation to Kingswood Tabernacle' near Bristol. He left Dursley with considerable goodwill following him and, after a short period at Kingswood, he returned to the U.S.A. and disappeared from view.

An inter-pastorate period throws heavy responsibilities on church officers and the bouyancy of its leadership at this time is seen in the decision to make the 1864 Sunday School treat a memorable event. For most of the Victorian era these annual treats were held nearby, on local hills — Stinchcombe, Downham, Cam Peak, Uley Bury — or on local farms, even in the school hall itself. 1864 was to be different. Here is Alfred Bloodworth's account of what happened on July 1st.

> 55 male scholars and 67 females and 18 teachers or substitutes, accompanied by 161 friends etc. making a total of 299, started from Dursley Station at 9.40 a.m. Arrived at Cheltenham Station at 11.30 a.m;Startedfrom Cheltenham Station at 7.51 p.m.; arrived at Dursley at 9.30 p.m. So about 8 hours were spent, and spent pleasantly, in Cheltenham. At noon we arrived at Salem Chapel Vestry and had a penny bun each — viz teachers and scholars and about 50 friends — and after singing the Doxology we, led by James Lang, teacher, by whom the various arrangements had been made, went to Pittville Gardens, where we arrived about one o'clock and where we spent 1¾ hours about, either in listening to the music or visiting the dome of the spa etc. and viewing the scenery from in it— or boating on the water or in walking and playing about the grounds. We then went to Jessop's Gardens where we arrived a little before 3 o'clock and spent there an hour, either feeding the monkeys — their various capers causing much fun — or in visiting with interest the fish, birds and various kinds of animals and flowers. Then left for Salem Chapel Vestry. . . where the scholars were supplied with tea and two two-penny buns each. After they had done, the teachers and about

Alfred Bloodworth and his wife *(Sidney and Ena Bloodworth)*

> 56 friends took tea. . . . We then went to the playgrounds of the British School in Henrietta Street from which we started for the railway station at about half past six. After spending about half an hour at that station we were taken to our destination — several singing on the way, some hymns and some, sad to say, viz male and female senior scholars, singing silly etc. songs. Our station yard was filled with parents waiting to receive us and the air was rent with our and their cheers as we arrived in the evening as in the morning when we left. Those who were not too tired repaired to the yard of the Tabernacle and sang the Evening Hymn to the tune Samson viz 'Glory to thee my God this night.' The banners were then collected and we separated for our homes, thankful to God that he had prevented the occurrence of any accident and for all the mercies of the day. Perhaps it should be mentioned that prior to starting in the morning we met at the school room at 9 a.m. and after (I) had given out 'From all that dwell below the skies' sung to the tune Simeon and engaged in prayer, Mr Lang gave an account of what would be the day's proceedings if the weather continued fine. The result of the day showed the excellence of the arrangements he had made.

Mr Bloodworth commented on the weather and roads. — 'fine but cloudy, the air cool, the roads not dusty, the dust having been laid the 2 or 3 days previously (by) rain! He also provided an account of finances, Bought of T. Simms confectioner, bread and biscuit maker, sole manufacturer for Cheltenham of Jones' patent prepared flour; Rich bread, cakes, Patent Luncheon Cakes:-

	£	s	d
24lbs cake (a) 5d	—	10	—
198 buns (a) 1d		16	6
300 buns (a) 2d	2	10	—
5 loaves bread (a) 3¼		1	4¼
	£3	17	10¼
Other expenses rail fare — children	8d		
— adults	1/4		
Visit to Pittville	1d		
Visit to Jessops	½d		
Other	¾		

Thomas Sims, baker, had once been a scholar at The Tabernacle Sunday School.

Alfred Bloodworth concluded his account by commenting that the children had returned to Dursley

> as happy as young larks (and) only too sorry that such bright excursions days as they spent in Cheltenham came so seldom. . . . Such joyous and happy occasions of social intercourse and of bringing the young and their seniors together and bringing them in contact with other persons and other places are calculated to enlarge and elevate their youthful ideas and prepare them in some measure for the future battle of life.

Today, with travel so commonplace, it is difficult to imagine the excitement such an expedition created. The Dursley — Coaley Junction Railway had opened in 1856. The Tabernacle Sunday School wasn't the only one to make use of the ease of movement it provided. In the same year, 1865, the Wesleyan Sunday School celebrated its sixty-second Anniversary on Whit Tuesday by travelling by special train to 'Draycotte' and to the home of Mr. and Mrs. A. Workman.[22]

Another event of significance for the Tabernacle took place in March 1865.

> An interesting and, for the town, novel meeting took place in the schoolroom when upwards of 100 of the parents of the scholars, in compliance with invitations from teachers, gathered at a free social tea meeting, being we believe the first meeting of the kind ever held in the town. This repast over, a mental and spiritual one was provided by the addresses being delivered by teachers and friends. The Rev. H. Jones of Uley presided and gave some practical remarks. Addresses were afterwards delivered by Mr. J. Lang on 'Parental Duty and Responsibility'; Mr G. Smith on 'Mother's Influence.'; Mr. A. Habbishaw. . . on 'Sunday Schools and their Work' and Mr. J. Barnes on 'The Advantages of the Right Training'. The Chairman then expressed a hope that this was not the last meeting of the kind. . . , an expression which was much applauded. Thanks were then given to the Chairman, ladies and friends; the hymn commencing 'Jerusalem, my happy home' was sung and the benediction pronounced.'[23]

Church records suggest that the organisers may have been a little disappointed at the response to their invitation:- Of sixty-eight possible fathers, thirty-two were present and of seventy-three mothers, fifty-five. Probably, as in the schools today, the parents they would really liked to have seen, didn't respond!

A major duty of a church secretary in the absence of a minister is to find a regular supply of people to fill the pulpit Sunday by Sunday. In the two years following the departure of Richard Bentley, Alfred Bloodworth records that he used a total of thirty-four ministers. Many of these were not local and he gives the home areas of some — Blackburn; Yorkshire; Clare in Suffolk; Western College, then at Plymouth; Staffordshire; Burton-on-Trent; Denbighshire; Beaconsfield; Essex; Nuneaton and even Stockton-on-Tees. Some of these must have attended 'with a view' to taking up the vacant pastorate but none satisfied the Tabernacle congregation, too many of them being 'sermon readers'.

Eventually it was to a relatively local man that they turned. Thomas Wallace, born 1803, in Perth of Presbyterian parents, had moved to live in Bath at an early age and came under the influence of the great William Jay of Argyle Congregational Church.[24] Later he studied for the ministry at the academies of Rowell, Northants, and Hoxton, London and began his career at Grantham. Moves via Petworth and Petersfield brought him to Bridport where around 1849 he and his family contracted typhoid fever. A daughter of four died and he was left debilitated for the rest of his life. After a period to recuperate he took the pastorate at Witney before retiring to Bath. It was from here that he came to take an occasional service at

Dursley and was so acceptable that he was pressed, and finally agreed, to become the Tabernacle minister. He was to receive £100 p.a. with prospects of an increase after the first year. His first Sunday in Dursley was on 5 November 1865 and he preached to large congregations. It was 'an anxious and laborious day — may there be large blessings'.

Wallace was a highly intelligent man and he brought with him considerable ministerial experience. He had published a number of items including *Devotional Retirement* and a Congregational Union of England and Wales prize winning essay *A Guide to the Christian Ministry*. His stay was a happy and affectionate one for himself and his congregation.

At the annual choir meeting supper in January 1866 works by Handel, Hadyn and Kent were sung. In April 1867 a well attended tea meeting listened to a lecture by him on The Holy Lord.[25] At a full to over-flowing Parish Vestry meeting in the same year, called to consider the proposal by W.J. Phelps Esq. of Chestal to divert the stream at Yellow Hundred, he spoke on the need to consider carefully, as many age old rights had vanished through enclosure. New walls and railings were erected in front of the Parsonage and burial ground in 1868, and a new heating stove was installed in the church. Two hymns written by Wallace were sung at the Sunday School Anniversary in the same year.[26] He preached at the Wesleyan Sunday School Anniversary Services when in 1868 they were held in the Tabernacle because the Methodist Church was being altered. It was after this occasion that the Wesleyan Scholars were reported to have marched to the grounds of Mr. Buston, Woodmancote Farm, headed by 'Garibaldi's Band' — presumably the Boulton Lane School drum and fife band.[27]

Thomas Wallace was in Dursley while much of St. James's Parish Church was being rebuilt.[28] Canon Madan, with the successful restoration

The Revd Wm Wallace, minister 1865–70 and the Revd Jason Jenkyns, 1871–79.

The Revd George Madan, honorary canon of Gloucester Cathedral, was Vicar of St. George's Church, Cam, 1835–1852, during which time he planned and built St. Bartholomew's Church as a chapel of ease. While at St. Mary Redcliffe Church he encountered great opposition to efforts to modernise services and in 1865 he returned to this area to become Rector of Dursley, a position he held until 1887 when he was succeeded by his nephew, N.W. Gresley. He died in Gloucester not long afterwards and his body was brought to Dursley by train for the funeral.

(Revd A.J. Minchin, Vicar of Lower Cam, 1974–82)

of St. Mary Redcliffe, Bristol, to his credit, became Rector of Dursley in 1865. He quickly set about restoring on a major scale his new church and reconsecration took place in April 1868 amid much rejoicing and before a great gathering of clergy and layfolk. The restoration cost nearly £*6000* of which the Canon, a much loved man, paid a fifth from his own resources.

Changes to the church included raising the roof, rebuilding the chancel on a larger scale and constructing an organ chamber. Before this the organ had stood in the middle of the long gallery which had spanned the nave in front of the tower. The north doorway of the church was blocked, because, it was said, the church was used as a short cut between Silver Street and Long Street. Apparently it was not unheard of for buckets of water to be carried this way from, what was then, a major supply, the Broadwell.[29]

Canon Madan also built himself a new rectory in 1866, now Dursley Court. This done he pulled down much of the old rectory, now 100 Kingshill Road, and converted it into a cottage for his servant.[30] It is of interest that Dursley's tithe barn once existed near to the old rectory — some 87 ft by 23 ft in size. In 1805 it was reported as being 'large, useless and greatly delapidated.' The rector, Timothy Vigor or Viger, wanted to demolish it as there was 'but a small quantity of glebe land' and 'but very little corn raised. . . in the parish'. It seems that its main use then was as a pig sty. An inspection team appointed by the bishop recommended that only part should go. What actually happened at this date is not clear.[31]

While touching on Parish Church affairs it is worth recording that in

The parish church of St. James before it was restored and altered by Canon Madan.
(from Bigland's 'Gloucestershire' 1791)

1871 'Old Natty' died at the age of ninety-one. In his younger days Nathaniel Thurston had been parish clerk and had led the church choir. He had also played the 'bass violoncello' 'which with other strings and wind instruments, combined with vocal power, formed the musical portion of the service.' This could take us back to the end of the previous century and on the available evidence it is a matter of debate as to whether St. James or the Tabernacle had the first church organ in the town.

Through age and infirmity Thomas Wallace returned to Bath at the end of 1870 to be greatly missed by people in the town of all denominations. He died in the city in 1889 aged eighty-five.

The Rev. Jason Jenkyns came in mid summer 1871 and at the usual tea meeting 300 were present, too many for the Jubilee school room to hold so that they overflowed into the church which, like the hall, was 'profusely decorated with evergreens, flowers, and mottoes'. At the public meeting that followed, Wesleyan ministers were present as well as many Congregational ones. Relationships with the Wesleyans have always been cordial but this was the first recorded occasion when their ministers have been present at an induction service.

Jason Jenkyns had received his ministerial training at Carmarthen College where he had distinguished himself as a Welsh preacher and here he came to be regarded as a young man of exceptional promise. After pastorates at St. Florence, near Tenby, and the bilingual Mount Pleasant Church, Pontypridd, he moved to Dursley, a man in his early forties. Affairs in the town were not easy. Its population was still falling, having already dropped by a third from its peak in the 1820s. Over the years the Tabernacle had changed from enthusiastic Methodistical evangelism which drew people in from a wide area to a more sober, though none the less, enjoyable and outward looking, Victorian respectability. Chapel building had gone on apace in local villages and the Tabernacle congregation one can assume, now came only from the town itself and its immediate environs. It had no known wealthy supporters. Trade in the town was still hard pressed from the declining population and was to be more so in the agricultural depression ahead. One man seems to have held the key to the future of Dursley in his hand at this time and this was Robert Ashton Lister. In 1867 he had begun a tiny engineering firm in rented premises. Slowly at first but with increasing rapidity it grew, providing more and more work for folk of the town and well outside it — and so more money for shopkeepers and the like. In the 1890s the population stopped its downward trend and began to climb sharply, though it wasn't until about 1925 that it acquired the same size as the peak years of a hundred years before — but all this is ahead of our story.

In an attempt to increase the income at the Tabernacle it was decided in 1870 to establish weekly collections as well as quarterly ones and for this end collecting boxes were placed near the door. Probably this is the origin of the present custom of announcing each Sunday the amount of the

The Tabernacle c. 1875, showing how it once stood alone in fields. The man in top hat and frock coat is almost certainly Jason Jenkyns who had had the building structure restored and altered only a short while before. *(Jeremy and Jonathan Pallister)*

collection of the previous week. It produced around £1 per quarter and undoubtedly helped but Jason Jenkyns frequently received short measure on his stipend. In February 1975 he received only £19 instead of £25. A 'friend' made this up to £20 and when a Mr. Baylis decided to pay his pew rent it reached £22. The deficit was made up in August but the uncertain position over income must have made budgeting at the Parsonage very difficult. On one occasion, in 1872, the burial fund was raided of £3 *6s 3d* to help out. Pleas to the congregation and the establishing of an annual minister's anniversary tea meeting improved matters eventually and from 1878 Jenkyn's stipend settled at a steady £120 p.a.

In the light of the financial problems it was a bold move to begin a complete restoration of the church, described then as being 'a very dingy and delapidated place.'[32] In 1873, for a cost of £400, the outside of the building was dealt with. It was re-roofed with Caernarvon slates. The main entrance was moved from the side to the end, and a vestibule built on. Windows were replaced with diamond paned glass and 'Bullock's Louvre Ventillators' were inserted. Once this was paid for, internal refurbishing was tackled. To raise funds a three day bazaar was held in 1879. It was

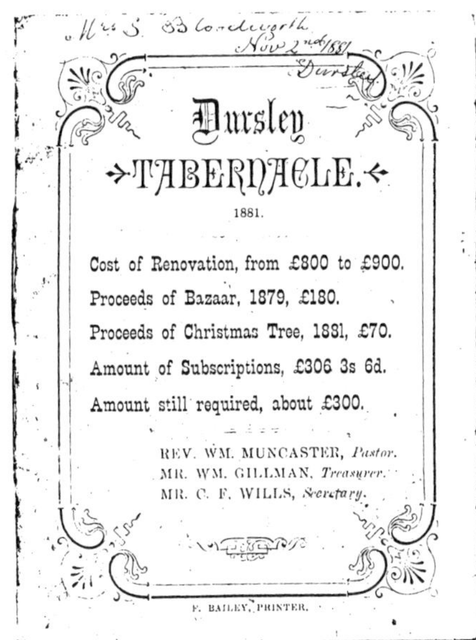

Mrs S. Bloodworth
Nov 2nd/1881
Dursley

Dursley
TABERNACLE.

1881.

Cost of Renovation, from £800 to £900.

Proceeds of Bazaar, 1879, £180.

Proceeds of Christmas Tree, 1881, £70.

Amount of Subscriptions, £306 3s 6d.

Amount still required, about £300.

REV. WM. MUNCASTER, *Pastor.*
MR. WM. GILLMAN, *Treasurer.*
MR. C. F. WILLS, *Secretary.*

F. BAILEY, PRINTER.

Money collected by Mrs S. Bloodworth	£	s	d
C. J. Tucker Esq, Bristol		10	0
R. Chapman Esq	5	0	0
Mrs S. Bloodworth	5	0	0
A Friend		5	0
A Friend		2	6
E. J. Bloodworth		2	0
J W Carr	2	0	0
Louie Bloodworth		1	0
Frederick G. Bloodworth		1	0
Willie Carr		1	0
Nellie Carr		1	0
	13	3	6

Recd. WM

The renovation subscription book of Sidney Bloodworth, later to become last Bailiff of Dursley.

opened by the Right Hon. Lord Fitzhardinge of Berkeley Castle and produced £180. A Christmas Tree spectacular brought in more money and with £250 to hand the second stage began. It was found that there would be required new galleries, ceiling, pews, flooring for the body, pulpit, heating apparatus, fittings etc. In other words the building was gutted. T. Thomas Esq., architect of Swansea, prepared plans and Mr. William Wibby of Gloucester got the contact to execute them. The transformation took four months in the summer of 1881 and cost between £800 and £900.[33]

The reopening services for the renovated church were held on Wednesday November 23 1881, but terrible winds and pouring rain kept many away.

The building was the showpiece of the town. Gone were the 'old fashioned plain pulpit; gone was all the decaying dull and 'antiquated' woodwork. Now all was highly polished golden pitch pine and red mahogany, black iron work touched with gold. The walls had been replastered and fresh coloured; the ceiling was beautiful with a rose flower centre piece; handsome gas brackets were there to replace whatever had been there before – probably candles. The new entrance doors were covered in scarlet cloth and had panels with gold moulding. On the wall behind the new pulpit, standing on a carpeted dais, was a new arch.[34]

The front of the Tabernacle much as it must have been in 1881 after restoration.

A view of the Tabernacle from the pulpit in 1981, probably hardly changed since 1881.
(Photo. David E. Evans)

It was a magnificent place. Although redecorated many times since then, and with the iron work around the dais removed, the hot air heating now produced by oil instead of coal, it is basically the same today.

We have no detailed picture of the interior before the transformation, but doubtless it was arranged spaciously as at present, to give all people an unimpeded view of the pulpit – except the unlucky few who, when the church was full, we know had to sit in a family pew with backs to it. The preached word has been a major element in Free Church worship from its beginnings and the pulpit's commanding position – the old one is believed to have been higher – is in line with centuries of tradition. As befits its importance it is one of the most ornate features of the church and is of pitch pine carved and cut away to reveal a mahogany background.

Little has been printed about Nonconformist chapels.[35] By writers of town guides and works on church architecture alike they are often ignored or dismissed in a few lines, while the parish church is extolled at length. Partly this must reflect the traditions of church and chapel. In the one the building itself is 'consecrated' and made holy; in the other it is 'opened' as a convenient assembly place, just as respected, but of value only when it has a living congregation. Many a town, however would be much less interesting without its chapels, not only visually as part of the backcloth of everyday living, but as expressing history, piety, aspirations and a vital confidence in God every bit as strong as that which emanated from the parish church and just as important in the life of the community. Some have good architecture and most are as lovingly and zealously polished and flower bedecked as any church. Dursley and Cam without their chapels would, in all respects, be much poorer places.

During the renovation period, services at the Tabernacle were held in the school hall and then this was also tackled, changing it from 'a barn, the walls . . . of which were by no means clean and the floor . . . not exactly even and straight' into something 'attractive, commodious and beautiful'.[36]

The pastorate of the Revd. Jenkyns witnessed a number of interesting events. In 1875 the Band of Hope was first recorded, to be followed two years later by the Good Templars and perhaps in these we can see the hand of temperance advocates Elizabeth Box and her daughter Frances, by then married to R.A. Lister, who was said to have one her best work at a time when drinking was increasing. The children of the Parish Church were by this time sending hampers of flowers to the poor in London in the spring and early summer months – primroses and violets.[37] These same children, 323 of them had their Sunday School treat tea in 1878 in the grounds of the new rectory (now Dursley Court) and games in the pump field opposite (now part of the rereation ground). 'Much of the amusement was created by a galvanic battery . . . and the contortions displayed by the children in their endeavours to seize a penny from a basin of electrified water was very diverting.'[38]

For the Tabernacle Sunday School anniversary in 1876 the Revd. Jenkyns procured Dr. Samuel Newth of New College, grandson of Adrian and in 1880 to be Chairman of the Congregational Union of England and Wales. For the occasion Jason Jenkyns had letters printed.

The Parsonage
Dursley
12th July 1876

Respected readers

Allow me to invite your attention to the accompanying announcement.

Having with some difficulty secured the services of so eminent a divine as Professor Newth, I hereby appeal to the leading residents of the district to sanction my success . . .

Your presence with that of your friends at Dursley Tabernacle next Sunday morning will greatly encourage the Minister and his congregation.

Best Wishes for both worlds
Your most respectful petititoner
Jason Jenkins

The appeal was successful and the collection of £20 was 'the largest ever known in connexion with this school.'

Jason Jenkyns moved to Anvil Street Chapel, Bristol in 1879. After three years, he left, intending to go to the U.S.A., but was dissuaded and

Banners were once the pride of Sunday schools. These typical survivors are from Kingswood Tabernacle. *(Photos. David E. Evans)*

agreed to form an English Church in Penarth. He retired from there with ill health in 1888 and died in London the following year.

1880 was a great year for Sunday schools for there were celebrations on a national basis to commemorate one hundred years of existence. The great tragedy was that animosity between Anglicans and Nonconformists prevented them from celebrating together. In the days leading up to the midsummer festivities the columns of the *Gloucester Journal* contained claims and counter claims from each side, that it had the honour of starting the first Sunday School. It was a matter of prestige and William King of Dursley was frequently referred to by the Nonconformist writers.

In Gloucester, county wide celebrations were held on one date for Anglicans and on another for Nonconformists. Each was great and joyful and festive, but one can only feel that Robert Raikes would have felt sad that his movement was riven with religious jealousy. It seems to have extended to Dursley as the Parish Church school took no part in the exuberant celebrations here – or maybe it was just felt that the county gathering was sufficient.

At two o'clock on 14 July 1880 some 600 teachers and scholars from many schools formed up and marched to the fields of Castle Farm (now the recreation ground), all wearing commemorative medals – Tabernacle, 110 children; Wesleyan with fife and drum band, 100; Cam Meeting, 105; Lower Cam Methodist 160; Coaley Methodist 89; and The Quarry Chapel

Cam Methodist Sunday School, with banner, in the glebe lands opposite the chapel c. 1900.
(Society Stewards, Cam Methodist Church)

about 50. There were games and then at four o'clock, tea. For the children, this was taken in the 'true primitive fashions on the grass', but many adults retired to the Tabernacle School Room. A procession later formed up in the following order:

Banner with portrait of Robert Raikes
Other banners
Large banner with words 'Sabbath Schools are England's Glory'
Eastington's fife & drum band
Ministers, laymen, children & teachers
Boulton Lane School fife & drum band
Rest of teachers and children

They made 'a brilliant stream of flags and banners, the whole procession beautifully relieved by a rich profusion of devices in flowers, fruits and grasses, most children having bouquets of flowers'. Up to the top of Woodmancote they went to halt while the bands played 'Hold the Fort,' the children joining in the chorus. Back down Woodmancote they paraded to the top of Bull Pitch. Another halt, another hymn and on to the Market Place, down and up Long Street and round to The Tabernacle. There, amid evergreens, ferns and flowers, children upstairs, adults below and overflowing into the aisles, a service began at seven o'clock. It was chaired by William Higgs of Gloucester, an international and veteran character in the schools movement. Several addresses were given including one from the Revd. Fredk. Gwynne of the Wesleyans. At the end it was all considered 'the most memorable day's proceedings Dursley has witnessed . . .'[39]

9

The Tabernacle goes into the Twentieth Century

The Revd. Jason Jenkyns left Dursley in midsummer in 1879 and was followed a year later by William Muncaster. He had been born in Carlisle in 1851, educated at Manchester Grammer School and Didsbury Methodist College of the same city, and Dursley was his first pastorate. He 'brought with him a force of education and literary capacity which raised the whole tone and character of the services which those who attended them will never forget'. Of him, it was later said, 'He had not the moral courage to preach a poor sermon'. Thus was his stay in Dursley characterized.

In 1883 the centenary of the Tabernacle's Sunday School was celebrated, or rather it was the hundredth anniversary of the settling of the school in church buildings, in reality the hundred and fifth year of the school itself. It was a big occasion on much the same lines as the 1880 school's movement event, a parade through the town with banners and the band of the Volunteer Rifle Brigade but with stops for photographs, none of which, unfortunately, seem to have survived. At a crowded public meeting several old scholars were present to recall early memories. Such were Mr. Higgins, who remembered being carried from Red Walk in 1824 on his father's shoulders to the school for the first time, and Mr. John Stiff, 'venerable, sterling, ninety years old and grandson of the Richard who 'sowed the seeds of the kingdom in the Forest of Dean' in the late 1700s. Again it was a great and memorable day.

School treats, harvest festivals, choir outings and other special occasions came and went each year. In September 1889, the choir with Mr. and Mrs. Muncaster, about thirty people in all, travelled in four horse brakes to Sharpness Point and there sat down to a 'substantial repast' in the pleasure ground. Boating, rambling and supper followed. Rain set in for the evening homeward journey but it was nevertheless accomplished in a 'very merry mood'. 1887 saw the Golden Jubilee of Queen Victoria's reign and Dursley was as excited and as lively as any town in celebrating.[1] The June day was 'gloriously fine' and peals of 'merry bells' rang out at times through it. Shops and houses were decorated with bunting and flowers, and, in the evening, gas illuminations on the sides of the town hall burned brilliantly in designs of the Prince of Wales feathers, a star and the letters

Sharpness Pleasure Gardens, often visited by Dursley folk. A band is playing among the trees. The occasion is unknown but is probably a Cam Methodist gathering.

'V.R.' Both the Parish Church and the workhouse bore Union Flags. The children of the three town Sunday Schools marched to the Parish Church for a service at 10.30 a.m. when the Rector preached and a collection was made for the town 'Coal Fund'. In the afternoon the children of the schools met again – at the farm of Mr. Buston in Woodmancote. They formed up in procession —

Rector and Mrs Gresley in pony carriages
Dursley Volunteer Rifle Brigade band
St. James's Sunday School
Tabernacle School
Wesleyan School

It was the largest procession seen for many years and was colourful with the usual banners and flags. After a tour of the town the company reached the fields of Castle Farm and dispersed for events which included attempting to climb a greasy pole for a leg of mutton worth ten shillings. No one succeeded in this.

At four o'clock there was a meat tea in 'an immense marquee' for 1600 and then more games. Fire balloons were released in the evening and then at nine o'clock, at the sound of a bugle, all ceased. Captain Graham called on the crowd to sing the National Anthem and then 250 volunteers, holding high flambeaux, together with the Rifle Brigade Band, led a procession up onto Stinchcombe Hill. It 'wound up the steep roadway, the moving light casting a ruddy glow upon the trees on each side and into the valley below.' At ten o'clock a flight of rockets from the Malvern Hills signalled the time to fire the beacon and soon it blazed into life joining the other thirty-five hill top fires that careful eyes could see.

In 1891 Christmas gifts at The Tabernacle totalled £9 *3s 0d* and this was distributed to the poor. These monetary distributions continued well into the next century though the number of recipients steadily declined.

Also in 1891, the organ was replaced by the present one made by the firm of Sweetlands of Bath. It was the gift of Mr. John Harding in memory of his wife Mary, a much loved Sunday school teacher. John was a man of some substance. In 1865–7 he demolished property in Kingshill Road and built himself 'The Agricultural Implement Warehouse' and adjacent to it, a house in which he then lived, Spring Villa,[2] now owned by Dursley Cricket Club. His ashes were buried in the Tabernacle vestibule in 1892 and a memorial stained glass window put nearby.

Ministers at the Tabernacle at the end of the century — William Muncaster 1880–92, Whitfield Watson, 1894–6 and John Thomas 1898–1902.

The Revd. William Muncaster departed from Dursley in 1892 for Brompton in Middlesex, and then Broadstairs. Here he died in 1921. He left the Tabernacle vigorous and confident and with a leadership strong enough to carry it successfully through the difficult years that lay ahead.

The Revd. Whitfield Watson came in 1894 – a keen gardener it seems, as his arrival coincides with unusual entries in the account books for manure, raspberry canes, stakes, grass seed and potatoes. He had begun his ministerial career as a Church of England evangelist in Birmingham and then acepted the pastorate of St. Andrews' Congregational Church in the same city in 1892.

The joy of his coming to Dursley was soon overshadowed by the death of his wife, after a long illness, seven weeks later. From this tragedy he seems never to have recovered and while he performed all the necessary functions

Robert Kingscote, one time keeper of the Bull Inn, staunch supporter of the Tabernacle, who was for over thirty years master of Dursley Union Workhouse. He and his wife Anne died within a few days of each other in 1893 and are buried in the Tabernacle graveyard *(Ron and Margaret Heathman)*

of his calling, it was without inspiration, it appears, so that in later years his short stay was looked back on as one that was less than successful. He left in 1896, lived in Gloucester without pastoral responsibility for two years, moved to a church at Kingston, Ireland and disappeared from history.

One organisation which made its appearances at The Tabernacle during Whitfield Watson's time was the Young People's Society of Christian Endeavour, in 1894, and this flourished for many decades. Indeed in spite of his bereavement, and, as it seems, his withdrawal from involvement in chapel life, that life went on. At Christmas 1894 the Sunday School had a party at which R.A. Lister J.P. gave each child a present from a Christmas tree laden with 'toys and knick-knacks'. This was in the year before he joined the church as a member.

A two day bazaar ws held in October 1895 at the Victoria Coffee Tavern in Silver Street opposite the parish church. The rector lent the church piano; Don Lusty, Tabernacle organist entertained with his string band and it was a great success putting £172 *9s 9d* in church coffers.

Shortly before he left, the Revd. Watson gave assistance at a serious accident.[3] One Fred Morgan a fitter for Listers, was returning from the Berkeley Hunt Show where he had been demonstrating Alexandra Cream Separators. At the top of the pitch before the Tabernacle he stopped his cart in order to fit shoes to the wheels for the descent, but the horse bolted, throwing his wife and the driver and himself out. The horse eventually stopped by Old Bell in Long Street. The adults were badly injured and it was their cries that brought Whitfield Watson from the Parsonage. The Constable appeared 'dragging Mr. Bloodworth's sprung waggon' and after both men had been put on, he pulled in the shafts and other men pushed from behind to take them to the Morgan's house in Union Street. The driver, with broken limbs, was later taken to Gloucester Infirmary. Mrs. Morgan, suffering two breaks in an arm and bad cuts on head and thigh, was taken to the doctor's surgery. All eventually recovered from their ordeal.

After five and a half years 'practically in a state of orphanhood, without a shepherd or guide', the Revd. John Thomas was inducted as Tabernacle minister. After training at Bristol Congregational Institute and ministries at Chepstow, London, Drybrook in the Forest of Dean, and Carlisle, Mr. Thomas had retired to Clevedon 'with a crushed spirit and with wrecked bodily health.' However the convalescent air of the Somerset Coast had reinvigorated him and in 1898, aged sixty, he came to Dursley. He was described as 'a quiet, gentle, gracious, kindly man with a strong interest in the temperance movement'. It is clear from church records that he had also the gift of inspiring others and his four years in the town were happy ones for his congregation – and for himself as he discovered here a marriage partner. The church he came to was 'united and peaceful' but determined not to bear again the burden of a ministry like the previous one, for it stipulated that it had the right to terminate a pastorate if affairs went awry.

A number of new organisations came into existence. There was the 'Sunshine Committee' which put flowers in the church for services (the first time this was done?) and distributed them afterwards to the sick and elderly. The 'Cottage Meeting Committee' in June 1898 had twenty-three active members, four cottages at its disposal and the prospects of more, and used Sankey's hymns. 'Working Bee' members received a penny each and made it increase and multiply. The Sunday School Committee, finding that some children could not attend through lack of suitable clothes, set about patching and distributing old, but otherwise wearable, discarded garments.

The church in 1898 had seventy-seven members but, then as now, the proportion that attended Church Meeting, a key part of traditional Congregationalism, was small – in March 1898, six men, including the minister, and twenty ladies Among those admitted to membership that month were the Revd. Robert Montgomery, his wife and Mr. and Mrs. A.J. Walters, bakers. Robert Montgomery had been inducted minister of the Baptist Church in South Street, Uley in May 1884 in the presence of a large congregation which included the Revd. William Muncaster of Dursley Tabernacle. In 1889 he published a history of the Baptists of Uley.

Early in 1898 the members of the Tabernacle decided that hence forth communion services should be monthly and alternately morning and evening, the pattern that exists today.

Two public affairs exercised the chapel's leadership in 1898. What part was the church to play in the management of the new Wesleyan School being erected by the Methodist Church and what part should it take in parochial charities? For the former it was agreed with the Wesleyans that the management committee should consist of the minister and six others from each church. For the Tabernacle the laymen for 1898–9 were

R.A. Lister, Engineer
John Kemp, Draper
George Smith, Senior Deacon and retired basket, sieve and chair maker
W.J. Grimes, Draper
R.H. Bruton, Gentleman of Prospect Place
John Sellick, Building Contracter

So far as the charities were concerned it was discovered that there were thirteen of these under joint control of Rector and both Nonconformist ministers. There was also a fourteenth, for bread, under the sole jurisdiction of the Rector.

Building work figured prominently in John Thomas's four years stay. On his arrival he and 'his wife' occupied rented accommodation for nine months as major renovations were beginning on the Parsonage. This was carried out by the two firms of Sellick Brothers and Sidney Bloodworth and Son. Like John Sellick, Sidney Bloodworth was a Tabernacle member. In 1884 he had been elected Bailiff of Dursley and was the last to hold the position. Between them they underpinned the Parsonage, inserted steel girders, laid on gas and fitted gas brackets, did work to windows and doors, put in new water cisterns, force pump, suction pipes and rising main, made alterations to the rainwater collecting cisterns in the cellar and installed a new water closet, possibly in anticipation of the piped water supply the town was about to get for the first time, though it was not laid on to the Parsonage until 1903. No mention has been found of a well but one is known to exist beneath the present kitchen.

In addition, a new range of classrooms, behind the Jubilee School Room, was built in 1889. In the hall itself, a platform was constucted at one end – probably with the railings and a pulpit which were removed in 1917. It, and the stairway were decorated. Total cost was just over £650. The original plan was for a suite of eight classrooms but became five in the light of the response to an appeal made by the Restoration Fund Committee. The appeal was in the form of an open letter to the public. It began by outlining the problems. Scholars on the roll numbered 180 and were split among twelve or so classes. Some used the Jubilee Room, eight or nine groups used the church and three occupied rooms in the unoccupied manse. More accommodation was needed for the children. The manse and church were being repaired and redecorated; in the latter a much needed improved ventilation system was being installed.

The appeal was for £1000.

> The Committee are conscious that in such a restricted locality as Dursley, it is not possible to raise so large a sum; they therefore confidently appeal to Sunday Schools and Church outside for assistance – especially as the main requirement is for the aid of the Mother Sunday School, not only of the County of Gloucestershire, but practically of the whole country. (The idea,

Mr & Mrs J.O. Higgs of Parsonage Street from whom Tabernacle members borrowed crockery for big occasions, c. 1890. *(Mrs E. Head)*

that it was William King's comment to Robert Raikes which brought about the Sunday School Movement, was greatly cherished.)

The Generous Help of fellow workers is earnestly asked; as also of Christian friends who sympathise with the efforts of Nonconformists in rural districts and small provincial towns, to maintain and extend the instruction of children and young people in the verities of the Christian Religion as taught in the Bible.

Early in 1899 'a large enthusiastic meeting was held in the Tabernacle' consisting of representatives of many Nonconformist churches in the area. It was called to consider the formation of a Dursley Free Church Council and after many speeches and on the proposition of Mr. R.A. Lister, seconded by the Revd. William Bailey of Sharpness, the Council came into being with the Revd. John Thomas as acting organising secretary. Later the council was extended to Wotton-under-Edge and so covered an area in the Severn Valley from Chipping Sodbury to Frampton-on-Severn.

Change came slowly to the Tabernacle in some things and small items were often big issues. In 1899 John Thomas proposed that the congregation should be invited to say aloud with him the Lord's Prayer. This idea was accepted but his introduction of sung 'Amens' to hymns did not find favour and was dropped. In following years the idea was mooted several times and in 1909 some members threatened to leave if the practice was introduced.

The question of how to obtain a sufficient and regular income was raised from time to time. In 1900 a letter was read from the Finance Committee to the Church Meeting saying that it could not see clearly a way out of the recurring annual deficit. Mr. R.A. Lister proposed and Mr. A.J. Walters seconded, that in that case it should be disbanded and financial matters placed in the hands of the Deacons. This was done. It is interesting to note that these short falls in income came about in spite of a regular income from substantial legacies. The 1829 bequest of £150 from William Smith had been added to at around the turn of the century.

Edmund Weight of Gloucester was a grandson of William King through one of William's daughters, Elizabeth, who incidently had been baptised by George Whitefield. Edmund's father is said to have been present at one of the conversations between King and Raikes on the subject of Sunday schools and subsequently had provided much information on the relationship between the two men. Church Secretary Alfred Bloodworth had corresponded with Edmund and as a result of Edmund's awakened interest in William King he thereafter gave £2 p.a. to the Tabernacle school and at his death in 1881 left £1000 to the church.

Mrs M. Jones at her death in 1900 bequeathed £300. Mary was the daughter of the Revd. William Bennett and had married a Dursley Inland Revenue Officer. George Smith, basket maker of Parsonage Street, teacher in the Sunday school for over forty years, lay preacher, much admired and loved, also died in 1900, leaving over £400 to the Tabernacle.

Mr. Tilton's bequest in 1899 was nearly £500. William Tilton had run an ironmongers shop and tinsmith works in what was, until recently, Durcan's shop in Parsonage Street, a building erected by his father, John Tilton, on the site of a blacksmith's workshop.[4] All these monies were invested and today still provide a valuable source of income. The yearly short fall income was made up either by sales of work, bazaars, tea meetings and the like or by Mr. R.A. Lister who quietly gave a donation to balance the books.

For many years boxes for weekly offerings had been placed by the doors. In 1897 these were replaced by bags, presumably held by sidesmen and immediately contributions jumped from around £3 a week to £9. In 1901 pew to pew collections were suggested but rejected. The idea was revised in 1903, accepted, resulted in a further big increase and a little later quarterly collections were discontinued.

Service times were discussed occasionally. At the turn of the century they were at 10.30 and 6.00. In 1905 it was proposed to change to 10.45 and 6.30, but this was rejected and it was not for many years that the change was made. Apart from two services at the Tabernacle, John Thomas held a monthly afternoon service and, in winter months, a fortnightly Bible Class at The Quarry Chapel.

Sunday was still a day set very much apart from the rest. Even Sunday newspapers were considered abominable. In December 1901 the officers and teachers resolved: 'Finding that attempts are being made to introduce into Dursley the systematic sale of Sunday newspapers, this meeting deems it its duty to record its protest against further desecration of the sanctity and restfulness of the Lord's Day, and expresses the hope that the inhabitants of our town and district will discountenance this aggessive movement by refusing to purchase such papers'. This, and others from Cam Meeting and other chapels, was published in the Dursley Gazette.

In 1902 The Tabernacle protested at the Government's proposed Education Act stating that the members were against any measure which —

a) removed rate supported schools from the full control of rate prayers.
b) provided public funds for sectarian instruction
c) placed Nonconformist teachers at a disadvantage by means of a religious test
d) discontinued the Board Schools which had done so much to raise standards in popular elementary education.
e) made any change in the staus quo without an 'appeal to the country'.

In the same year members were incensed by the leaders of the Parish Church. 'This meeting of the Members of Dursley Tabernacle Church and Congregation sincerely regrets that a Christian Thanksgiving Service in which the three denominations in the town could cordially and on terms of fraternal fellowship unite on Coronation Day, is deemed impracticable by

Mr and Mrs John Morgan, c. 1900, outside their cottage at the end of Prospect Place, now demolished. *(Mrs E. Head)*

the representatives of the Episcopal Church'. The motion was proposed by Mr. R.A. Lister, seconded by Samuel Workman Esq. of The Quarry and carried.

A year later December 1903, the Church tilted at strong drink. In a resolution to the local Justices of the peace it stated 'We believe the number of houses licenced for the sale of intoxicating liquor in the parish of Dursley to be in excess of the needs of the population and we pray your Lordships to make use of any opportunity that presents itself for reducing their number.' For the record, in 1901 the parish population was 2372 and there were, in 1903, fourteen public houses – Old Bell, Star, Railway Inn, Fox & Hounds, Kings Head, Broadwell Tavern, Bell & Castle, Crown, Lamb, licenced premises run by Wintle Brothers in Long Street, New Inn, Carpenters Arms, Cross Keys and The Bull. The last four were 'tied' to Thomas W. Elvey, whose brewery was on the left as one entered the bottom of Boulton Lane.

The Revd. John Thomas left Dursley quietly and with no fuss at the end of 1902. He retired to Bristol and his membership was transferred to Sneyd Park Church – 'Mr Thomas is a living epistle and needs no letters of commendation from us . . .' He died in 1915 aged seventy-three.

In 1904 there died John Morgan, aged eighty-three, and a member of the Tabernacle for nearly fifty years. His employment had been at Rivers Mill in the time of George Lister and at the Tabernacle he was for long chapel keeper and organ blower. His diminutative wife was a kindly person and one for whom she showed great concern was Old Daddock, a tramp often to be seen on the Town Hall steps. In winter he slept at the workhouse and in the day Mrs. Morgan would give him a hot drink. At her death she worried over who would look after the old man when she had gone.[6]

After a long interpastorate period, Arthur Haig, who had preached at the Tabernacle while a student at Western College, Bristol, came in 1905 to Dursley. Here he was ordained a Minister of the Gospel and inducted to the Tabernacle pastorate. His was a lively and happy ministry and in reading Church minutes and other documents one has the impression of a young man, full of ideas dancing light footedly round rather solemn, slightly bemused Deacons and other Church officials. One of his conditions for taking the pastorate was that a bath with hot and cold water should be fitted in the Parsonage – but he had to pay the water rate for this, ten shillings per annum which at this time was separate from the general water rate. In 1906 he married, and as a wedding present, the Church furnished his drawing room.

Services at the Tabernacle were well attended and Mrs. Nellie Head now aged ninety-one remembers well sitting in a crowded gallery. 'Sunday best' was normal, the ladies in long Edwardian dresses and among the wealthier men top hats were not uncommon. However though attendance was high, actual membership numbers were comparatively small – around ninety for most of the decade. The Church Meeting which heard of Arthur Haig's acceptance of the call to the Tabernacle numbered thirteen; the first such meeting of his pastorate, twenty two. Yet this is deceptive. Church life was not just Sunday observance, it flourished all the week and provided particularly for younger people.

The Young People's Society of Christian Endeavour, a strongly anti-drink organisation founded nationally in 1881, was very active. Begun in the Church by the Revd. Whitfield Watson, who ran it according to his ideas unaffiliated to the national union, it was remodelled to a standard pattern by John Thomas in 1894. Its weekly meetings were largely devotional and each usually centred on a paper read by an invited adult. In August 1904 for example topics were 'The Building of Character', 'The First Fruits of God', 'The Blessings of the Better Covenant', 'Missionary Books I have Read' and 'The Duty of Winsomeness'. It was however practical as well. Its members visited the sick and aged – wild flowers were sometimes picked and taken, it distributed literature of a moral kind and it ran devotional meetings for children at The Quarry Chapel in the winter months, and at the Bowcott Mission. The Mission closed in 1909. In 1906 its members collected ten shillings for the unemployed of West Ham.

Cam Meeting and the Wesleyan Methodist Churches also had Christian Endeavour groups and joint meetings were sometimes held. District rallies were attended and were reached by horse brake or frequently in cycling parties. On August Bank Holiday Monday in 1907 the Mid-Gloucestershire Union held a great convention on Stinchcombe Hill and in the following March a very successful 'Public Temperance Demonstration' was held in the town in support of the proposed new Licensing Bill being considered by Parliament. Chairman was R.A. Lister and the meeting met with not a little opposition.

Later in 1908, a sewing circle was formed among Endeavour members, to repair and make up garments for the poor, and flowers were sent to an East London Mission. Also for young people a Tabernacle Guild was formed in 1905. This seems to have been more of a social gathering and by 1907 it had 147 members. Its programme included rambles or horse brake outings in the Summer and in Winter, lantern lectures were sometimes organised in local villages and hamlets. Presumably the Church's magic lantern was used for these. An acetylene model was bought in 1906, lime light being considered too expensive.

Another activity was considered in 1908 – the formation of a Boys Brigade Unit. This idea was changed eventually to Boy Scouts on the grounds that they did similar work but had a cheaper and more attractive uniform. Thirty-two were enrolled in December. George Bloodworth seems to have been the first Scout Master soon to be followed by Arthur Haig himself. The Church provided all the uniforms and Mrs. Head can remember playing the piano for their exercises in these early years.

The Tabernacle has quietly taken pride in having a very early Sunday

Tabernacle Choir outing — probably to Framilode Tea Gardens c. 1910
Back row – W.J. Ashworth, Mr. Watts, Revd Arthur Haig, Ernest Kemp, W. Henry Allen
3rd row – Margaret Kemp, John Kemp, Samuel Workman, Percy Derrett, ?, Sidney Bloodworth, Mrs Allen, ?.
2nd row – Mrs Haig, ?, ?, Mrs Griffin, Nellie Workman (later Mrs E. Head) , Alice Earl, Mrs Ashworth.
Front, ?, ?, ?, Miss Gardiner, Mrs Percy Ashworth.

School. It should also take similar pride in the knowledge that it formed the first Scout Troop in Dursley and one of the earliest nationally. When in 1912 the Revd. Arthur Haig left Dursley, leadership was assumed by Percy Ashworth and then, when he resigned a year later, by Bruce Champion. Bruce, an Anglican, requested that the Troop move to neutral premises. As the 1st Dursley Group it still fulfills a vital need among boys of the town, as does the 3rd Dursley which separated from it in 1937/38. In the inter-war years another Scout Troop was formed at the Tabernacle – the 2nd Dursley but this is no longer in existence.

The Sunday School flourished. In 1908 it had 170 scholars and fourteen teachers. Its main meetings were on Sunday afternoons but morning sessions were also held before public worship. A kindergarten service was held during morning worship for tiny children. For the children, the library still operated – '250 healthy and interesting books to fight bad literature with good.' A teachers' section of the library had been formed. To

The 2nd Dursley Scout Troop c. 1935. In the middle row are G.S.M. L.G. Barnett and A.S.M. G. Phillips.

help young people speak well the Revd. Haig ran an elocution class.

It had 171 children on its books in 1911 and 22 teachers. Average attendance was 43 in the morning and 131 in the afternoon and 107 children belonged to the clothing club, secretary of which was Percy Hicks. By 1914, 227 children met in 19 classes and it is not surprising that a new school hall was opened. This, built by Sidney Bloodworth for £800, was declared open by Sir Ashton Lister in July 1914 but was only part of the original plan which was to build also a new manse.

Not all the children were well behaved and one suspects that some attended only because of parental or social pressures. In this the Tabernacle was not alone. An illuminating minute of Cam Methodist Church of this period stated that 'a company of Gentlemen (must) look after the bad conduct in the gallery – card playing and novel reading must at any cost be stopped!'[7]

Long prayers and sermons could not have been attractive to children and Mrs Head can remember how they would relieve the tedium sometimes, by giggling at the animated, but to them funny, expressions assumed by those leading prayers. Idly doodling on gallery pews would have served the same purpose.

A Tabernacle Sunday School treat on Stinchcombe Hill c. 1910. One regular joy for children was to chase a fleet footed teacher and try to snatch small bags of sweets stitched all over his coat *(Mrs M. Talboys)*

Children on the Broadway c. 1910, a route to Stinchcombe Hill which has seen countless parties of merry makers pass up and down it. *(Mrs D. Deane)*

Sunday School sports, held usually on a mid summer week evening, and treats were yearly high lights. Sometimes treats were held in the Victoria Hall but usually they were on Stinchcombe Hill – games tea and always fireworks at the end. In 1900, eleven shillings, a considerable sum, was spent on them; in 1911 100 chinese lanterns were accepted from the Coronation Committee and used at dusk on the homeward journey instead of the customary 'coloured fire'. In 1904 a 5/- gratuity was paid to 'Mr Lister's servants' for helping. The Lister Band sometimes played; Sidney Bloodworth's wagon, horse and man were usually hired for drives around the hill and Mr Buston's waggonette was used for general transport; the Scouts put up swings and the Choir was often invited. All this continued through the war, though in 1917 no food was provided at the request of the local Food Controller, nor were there fireworks that year. Younger school teachers were also missing as many had joined 'Kitcheners Army' or the Territorials. Sadness came in 1918 when teacher Doris Wyatt was killed in an accident at Listers. By this time the school seems to have been wholly a Sunday afternoon affair.

Other Sunday Schools of course had their treats. On at least one occasion the Cam Meeting School used Bertie Workman's Draycott Flour Mills Sentinel steam lorry to take the children up on to Selsley Common – and they returned blackened by the smoke![8]

The Sunday School movement as a whole was strong and in 1908 it was decided by the Dursley and Wotton-under-Edge Free Church Council to form a local auxiliary to the Bristol Sunday School Union. Schools in local villages affiliated to the Bristol Union formed the nucleus and these were joined by those at The Tabernacle and Cam Meeting. The school at Dursley Methodist Church joined in early 1909 and that at Cam Methodist in 1910. By 1912, when the Annual rally was held at Dursley Methodist Church, the auxiliary had 22 schools, 1718 children and 250 teachers. It was from the beginning very active in promoting schoolwork. Thus in 1910, when the Annual Raly was at The Tabernacle, a practical session was run by a Miss Grimshaw from Bristol, using thirty 6 to 8 year olds and nine teachers. This lasted an hour 'with no sign of weariness, and consisted of a welcome song, prayers, scripture reading, nature talk, birthday greetings, marching exercise, a missionary collection and a story – 'Peter's escape from prison'. The children afterwards executed their impression in drawings fearfully and wonderfully made. A new hymn was taught and a name received on the cradle roll"

A prominent member of the Auxiliary was George Montgomery. In 1911 he was elected President and in his term of office he was frequently absent from Dursley, his 'predigious perambulations' taking him out to the other schools and churches. In 1912 he was awarded the national Sunday School Union's Silver Medal for first place in an examination on 'Scripture History and Doctrine'.

An adherent, later member of the Tabernacle in this period was Bertie

The shop of George and Ebeneezer Montgomery, sons of the Revd Montgomery, late nineteenth century pastor of Uley Baptist Chapel. The two brothers are remembered today for their tireless work at the Tabernacle, George particularly with the Sunday school. Ebbie played a big role in the Comrade's Circle, a group of young men who met regularly for Bible study before Sunday morning worship. Sometime after this picture was taken he left the shop and became manager of the local Labour Exchange and many young people coming to work in the town in the 1930s had good reason to be grateful for what he did for them, which went far beyond the call of duty. Here Ebbie is far right, George is next to him. *(Robert Montgomery)*

Bruton who came to Dursley from Shortwood Baptist Chapel. By 1890 he was running independently of any church, a Bible Class for young men and for many years this met in the Town Hall. He became a Sunday School teacher but his Bible Class retained its separate identity in spite of several attempts by him and the Tabernacle to find a way of linking up. He was a great admirer of William Tyndale and published several items about him. By the time he died in about 1930 he was a Director of Cam Mills. Anyway his bequests were his clothes and wearing apparel to the Mill for distribution to needy employees, £1000 to the British and Foreign Bible Society and £250 each on trust for upkeep of the Monuments at Vilvorden, near Brussells, where Tyndale was burnt at the stake in 1536, and North Nibley.

Mr A.H. Bruton was also interested in history and collaborated with Ebbie Montgomery in producing, for the centenary of the building of the present Tabernacle, a booklet 'Another Milestone' (1908).

One proposal made by Arthur Haig just before he left Dursley was that all groups in the church catering for young people should come within an umbrella organisation called The Young People's Institute. This merger was extremely successful and in 1911, jointly with a church in Halifax, Dursley Tabernacle won the prize of the Congregational Union of England and Wales for the best winter programme for young people.

Tabernacle activities were not confined to young people. In 1905 soon after his arrival Arthur Haig initiated revision of the church rules. Unfortunately what they were before is unknown but three points from what they became are of interest.

Membership. 'This Church shall consist of persons who have professed and given satisfactory evidence of faith in, and loyalty to, the Lord Jesus Christ'.

Discipline. 'In cases which call for discipline, members of the church shall be dealth with according to the principles laid down in I Cor. 5, 11–13 and Gal. 6, 1.'

Diaconate. The Deacons' terms of office were two years, half to retire annually. Election was by ballot before the April Communion Service. Each member received before hand, a ballot list of *all* male members of the church over the age of 21 and from this each made his selection. If elected, a member was permitted to decline to serve. The rules allowed for six

The Revd Arthur Haig, minister 1905–12, and the Tabernacle as it was in his time.

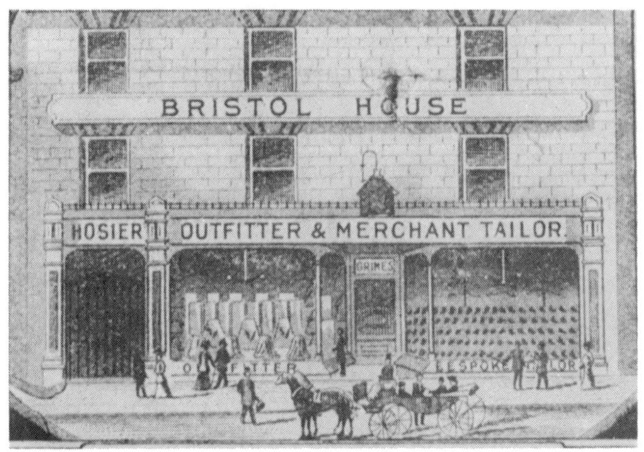

Shops of three of the many tradesmen who supported the Tabernacle in Edwardian times; Grimes, Stowers and Kemps.

Deacons to be elected but in fact for many years the number remained at four.

In 1906 over 80 people gathered one September evening on what were then the extensive lawns in front of the Parsonage. The gardens were festooned with fairy lights and chinese lanterns and in these delightful surroundings with only the occasional crunching of cart wheels, they listened to a concert of songs, recitations and an instrumental quartet.

The centenary celebrations of 1908 had a climax in June when Dr. Alfred Gavrie Principal of New College, London, took the celebration services. There was a 'thanksgiving day' and on this was held a tea party which spread from school rooms out onto the Parsonage lawns. Centre piece was a 'very handsome . . . cake generously presented by Messrs. A.T. Walters and Son. This bore several inscriptions including the text 'Unto Thy Name be the glory, both now and forever'; and the names of the ten ministers who have occupied the Tabernacle pastorate during the century. The cake, which was greatly admired, was a fine example of the confectioners art and it was decorated with portraits of the pastor and deacons, and a picture of the Tabernacle.'

The booklet 'Another Milestone' produced for the occasion has been alluded to already. In it, Mr. E.C. Montgomery described the Tabernacle as it then was.

There were 15 lady 'visitors' and a sewing class for mothers who could not attend Sunday services. A Missionary Auxiliary existed to raise money and interest in work overseas and this had been supported for ten years by the Watchers Band, a group of people who prayed regularly for it. A Missionary Study Circle provided knowledge of places overseas where work went on and, since the first 'John and Mary Dursley' had been adopted, a succession of Mary's had been supported at Bangalore High School in India.

The choir numbered 28 people; Church membership stood at 85 and though an increase of 33 on 1905 when Arthur Haig arrived, it represented only a small proportion of the regular congregation which at this time was probably around the 400 mark.

Prayer meetings, a week night preaching service, support of the International Bible Reading Association (111 members), the Bible Society, the Evangelical Alliance, Dr. Barnardo's Homes, the District Free Church Council and the Sunday School Union were all part of the chapel life.

In 1909 the use of individual communion glasses was adopted. These were given by Mrs W.H. Allen, a much loved member.

'The World Petition' of the Peace Society was debated in 1911 in church meeting, signed and sent to the Society and a resolution was sent to Sir Edward Grey, Foreign Secretary, supporting the proposed treaty of peace between Great Britain and the U.S.A.

The Revd. Arthur Haig left Dursley in 1912. At a farewell gathering in April he was presented with a purse of gold of £40 in value – a consider-

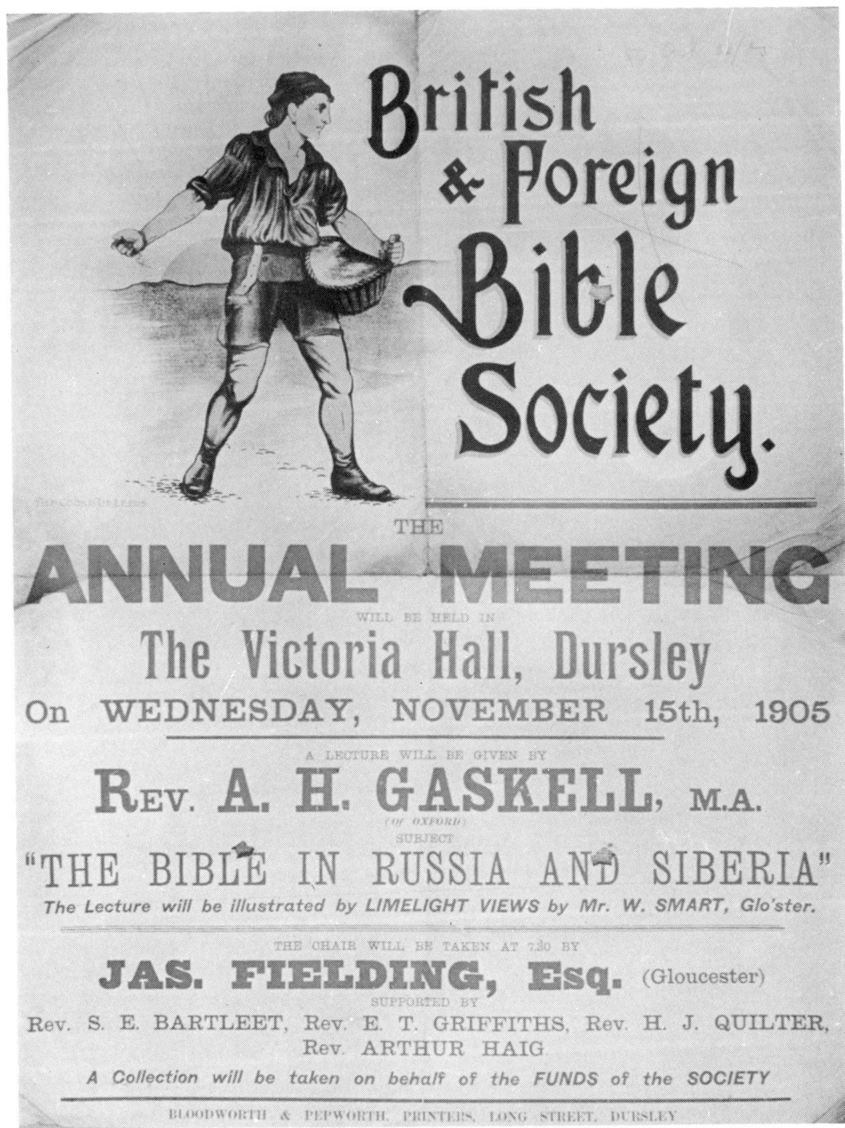

British & Foreign Bible Society.

THE ANNUAL MEETING

WILL BE HELD IN

The Victoria Hall, Dursley

On WEDNESDAY, NOVEMBER 15th, 1905

A LECTURE WILL BE GIVEN BY

REV. A. H. GASKELL, M.A.

(OF OXFORD)

SUBJECT

"THE BIBLE IN RUSSIA AND SIBERIA"

The Lecture will be illustrated by LIMELIGHT VIEWS by Mr. W. SMART, Glo'ster.

THE CHAIR WILL BE TAKEN AT 7.30 BY

JAS. FIELDING, Esq. (Gloucester)

SUPPORTED BY

Rev. S. E. BARTLEET, Rev. E. T. GRIFFITHS, Rev. H. J. QUILTER, Rev. ARTHUR HAIG

A Collection will be taken on behalf of the FUNDS of the SOCIETY

BLOODWORTH & PEPWORTH, PRINTERS, LONG STREET, DURSLEY

One of the first ventures in which Anglican, Methodist and Congregational Churches in Dursley worked together. *(Jeremy and Jonathan Pallister)*

able sum when local workman earned perhaps £1 per week and a measure of the great affection he had gained from his congregation.. He moved to Stone in Staffordshire then Chatham in Kent and from 1920 to 1939 he was a Royal Naval Chaplain. During the period of World War II he ministered at Bude, Cornwall, then spent two years at Margate before retiring in 1947. He died, aged 94, in 1970 at Fen Place, Sussex – a home for retired Congregational Ministers.

Within a few months he was followed at Dursley by Frederick Ives Cater, A.T.S. who was born at Sudbury, Suffolk and who trained at New College. Before moving to Dursley he spent eleven years at Oundle, Northamptonshire and while there published a history of the county's Nonconformists.

The Revd Ives Cater, minister 1912–19.

Charlie and Bessie Webb near their home at the far end of Woodmancote in 1914. Charlie's great grandfather helped to build the present Tabernacle and his grandfather was carried as a baby to the opening services. Charlie, also, was a loyal member of the church and was very upset, as doubtless other elderly folk were when, after the last war, the church was redecorated and the painted Lord's Prayer behind the pulpit was covered over. He died aged 88 in 1967. *(Mrs C. Pyle)*

His ministry took the church through the years of World War I. Activity continued much as in peace time until towards its end, though saddened and shot through with concern over local people embroiled in the conflict in Europe. Some never returned and their names are to be found on a memorial in the church vestibule.

Blackout was put up in church and hall in 1916. An urgent cash collection was made in 1917 for Prisoner of War Fund parcels and economies had to be made in the use of lighting and fuel. In this year too Ives Cater informed the Church that he had joined the Gloucestershire Volunteer Regiment and might have to leave suddenly. He also took up munitions works – almost certainly at Listers – for six half days a week. In both actions he was supported and commended by his congregation.

Ives Cater left Dursley in 1919 for Burslem and then in 1928 he moved to Over, Cheshire where he died four months later. His family still has contacts with the Tabernacle and this continuing connection with a well loved man is a delight to the Church.

An interesting picture from St. James's Church in 1904. In that year the bells were re-hung and they are seen here after their removal from the tower with their old wooden supports. By comparing this with pictures taken later it can be seen that restoration work on the bells was done without moving them from these position. Standing bare headed on the right of the doorway is Canon Bartleet, rector 1899–1911.

(Mrs L. Trollope)

10

The Last Sixty Years at The Tabernacle

The inter war years at the Tabernacle were covered by three ministers.

First was Ernest Knight B.D. 1921–24. Born in London, he took his degree at the Congregational College, Montreal, trained for the ministry at Western College, Bristol and was ordained in Perth, Western Australia where he stayed 1908–12. He then became pastor of the Union Chapel, Calcutta and while there travelled by horse and foot through the Himalayas to the Tibetan border. In India during the war period he was a United Board Chaplain to the armed services. After his short stay in Dursley he spent 23 years at Boscombe, Hants, before moving to Bournemouth, where he died in 1955.

Secondly came Harold I. Frith M.A. 1926–31. Born Yardley, Birmingham, he trained at the Lancashire College and Manchester University where he gained several prizes. He came to Dursley after a year on a research scholarship at Mansfield College, Oxford.

After leaving Dursley he spent three years in Reading, at Park Church, and then until 1947 he held pastorates in Hampshire. From 1945 to 1959, when he died, he was secretary of the Hampshire Congregational Union. For several years he held the position of lecturer in Biblical and historical theology in the then University College, Southampton.

Thirdly there was Frank Shepherd B.A. 1932–43. Born in Rochdale and trained at The Lancashire College, Dursley was his first ministerial post. Later he held pastorates in Shipley, Yorkshire; Cleveleys, Lancashire; Olton, Warwickshire and Manchester. He died in Buxton in 1972. He was the first Tabernacle minister to preach in the Parish Church in Dursley.

All these men were people of distinction and their qualities, diverse though they were, kept the church alive and it flourished. Nationally the period was difficult and in the churches there were great problems to face upto. The 1914–18 war had been a water shed and life post war, more mobile and less parochial, was very different to the more stable, static and structured order that had existed before.

Rapid secularization of Sunday was one outcome of this change and by 1925 Sunday schools in general were lamenting falling rolls. By 1933

Ministers of the interwar period. Ernest Knight, 1921–24; Ingram Frith, 1926–31 and Frank Shepherd, 1932–43.

churches were expressing concern at the lack of religious education in the 'average home' and at the wide variations, from excellent to perfunctory, it received in day schools.

The Tabernacle school followed the national pattern but the effect was delayed. In 1921 with 177 scholars, it asked Sir Ashton Lister to use his influence with the County Council to get a sign of motorists erected in the Kingshill Road saying 'Sunday School'. Five years later the roll had increased to 196 with an average attendance of 150 but thereafter numbers fell until in 1935 the usual attendance was about 80, a figure maintained roughly until the end of World War II.

Sunday school anniversaries became great ocasions and outstanding preachers and personalities were frequently booked over a year ahead. For example, in 1944, Uncle Mac of the BBC (Derek McCullock) agreed to come, though at the last moment he had to withdraw. School Treats continued, still mainly in Stinchcombe Hill, but sometimes on local farms and even at Weston-super-Mare.

In 1919 the Church sent a resolution to the Government urging that war time restrictions on the manufacture and sale of intoxicating liquors be continued 'in view of the great advantages to the efficiency and moral well being of the nation and to public health and order.'

The 1920 Lambeth Conference brought forth another resolution recording the Church's appreciation of the spirit of the Established Church in setting out its Manifesto on Reunion and urging the Congregational Union to give it 'sympathetic and prayerful consideration without delay'.

Sir Ashton Lister and Ernest Barrett, headmaster of the new Dursley Secondary School, at school sports c. 1925 *(Miss K. Kemp)*

John and Charlotte Kemp with their children c. 1895.
Back – Margaret, Herbert & Arthur
Front – Mabel, Alfred, Ernest & Katherine *(Miss K. Kemp)*

It was in this year also that the free will offering envelope scheme began.

Mr & Mrs Ernest Barrett joined the Church in 1921, transferring membership from Lewisham. Mr Barrett was the first headmaster of the new County Secondary, later Grammar, School in the town. It opened that year in the house at Rednock that had once belonged to George Harris, the clothier the Tabernacle had had such close dealings with in the early nineteenth century.

John and Charlotte Kemp celebrated their Golden Wedding in 1923 and they received from the Church an illuminated address.

John,[1] son of a Torrington, Devon, brewer, became an apprentice draper in Stroud in 1859. In 1873 he married his employer's daughter at Rodborough Tabernacle and settled in Dursley where he had a shop, London House, now demolished, in the Market Place. To younger people John and Charlotte seemed very correct and a little formal but both were tireless workers at The Tabernacle.

John became a Deacon in 1881 and was for many years both treasurer and secretary. The latter post he gave up in 1914 when he was presented with 'a handsome Parisian Clock Suite in onyx and guilt . . . and a pedestal rose bowl of enchased silver and glass'. Of him, Sir Ashton Lister, who could not be present wrote:–

> All you can present to Mr John Kemp is the merest token of our gratitude, regard and esteem: our debt to him as a Church and congregation is far beyond our means to discharge.

John Kemp retired from being treasurer, after 22 years, in 1921 and in 1928 he and Samual Workman were made Life Deacons, the first in the history of the church so far as is known. John died a few months afterwards aged 84; Charlotte lived until 85 in 1933.

Samual Workman, who lived at The Quarry, was also an outstanding figure both at the Tabernacle, where he can be remembered sitting near the front of the church timing the entry of the minister about to take the service, and at the Quarry Chapel where he was prominent in its affairs from its early days. He married three times, died aged 93 in 1929 and is buried in the Quarry burial ground.

Samuel's son, George, a builder, helped in the great restoration of the Tabernacle in the 1870s and 80s. His daughter-in-law, George's wife, Annie, is remembered for being the first lady in Cam to ride a bicycle, her appearance on a 'boneshaker' scandalizing the community.

Developments in cycle design led to a craze for cycle riding in late Victorian times and drew the attention of writers for the religious press.

> The mere act of riding a bicycle is not in itself sinful, and if it is the only available means of reaching the church on Sunday it may be excusable. On the other hand, if walking or riding in the usual way is discarded for the sake of the exercise or exhileration bicycle riding affords, it is clearly wrong. Besides, dignity of action and a noble decorum should be inseparable from the high office of Sunday school teacher, and anything that impairs the dignity of that office necessarily impairs the influence as well. Bear this well in mind' ('Home Companion', 1885, notes for Sunday school teachers).
>
> The bicycle is a thoroughly Christian machine, for it improves the temper, discourages dissipation, makes a man look on the bright side of things and puts vivacity into his religion. In known from experience that a minister can preach better on Sunday if he rides a bicycle on Saturday' ('Ipswich Nonconformists', 1894).[3]

Castle Gardens to the South of the Tabernacle were bought in 1926 for £256 of which £100 came from Sir Ashton Lister. It is not clear why the ground was bought – perhaps with a view to future development or perhaps to protect the environment of the chapel. Ten years later it became known that the local council was intent on building a car park on Castle Farm land and it was feared that the gardens would be acquired compulsorily to provide access from Parsonage Street, with all the possible noise and nuisance this could bring. At the same time the GPO was looking for a site for expansion and it was decided to offer Castle Gardens for this use. The offer was acepted and the present main post office erected.

1927 saw Tabernacle members making three public protests. The first, published in the Dursley Gazette, was against the evils of gambling. The second was directed at the Territorial Army for using Cam Long Down rifle range on a Sunday. No satisfaction was received as a result of this and the matter placed in the hands of the County Congregational Union.

The third, sent to the local Member of Parliament, protested at the suggestion revision of the Book of Common Prayer, calling it 'great danger to Protestant principles'. As it happened the revision was rejected by Parliament but satisfaction was short lived for a second revision was submitted the following year. Again a resolution was sent condemning this as 'a menace to the Protestantism of both Church and realm.'

In 1929 clothing was sent to distressed miners and on May 26th a united service was held on Cam Peak. May Day gatherings on hill tops have a long history stretching back to pagan times. When Cam Peak was first used for Christian worship is unknown but in 1908 a reference to a May morning meeting with Cam Meeting may refer a hill top service. It is recorded that the event developed out of the ancient custom of May Walking.

Another Springtime annual event was a long walk on Good Friday followed by an evening service. On one occasion, at least, this went over Cam Long Down and along the Cotswold Edge to Stroud from whence a bus was used for the return. Long walks were not uncommon social occasions. The late Gladys Kendall described on one occasion how the choir had walked to one of the River Severn ferry points near Saul, crossed, had tea on the far side and returned via a ferry near or at Purton.

Sir Ashton Lister, great benefactor of town and Tabernacle, died in 1929. Although he became a man of wealth and standing in the County he developed none of the arrogance and pomposity which sometimes goes with rise in fortune. His home at The Towers was an open one and church meetings were sometimes held there. When the Revd. Harold Frith and his young bride came to Dursley in 1926 they were made very welcome in his home while the Parsonage was being renovated.

A staunch adherent of the Tabernacle – he was member from 1895 – he became a trustee in 1899 and frequently, quietly, set the church finances straight when they went into the red. He had a passionate interest in young people and supported youth activities where he could. For a while he became a total abstainer from intoxicating liquor in the hope of setting an example to younger folk and for most of his life he was a strong advocate of temperance.

One reason for the long and happy association of Sir Ashton with the Tabernacle and, indeed, could account for the strength of the church itself, could well be that like him, most of its members would have been Liberal in political conviction. The town at the turn of the century was a Liberal stronghold and if the Established Church could be considered the Tory Party at prayer, much the same could perhaps be said then of Liberals and Nonconformists.

The Revd. Harold Frith preached a funeral sermon to a crowded church and Robert Ashton Lister was buried in the Tabernacle graveyard by his wife who died in 1911. In 1980 a simple plaque to his memory was placed in the church above the pew he and his wife regularly occupied.

Church activity abounded in the inter war years – choir practice, recitals and cantatas; Comrades'Circle; London Missionary Society, Watchers Prayer Union, Temperance, League of Nations Union, Home Churches Fund, Free Church Council, Medical Mission and County Union meetings; garden parties and bazaars – often two day events, gift days – the extraordinary sum of £605 was raised in 1926 towards a £1000 renovation scheme; Girls' Fireside Club; Sunday school; week night services in winter and occasional open air services in summer – usually on Stinchcombe Hill; united services with the Methodist and Anglican churches; toy service, monthly Church Meetings and of course weekly Sunday services, morning and evening. Great support was given to the Y.M.C.A. in Long Street where a hall, hostel and boys' club provided much needed facilities particularly for youths coming into the town to work. It also provided a social centre where young people of both sexes could meet. This venture survived the Second World War but fell a victim to the post war slump.

A commemoration service for the life of George Whitefield, organised by the local Free Church Council, was held on Stinchcombe Hill in July 1934 and in the same year a companionship scheme was set up among Congregational Churches in the county. Under this larger and smaller churches were linked, each supporting and visiting the other for a year.

A Tabernacle outing in a charabanc with Eddie Jones – probably bound for Weston-super-Mare. *(Mrs M. Talboys)*

Comrade's Circle Concert party, Christmas 1927.
Back — ? Preater, Oliver Vinton, Reg Butcher
Middle – Ray Norville, ? Milliner, Ray Owen, Reg Spurling, Tom Spurling, Lawrence Barrett, Ebbie Montgomery
Front — Arthur Grigg *(Ray Owen)*

Many happy outings by coach for Dursley people resulted from this scheme and it continued until the inauguration of the United Reformed Church in 1972.

A letter of thanks and goodwill was sent from the Church in 1935 to Anthony Eden, the British Minister for League of Nations Affairs, because of his great efforts to prevent the outbreak of hostilities in the Italo – Abyssinian dispute.

The news that another secondary school might be built in Dursley was considered by the church in 1936. The view was expressed that it should be a Council School, as against a Church School, and steps were taken to inform the authorities of this view.

New housing estates around the town, Kingshill, Olive Grove and Highfields in part, brought many newcomers into the area in the same and following years and, with the other churches in Dursley and Cam, a contact and visiting scheme was brought into operation.

In 1937 a London Missionary Society Pilots Group was begun and in the following year a collection was made for the Relief Fund for Czechoslovakian Protestant Churches and another was made in 1939 for Jewish refugees.

1939 was a full year. The Dursley Welsh Society met on Tabernacle premises and held a St. David's Day celebreation. Open air services, at the invitation of the Rector, were held on Stinchcombe Hill jointly with Methodists and Anglicans. A meeting with the British Organ Blowing Company resulted in muscle power giving way to electric. The centenary of the martyrdom of John Williams was commemorated.

Overall, however, hung the threat, and then the actuality, of war. In August the Ministry of Labour was given permission to use Tabernacle premises during a national emergency. Then came evacuees from Birmingham. The ministers from the three town churches visited the schools, including the built but unopened new secondary at Highfields, to sort out children with denominational backgrounds and share out the rest for Sunday School purposes. Soldiers began to appear in the town.

The Birmingham evacuees did not stay long. The contrast between city life and that in a small country town was too great and before long they were drifting back leaving memories with many of those who boarded them which remain vivid to this day.

In the summer of 1940 children and staff of Harwich County School came to Dursley and used Tabernacle rooms for teaching purposes for some three years. In the Autumn, the King's Own Scottish Borderers came for Church parades. The Dursley Public Assistance Institution (formerly Workhouse) in Union Street was closed and the elderly folk in it transferred to Northleach and Stow-on-the-Wold. As with the other town churches, the Tabernacle had had close links with the Institution for many years, visiting, putting on concerts and so on. Closing it resulted in splitting up close friendships among the inmates and protests were made over this by church folk.

The Dursley and District Spitfire Fund appealed to the churches for support but all three replied that they were unable to do so as corporate bodies but doubtless many of their members would. An agreement was made that if any one of the three town churches was destroyed by enemy action, hospitality would be extended by the others.

By 1941 the Tabernacle had its own Youth Squad of First Aiders, its Fire Watchers, was receiving sadly news of killed or wounded service men and women, and had opened its rooms to troops in the town for reading writing and relaxation. Service personnel came and went rapidly but the open house policy continued for most of the war. In 1942 it was recorded that the ladies of the church were providing 'some sort of refreshment' for the troops out of their own rations.

In 1942 the church railings went for the war effort. Compensation was received in 1950 – £1 *5s 0d* (£1.25) 'Feelings of stupefaction were felt at

MOTHERS' DAY SERVICE

SUNDAY MORNING, MAY 14, 1944.

OBSERVED BY

MEMBERS OF U.S. ARMY (together with) MEMBERS OF THE LOCAL CONGREGATIONAL CHURCH

PROGRAM

ORGAN PRELUDES: Majestic Sweetness; Whispering Hope.

DOXOLOGY.

LORD'S PRAYER.

HYMNS (two verses of each) accompanied by MISS DRESHER at the piano.

1. Have Thine own Way.
2. Standing on the Promises.
3. Sweet By and By.
4. The Old Rugged Cross.
5. Let the Lower Lights be Burning.
6. When the Roll is called up yonder.

SCRIPTURE .. .. .. S. SGT. WARREN BLAYLOCK, U.S. Army

SPECIAL SONG—"Thanks be to God" .. By GIRLS' JUNIOR CHOIR

OFFERING. (The loose offering this morning will go to the Sunshine Home for Blind Children. Those of us who have each year given to our mothers some present or remembrance on Mothers' Day, but who will not have that opportunity this year due to our being away, will welcome this privilege of making an offering to-day to this Home for Blind Children and we know our mothers will be made happy by our doing this).

SPECIAL SONG—"My Mother's Bible" .. .. by U.S. ARMY NURSES

ANNOUNCEMENTS .. .. CHURCH SECRETARY

SPECIAL SONG .. .. U.S. ARMY SOLDIERS

SERMON .. .. CHAPLAIN HINSON

HYMN—"Blest be the Tie that Binds" (First Verse)

BENEDICTION.

A Prayer for Mother.

Lord Jesus, Thou hast known
A mother's love and tender care,
And Thou wilt hear while for my mother most dear
I make this Sabboth prayer.
Protect her life, I pray,
Who gave the gift of life to me;
And may she know from day to day the deepening glow
Of joy that comes from Thee.
I cannot pay my debt
For all the love that she has given;
But Thou, love's Lord, will not forget her due reward—
Bless her in earth and heaven. Amen.

—*Van Dyke.*

To those who are not accustomed to observing Mothers' Day as we are in the United States, we would like to explain that: Mothers' Day is observed in the United States of America on the second Sunday in May each year. Special Services are held in the Churches to commemorate the occasion. And people in general try to do something on that day in honour of their mothers whether they be living or dead. Ordinarilly, people wear a red flower that day if their mother is living, and if their mother is not living they wear a white flower.

A SALUTE TO WOMANHOOD.

We consider it a great privilege to honor womanhood in general and Motherhood in particular. Almost without exception we who are in the Military Service have a mother, a wife, or a sweetheart somewhere. We know that they are praying for the war to soon be over and that they are waiting and serving for our early return. We feel that they have the most difficult part of the battle to wage and that their burden is the heaviest to bear. It is because they are doing their part so well that our part is made easier and we are encouraged to use our full strength and talents to make the world a happier and safer place for them to live.

To the women in the Service with us and to those in the community around us we wish to thank you for every act of kindness that contributes to the happiness of our stay here. We are happy to have the privilege of worshipping God with you and to have you join us today in honoring Mother.

this princely munificence . . .!' In 1942 also, occurred the remarkable visit to the church of Dr. Carl Scweitzer 'the eminent Divine of the German Confessional Church'.

More pressure on church accommodation came in 1943 when the children from Harwich were joined by a class from the Dursley Council School (now housing Dursley Technical College).

The year also saw the departure of its minister Frank Shepherd and the assumption by the Gloucester and Hereford Congregational Union of trusteeship for buildings and land. Up to this time trustees were private individuals.

From late 1943 onwards American soldiers were to be seen in the streets of Dursley and they proved popular, particularly among the children who found their gum irresistable. With the troops came two Chaplains. The Revd. Barsh was offered use of the Methodist Church for parades and the Revd. Hinson of the American Evacuation Hospital Unit, the Tabernacle. Both offers were gratefully accepted and both chaplains took services frequently at churches in the area including The Quarry.

One great day was May 14th 1944 – America's 'Mothers' Day'. Such was war time security that even the order of service printed for use at the Tabernacle was wrapped in anonimity! Then as suddenly as they had appeared, the Americans left, as did most other troops, and the D Day landings in France got under way – but not before Pastor Hinson had received a presentation from Tabernacle members. An appreciation of the kindness shown to the American troops came a little later when the Revd. Hinson, working an 18 hour day within the sound of the Normandy battles, found time to pen his gratitude.

In the Autumn of 1944 Tabernacle rooms were used for one weekend as a reception and rest centre for mothers and children being moved from areas in southern Britain likely to be hit by German flying bombs. These evacuees were cared for by local folk. This was not the first time Dursley had been a haven in time of threat and at least one town – Eastbourne – has a Dursley Road to commemorate the fact.

With so many of its members and adherents away in various parts of the world, fighting, the church in 1943 decided to duplicate monthly news-letters to provide closer contact. They were written in turn by a large number of people – some were morale boosting, some just newsy, but all were appreciated by the recipients.

In 1943 £180 was raised for the 'Sunshine Home for Blind Babies' – a sum which included money collected while carol singing at '233 stations' around the town over 15 evenings at Christmastide. Generous givers were the Americans who seem not to have experienced this custom before. Support for the Sunshine Home had begun in 1928 and by 1952 £2,657 had been sent. Chief activist in this was Ernest Kemp, a choir member with a strong mellow bass voice.

Anyone entering the Tabernacle in the late 1930s who glanced up to the

Ernest Kemp enjoying a visit to the Sunshine Home for Blind Babies.

back gallery to see who was making the organ sound out might well have been surprised to see a very youthful figure seated at the consol. This would have been Jack Dobbs, a Berkeley lad, then a pupil at Dursley Grammar School and for four years official church organist. Jack went on to Cardiff University to take a degree in music and after a period in Durham is now at Dartington hall, Devon. In 1945 he was invited by the compilers of the new post war hymn book, 'Congregational Praise', to compose a tune for a hymn with a difficult metre 'We sing of life, God's glorious gift to man.' This he did with the voice of Ernest Kemp in mind and, out of gratitude for the understanding and affection with which he had been surrounded in his youth, called it 'Dursley Tabernacle'.[4]

Services have been broadcast from the Tabernacle on several occasions. The most recent was in 1978 when the church celebrated the 200th anniversary of William King's Sunday school and Jack Dobbs' fine, joyful tune was one of those included. Another of his hymn tunes, 'Teilo Sant', is also to be found in 'Congregational Praise'.

Irene Norville, for many years church choirmaster began a very success-

"DURSLEY" ALPHABET

A is for Adams, the musical vet.
B is for Bailey's, who print the Gazette.
It's also for Bloodworth, with well-equipped shelves—
If you don't take my word, go and see for yourselves
C stands for Champion's, for carpets and rugs,
And also for Cope, who sells med'cines and drugs.
D's for a fruit shop, by name it is Deane's.
E's Ellett's, for papers, books and magazines.
F's for the Doctors—Fayle, Falconer and Fraser,
And Fowles the optician, a "posh" type of glazier.
G's Giddings, who's busy both winter and summer
As house decorator, contractor and plumber.
H Canon Helm, whom one's happy to greet,
And Hancock with limited portions of meat.
And if to augment that small ration you wish,
Hamblett's, I'm sure, would supply you with fish.
One more H is Holmes, with a knowledge of amps,
He sells all things electric, from sets down to lamps.
I might have been awkward about which to talk,
But the Iveys will make you in comfort to walk.
J's for Jones—Angus—' his reverence ' to you,
He does all (and more) he's expected to do.
K is for Kemp, you might possibly know 'im,
He takes the blame for concocting this ' poem.'
It's also for Kingham—he's in the ' K ' batch—
'Tis he who looks after (or looks *for*) your ' thatch.'
L is for Lister's, a firm of renown,
Undoubtedly they're the back-bone of the town.
M's for Montgom'ry, at tail'ring no fool,
These brothers spend Sundays 'twixt Church and the School.
N is for Norville, in music well versed,
O's the Old Bell, where one quenches one's thirst.
P is for Pugh, suites of furniture selling.
Q's formed for sweets of a different spelling.
R stands for Robinson's fruit, flowers and seeds,
S is for Shapland, who bakes for our needs.
T is for Talboys—a blacksmith is Ted—
But with no spreading chestnut tree over his head.
U *was* for Urch's, who made cakes galore.
(It's Fearis's now, so 'tis Urch's no more).
V is for Vigus—he attends marriages.
He now sends cars, where *we* used to have carriages.
W's Wilcox's, farmers, they're brothers;
These are but two, of course there are others;
There's Workman, Webb, Wintle, Wood, Wainwright & Wilkes.
At the latter, with luck, you get nylons and silks.
X stands for *ex*clusions—they can't all be said,
Y Z pass unchallenged—they need a ' wise 'ead.'

There are no letters left, so my nonsense is done;
I hope it has caused a few moments of fun.
Some names are left out, but there's no slight intended,
The grey matter just won't be further extended.

Composed by Ernest Kemp as a Tabernacle money raiser.

DURSLEY TABERNACLE. (10 10. 10 10. 10 10.) JACK P. B. DOBBS, 1922–

(by courtesy of Jack Dobbs and the United Reformed Church)

ful town Male Voice Choir in 1944 and at the end of that year the toys given to the church's children at a party were mainly home made.

The joyful flag bedecked atmosphere of the town on V.E. Day in 1945 was saddened by the new of the death of Deacon, Corporal Oliver Vinton, Later in the year khaki and two shades of blue appeared with increasing frequency in the congregation and a welcome home supper was organised. Towards the end of the year a 'Thanksgiving and Welcome Home Savings Week' was held in the town. Highlight was a day when Group Captain Leonard Cheshire, V.C., D.S.O. took the salute at a march past of servicemen headed by the band of the 12th lancers – among them members of the crew of Dursley's submarine. Fireworks and a torchlight procession ended the day.

The war with Japan had yet to be won, however, and so had the climb out of the austerity the years of fighting had brought. To help the Tabernacle face and adapt to the present world three ministers have come.

Angus Jones 1945–61. Trained at Yorkshire United College, Bradford, he ministered at Malvern Link Countess of Huntingdon's Church before coming to Dursley. While here he was for seven years secretary of the

Tabernacle Minister and Diaconate 1959.
Standing – Percy Hicks, Stanley Wilcox, John Wilcox, Jim Fowler, Dick Phillips, Ken Green, Fred Perry
Seated – Frances Summers, George Montgomer, Revd Angus Jones, Ebbie Montgomery, Nell White, Joan Kingham.

Dursley Tabernacle celebrated 200 years of childrens work in 1978. Among the special events was a social at the Lister Hall and seen here cutting the bi-centenary cake are: Mrs and Mr Cornock, Mayoress and Mayor of Dursley, Sheila and the Revd Glyn Jenkins, George Timbrell, master baker, the Revd Frank and Pat Nun and the Revd Angus and Joyce Jones. *(Dursley Gazette)*

Gloucestershire and Herefordshire Congregational Union. After 12 years at West Orchard Church Coventry he moved to Grange over Sands, Lancs from which church he retired in 1979.

Frank Nunn B.Sc., B.D., 1961–71. Trained at Lancashire College, his first pastorate was at Knowle Park Church, Bristol 1955–61. Now at Central Church, Sheffield.

Glyn Jenkins B.A. B.D. our present minister and his family settled in Dursley in 1972. He trained at The Northern Congregational College before becoming pastor at Milnrow and Littleborough Churches Rochdale, Lancashire. His ministry in Gloucestershire was at first to Dursley Tabernacle and The Quarry Churches but in 1976 this extended to include Sharpness U.R.C.

One of the ideas he brought with him from the north was that of a 'procession of witness'. This was put to the ministers of the other churches of the town, readily accepted and the Good Friday procession to Cam Peak, based on the Roman Catholic 'Stations of the Cross', has been a regular ecumenical event since then.

These three most recent leaders of The Tabernacle are part of a long succession of men of high calibre who from its earliest days, have been

These Cam Peak services were begun by the Revd. David Truss of Cam Meeting in about 1902

The ecumenical Good Friday Process of Witness 1981. Carrying the heavy wooden cross, made by R.A. Lister & Co. Ltd, past St George's Church, Upper Cam. . . .

The Revd Glyn Jenkins leads meditation at the sixth Station of the Cross outside Downhouse Farm. . . .

. . . After the Cross was erected on Cam Peak — The Revd Lee Jong Hun of Korea, Revd Glyn Jenkins, (Tabernacle U.R.C.) Revd Canon Eric Hoskin, (St James's Parish Church), Revd Basil Venner (Dursley and Cam Methodist Churches) Miss Joan Kingham, chairman of Dursley Council of Churches 1981. *(Photos. David E. Evans)*

Informal talk before the United Evening Service at the time of Christian Aid Week 1981. Fred Perry, Tabernacle Church Secretary; Mrs Newbigin; Revd Basil Venner; Revd Glyn Jenkins; Revd Dr Lesslie Newbigin who preached. *(Photo. David E. Evans)*

called to minister in a distinctive way in the town. The gifts they have brought have been diverse but a thread of strong spirituality and leadership has run through their pastorates and this has shown itself in the strength of the congregation. Records of the activities of the church from the beginning of this century until now are full and detailed. They deserve careful appraisal to show how the church has coped with the great revolution in social structure and religious outlook England has undergone in the last 80 years. From a largely Christian, ordered and fairly static society, through a period which has brought more exciting, or frightening, inventions and situations than the span of a common man's life has ever seen or experienced before, including two global wars, we have become a highly mobile, restless, mainly irreligious people. All of our town's churches have had to adapt in a positive way to survive and maybe the story of how they have done this will be written in full in the future. Possibly it will be written from the stance of a more united Church for the massive fall in church attendance generally has had one good effect – it has helped to strip away much of the over confident, denominational arrogance and intolerance of previous ages – apparent to some extent even in placid Dursley. As 'comrades in adversity', adherents of different church disciplines are learning slowly to accept each other simply as Christians.

The ecumenical movement is real. Methodists and Anglicans have faced the issues of union. In 1972 the United Reformed Church in England and Wales came into being through the joining of the Congregational Church in England and Wales and the Presbyterian Church of England. The Tabernacle and the Quarry Chapel, but not Cam Meeting, are within the fold of the U.R.C. and union extended in 1981 to the Churches of Christ. The United Reformed Church sees itself, not as end, but as a spring board for greater church unity. It was in the van in promoting 'The Ten Propositions for Unity' which have led to the covenant proposals that are being considered by the the Church of England, the Methodists, the Moravians and the United Reformed Church.

One thing is certain and that is that the Tabernacle, like other churches must continue to change and adapt its presentation of the great central truths of the Christian faith, without compromising them, to match the times in which it exists. Without a positive approach it will wither, lingeringly, to extinction, left behind by the exciting, vibrant, God created world outside. It came into existence because two young men, George Whitefield and Thomas Adams, were not afraid to be in and to challenge the godless society into which they were born. They, and others of their ilk at the time, did so without the comforts of a centrally heated meeting house with all 'mod cons' but went to the people on commons and in market places in all winds and weathers. In its present minister Tabernacle folk are fortunate indeed to have a man ready to lead them vigorously to face up to the problems of spiritual life today.

They are fortunate, too, in the quality of the lay men and women who

A delightful study of age and youth in 1978. Percy Hicks, here 88 years, a member of the Tabernacle since boyhood, and Tracey Rogers, 2 weeks. Percy died March 1982. *(Photo. Ron Jones)*

A Sunday morning's congregation in 1979 *(Photo. Ron Jones)*

Easter Sunday 1981. The Revd. Glyn Jenkins receives into membership of the church Dr and Mrs M. Freeman, Mr and Mrs P. Rudge, Mrs E.M. Fowler, Mrs S. Simpson, Mrs V. Harding. Elders helping are Ernest Powell, Margaret Pengelly, Fred Perry and Bob Faraway.

After Easter Sunday morning Family Communion Service 1981 *(Photos. David E. Evans)*

have played a leading part in church affairs in local and in wider fields, and continue to do so – lay preachers, Sunday School now Junior Church leaders, secretaries, treasurers, Deacons now Elders, organists, organisation leaders, chapel keepers now caretakers, ladies whose tea brewing has invigorated many a meeting and so on.

It is in the nature of things that in reciting the history of the Tabernacle it is the names of men who have been almost exclusively mentioned. There is no doubt, however, that shadowy though they are in chapel records – the first woman Deacon wasn't elected until the time of World War I – the women of the church have played and still play a vital role which must not be under-estimated. For her freshness and vitality in her own right, as well as for her support of her husband, the church today is deeply in debt to Sheila Jenkins, the present 'Lady of the Parsonage'.

It was in the pastorate of Angus Jones that Robert Murray in Dursley, now M.A., B.D., felt the call to the Christian ministry. He trained at New College and since 1974 has been minister of Braintree U.R.C., Essex. To commemorate in 1980, the bicentenary of Robert Raikes' first Sunday School, his church performed 'Raikes Progress' and Robert and children from the church were pictured acting it in 'Reform'.

Author of the play is Charles Jukes, frequently actor-producer in The Tabard Players, Dursley Tabernacle's drama group. It was written in 1978 to mark the bicentenary of its own Sunday School, formed by William King, and it was performed at the U.R.C. West Midlands Provincial Family Day at Gloucester that year.

William King, John Dando, Adrian Newth and men of their like had a strong Christian faith, awakened, or at least brought to flower, by the enthusiasm of George Whitefield. So far as can be discovered, today, Dursley Tabernacle is the strongest of the churches in England (and perhaps in an even wider sphere) which can trace their origins directly to Whitefield's powerful evangelism. For nearly 240 years the society which began as a meeting of his followers in a cottage in the hamlet of Stancombe has witnessed to the Christian faith and in that faith its present members look to the future with confidence.

Our family at the Parsonage, the Jenkins; Glyn and Sheila and their children Bronwen, Graham and Matthew, 1981. *(Photo. David Evans)*

Addendum

The Reverend William Havergal in Coaley and Dursley, 1820–1822

William Havergal was born at High Wycombe in 1793 and made the usual progression of schools and university to become a curate in the Church of England. His first charges were two parishes widely separated, one in Bristol and one near Taunton. Following his marriage be became curate at Coaley for a short while, after which he moved to Worcestershire. He died at Leamington in 1870. His fame rests on his contributions to church music and many of his hymn tunes are still sung today.

He described Coaley as being 'one of the parishes long considered as one of the dark and neglected parts of Gloucestershire . . . three miles from Dursley, an uncommonly pretty place, dairy country, but some cloth and edge-tools are manufactured . . .' He went to Coaley at the request of the Bishop of Gloucester, whom he described as 'a fine sun' in an 'Artic sea' of a diocese, and there was in sole charge, with a lectureship in Dursley. In a letter to his mother he wrote;

> 'The Bishop of Gloucester is very solicitous I should take the lectureship as Dursley is an important sphere and he longs to get the truth preached in it'

From this it sounds as if Dursley too was neglected under its absentee rector a situation which would help to account for the prosperity of the Tabernacle and Wesleyan chapels at this time. In another letter Havergal wrote;

> 'I preach at Dursley once on Sundays and each other Thursday. The middle and poor people hear me gladly but the wealthy and gay, though not hostile or unkind, are stout in prejudice and worldliness. But I 'plow in hope'

Two years later in May 1822 he wrote;

> 'About three months ago notice was given me that my services were no longer required at Dursley. The ostensible reasons were that the incumbent's better health would allow him to take the evening duty and that he could no longer afford to engage help. But I suspect there is a feeling you can better imagine than I can describe. The parish began to arouse and individuals to inquire. The church was filled when I preached; some Dissenters, alas! found their way into it, and sixty subscribers to the Church Missionary Society had been readily obtained by some of my friends. At this juncture the Vicar of Coaley (who lived in Bath) apprised me of his intension to resign or exchange . . .'

From this it would seem that Havergal's enthusiasm was resented by some, perhaps the wealthy, and maybe Vicar of Coaley and Rector of Dursley acted together to get rid of this young man. In the event he moved to Worcestershire. His Dursley hearers set about collecting for a farewell present of a silver basket but, possibly fearing that this would lead to more trouble in the parish, he dissuaded them from doing so, an act commended by his bishop. From his Coaley parishioners, however, he accepted a silver tea pot.

Although William Havergal was in this area for less than three years he engendered deep affection. When his daughter revisited Coaley some fifty years later she found that he was remembered vividly and she recorded much of what she heard.

> "The congregations were wonderful. The church that was so empty hadn't even standing room. I've seen the road lined with horses, gigs, and carts from all parts. When the people knew he was going away they thickened to hear him; and the last sermon! not a dry eye in the church. I can show you the hymn-book Mr. Havergal made for us. We used to say, 'Mr. Havergal is all music.' Old Thomas Cam, the clerk, was so too; and they did have such talks. The new hymn-book was so liked that my little cousin George took some eggs to the vicarage to get one. Mr. Havergal was out, but George soon had one. The school children loved him dearly. He was the one to keep a parish right, for they took all their quarrels to him and he squared them all."

> "I was a stiffish lad of fourteen when Mr. Havergal came to Coaley, and I went with my father to work at the vicarage garden. The vicarage was new, for the old one was pulled down after the last parson had hung himself in it. The garden was covered

with rubbish. I remember Mr. Havergal would work along with us sometimes, and he could put his hand to anything. He was a lithesome man — not a lithesomer in England. Such a one to be up in the morning; and he'd set the vicarage windows open, to let out the night air. And to see him walk! why he'd be at Dursley in twenty-five minutes, and its three miles. He never touched the stiles; he'd go clean over them. When I heard you were come to the village, miss, I said to my missus, 'Her father did what few would do now-a-days.' There was a poor fellow, Joe Ford convicted at Gloucester for horse-stealing. He was condemned to die, and when the 'Size was over Mr Havergal travelled every day to see him, though it's fourteen miles, and he mostly walked it. From his condemnation to his execution Mr. Havergal saw him daily. His body was buried under the church tower; there were over three hundred at the funeral, and Mr. Havergal addressed them from the grave. The text of the sermon the next Sunday was, 'The way of transgressors is hard.'

Details of the triple hanging can be found on page 87.

"I remember how people said 'Mr. Havergal do be in and out of the houses all the week, and that fetched them to church on Sunday; and he do be as frequent to Dissenters as to the t'others.' Why, the head man at the chapel turned over to the Church!

"The old clerk, Thomas Cam, was a musicianer; he made pieces that were sung at Gloucester College. Mr. Havergal and he had mighty turns at it; and what seemed so curious to me was, that they both made tunes in their heads without stopping to play them."

Coaley Peak is one of the juttings of the Cotswold range. The long narrow lanes leading up to it are almost impassable in winter; not only "oxey" and clayey, but with water-springs over-flowing the path. But through mud and water ankle deep did the pastor go after his flock. An old man remembered one night when, he said, "There was awful fighting highish up, quite at the hills. They ran to the vicarage and called him, though long past midnight. Up he went; he wasn't the sort to mind a journey night or day to do good, and he had some One to watch over him. They say when he got up to the fighting they soon dropped their hands, and he reasoned them into lambs, and got 'em all to shake hands and go home."

"The old church was crowded then. Mother told me she often stood three Sundays running. Mr. Havergal preached then; a good minister he was, beloved by all far and near. They travelled from Uley and Dursley and Kingscote to hear him. He preached the Gospel and that's the doctrine to fill churches."

"Mr. Havergal led the rabble of Coaley as asey as a shepherd leads his she'p dog. There was plenty of rabble when he cum'st to Coaley; and when he took to us, them that wudna hearken to nons't, ud hearken to him. There was one particular bad fellow, not over eighteen. Mr. Havergal got him put in the stocks a few hours, just as long as he thought needful to soften him. Then he took him to the vicarage, and gave him a good supper and good advice. He'd hearken to no one; but in course he hearkened to Mr. Havergal, for no one could go agen him. When my father was ill, that good parson came again and again, and he'd administer medicine to sowl as well as body—aye, a sight of medicine he guv for nothing—up till ten a night folks went for his mixtures. I remember Coaley church was cram full, not a standin' empty. He was a plain-spoken man, preaching the Gospel, and that 'all our righteousness was as

> filthy rags.' He's in my eye now—a very upstanding man, not his fellow in the pulpit, I knows."

The reference to Havergal's medical skill is interesting. It is said that he was good at treating burns and broken bones and that his medicines were better than the doctor's. Some of his parishioners indeed would not take the doctor's mixtures until Havergal had first tasted and approved! This must have been annoying to the doctor but nevertheless the two were on good terms and Havergal was invited to send to the doctor's house whenever he needed fresh supplies.

> My beloved father was voluntary chaplain at the workhouse (at the top of Boulton Lane, Dursley). "Mr. Havergal went of his own free will to comfort and instruct them. He used to take a three-legged stool and sit down among them as freely as if he was in a palace. There was one poor creature, Kate Twirling, who had been ex-communicated out of the Church. 'Twas stricter rules in those days. Poor thing! she had been a beautiful girl, but so bad. Mr Havergal could not rest till he brought her back to the Church; and he knew that was not enough; ah, it was to Jesus he tried to bring us all. I remember after Kate died it was found that great property belonged to her. Never mind, Mr. Havergal showed her the true riches. All he did was out of love to God and free good-will to man."
>
> Another man told me that when my father first came to Coaley, as soon as ever church was over the game of fives was played against the tower walls; but for shame they could not play after hearing such sermons. An old pilgrim, John Stiff by name, remarked: "Aye, he preached the Gospel and the marrow of the Gospel. There was mighty little of that in the Establishment then. I used to walk five miles to hear Mr. Havergal preach. And all the Dissenters turned to Church. Ah, he preached Christ and he lived Christ, and now he's with Christ for ever. He was the first to tell us about the missionaries."
>
> "His sermons were the means of my dear father and mother's conversion, but I did not then know the Lord myself. I remember the effort made by my crippled father to go and hear him. How well I recollect your father's beaming face! He was so full of the love of Christ, it shone in every feature. Precious man! every one loved him, every one looked up to him, for his life preached. And it was not only his own parish he cared for, but many others; and it was Mr. Havergal who first held missionary meetings in Dursley, Uley, and other places. His correspondence was much blessed to me."

Dursley's Castle

Various accounts about the castle have come down to us and its remains — substantial foundations — were still to be seen at the end of the 1700s. The site of the castle is unknown and the only information we have is that it was just to the north of the town centre. In 1978 it was decided to plant a tree at each end of the lawn outside the Tabernacle to commemorate two hundred years of work with children at the church. Attempts to dig a hole at the post-office end of the lawn were thwarted by the present just below the turf of big dressed stones and so both t·ees were planted at the other end where the soil was deep. No attempt was made to investigate the stones but it seems likely that they were present before the Tabernacle was erected and it is interesting to speculate as to whether they form part of the castle remains or not. Against this idea is that Tabernacle records make no reference to the castle but then we have no description of the building of the church at all, except that stone came from Granny's Tump Quarry. On the other hand, land with foundations showing was probably of little value agriculturally but *could* have been used as a building site. So — is Dursley Tabernacle built on the site of the old castle?

Josiah Woodward D.D., 1656–1712

Josiah, a son of Joseph Woodward, minister of St. James's Church during the Puritan Interregnum, was aged about six when his father died — old enough to be influenced by his father's piety. He entered the Anglican ministry, was appointed by the East India Company to the London parish of Poplar in 1679 and in 1711 became Rector of Newchurch, Kent, and also curate of Maidstone where he died and was buried (It must be he who was the 'Dr. Woodward of Maidstone' and not Joseph as previously stated).

In 1697 Josiah published "An Account of the Religious Societies in the City of London &c" which quickly ran to seven editions and was translated into German. In it he described the Anglican societies, first formed in 1678, which were a reaction to the moral and religious laxity of the period. Members met to strengthen faith and to perform works of charity. Woodward fostered such a society in Poplar. The S.P.C.K. was created in 1698 and soon began distributing widely abstracts of The Account. The book exercised considerable influence on Anglican religious life at the time and, later, on the beginnings of the Evangelical Revival. Samuel Wesley at Epworth began a society after reading the book and his son John grew up with it. George Whitefield acknowledged his debt to Josiah when writing of his first society, that at Gloucester in 1735.

Thus the son of a Dursley Puritan and grandson of a Cam tanner played a significant part in the evolution of Methodism, Wesleyan and Calvanistic.

(References: Dr. Woodward's 'Account' with introduction by D.E. Jenkins (1935)
Introduction to 'John Wesley in Wales' by A.H. Williams (1971)).

References

Sources of Information

Unless otherwise stated the information contained in this book was taken from minute, account and other books in the keeping of Dursley Tabernacle U.R.C.

Abbreviations:
- G.R.O. Gloucester Record office
- G.C.L. Central Library, Gloucester
- T.H.C.S. Transactions of the Congregational Historical Society
- G.J. Gloucester Journal

References – Chapter I

1. *Dursley and its Neighboughood*, Revd. John Blunt, 1877, p. 61.
2. Sermon of John Owen, quoted in *Cromwell – Our Chief of Men*, Antonia Fraser, 1973, p. 46. See also *The English Church 1640–1660*, W.A. Shaw in 2 vols, 1900.
3. Blunt, op. cit., p. 84.
4. Fuller, quoted in *Sunday, its Christian and Social Significance*, William Hodgkins, 1960, p0. 49.
5. *Practical Works*, Baxter, Vol. III, p. 746.
6. Blunt, op. cit., p. 82.
7. The full statement will be found in *Confessions of Faith*, 1855, Dr. Williams' Library, ref. no. 5105.
8. Blunt, op. cit., p. 61. *Godfrey Goodman, Bishop of Gloucester 1583–1656*, G. Soden, 1953, pp. 155, 156, 391. Walkers *Sufferings of the Clergy*, revised by A.G. Matthews.
9. *Nonconformist Memorials*, E. Calamy. *Great and Good Men of Gloucestershire*, J. Stratford, 1867. *In Days of Old*, J. Starley, 1912. *Wotton-under-Edge*, E.S. Lindley, 1962, p. 239.
10. G.C.L. *Hockaday Abstracts*.
11. *A Collection of Sufferings of People called Quakers*, J. Besse, 1743.

References – Chapter II

1. *Uniformity and Nonconformity*, Congregational Historical Soc. Trans. supplement, April 1962. *Worship and Theology in England 1690–1850*, Horton Davies, 1961. *Dissent and Parliamentary Politics in England 1661–1689*, D.R. Lacey, 1969. *Freedom after Ejection 1690–1692*, Alexander Gordon, 1917.

2/3. Woodward and Stubbes. *Calamy Revised*, A.G. Matthews, 1934. Stratford, op. cit. D.N.B. Stubbes and Col. Birch – See Lacey above. Stubbes' son, also Henry, had a remarkable career, becoming second keeper of the Bodleian Library until expelled at the Restoration in 1660. He thereupon set as a physician, securing a royal appointment in Jamaica. He was drowned on the way to Bath in 1676 and is buried in Bath Abbey. See *A Seventeenth Century Defender of Islam — Henry Stubbe,* P.M. Holt, published by Friends of Dr. Williams's Library, 1972.

4. Calamy Revised, op. cit.
5. So described by the Vicar of Corsham, Wilts in 1674: Salisbury Diocesan records.
6. *Religious Developments in Wales 1664–1682,* Thomas Richards, 1923.
7. Calamy Revised, op. cit.
8. Private letter from the Revd. Dr. G.F. Nuttall.
9. *History of Castle Green Congregational Church, Bristol,* published by the church, 1967.
10. Stratford, op. cit., p. 180.
11. *Collection of Sufferings of People called Quakers,* J. Besse, 1743.
12. Bishop Compton census returns.
13. *Gloucestershire Studies,* H.R. Finberg, p. 155.
14. Gordon, op. cit.
15. G.R.O. QS 02.
16. *The Up to Date History of Cam Meeting,* published by the church 1962.
17. *Gloucestershire Woollen Mills,* J. Tann, p. 119.
18. ibid.
19. G.R.O. QS 02.
20. Cam Meeting burial registers, G.R.O. D 3567 1/39.
21. *The History of Cheshire,* Ormerod, 1882, vol. 3.
22. The John Evans List of Dissenting Ministers and Congregations 1715–1729 in Dr. Williams's Library, London.
23. Reports of the Charity Commissioners 1824–1868.
24. Evans List, op. cit.
25. *Pages of the Past, Thornbury,* H.W. Phillips, 1978.
26. Records of Southgate Congregational Church, Gloucester, held in the U.R.C. archives, Leamington Spa.
27. G.R.O. QS 02.
28. G.R.O. D 3567 1/39.
29. ibid.
30. Horton Davies, op. cit.
31. as 16.
32. G.R.O. QS 02.
33. ibid.
34. as 16.
35. G.R.O. QS 03.
36. Deeds in custody of Twemlow Trust.
37. G.C.L. cuttings book 1873–78.
38. S.P.C.K. letter books.
39. ibid.
40. ibid.
41. as 36.
42. ibid.
43. ibid.
44. ibid.
45. ibid.
46. ibid.
47. G.R.O. D 2831/13.
48. ibid.
49. as 36.
50. as 16.
51. ibid; also Surman Index in Dr. Williams's Library.
52. G.R.O. GDR 285 B(1).

53. G.R.O. GDR 397.
54. G.R.O. GDR 381.
55. Thompson List of 1772 in Dr. Williams's Library. *Letters to Dissenting Ministers and Students,* Job Orton, 1806.
56. Orton, op. cit.
57. Stated in a memorandum sent to Dursley Tabernacle in 1900 from Memorial Hall Library, London, quoting from Joshua Wilson manuscripts.

References – Chapter III

1. Printed in *Dissent and the Wesleyans,* Donald Davie, Journal of the U.R.C. History Society, October 1977.
2. Works of Thomas Secker, Vol. 5.
3. *English Men and Manners in the Eighteenth Century,* A.S. Turberville, 1957. *Worship and Theology in England 1690–1850,* Horton Davies, 1961.
4. For the reader interested in George Whitefield the two volume biography by Arnold Dallimore is essential. Vol. I, 1970; Vol. II, 1980. Other sources of information on Whitefield: His *Journal* and *Works; Letters of George Whitefield,* 5 vols., 1771; *Memoirs of the Life of George Whitefield,* 8 vols., 1772; *George Whitefield the Awakener,* A.D. Belden, 1930.
5. Cole: *History of Southgate Congregational Church, Gloucester,* T.J. Lander. *Great and Good Men of Gloucestershire,* J. Stratford, 1867. *George Whitefield's Curate: Gloucestershire Dissent and Revival,* Dr. G.F. Nuttall, 1976. Records of Southgate Congregational Church, Glos, in the U.R.C. archives, Leamington Spa.
6. Nuttall, *Whitefield's Curate,* op. cit; also Theological Magazine, January 1801.
7. Dallimore, op. cit., Vol. 1, p. 439.
8. For example Devonport in 1763 soon to be followed by Exeter and Gosport. See *Whitefield and Congregationalism,* C.E. Watson, T.C.H.S., Vol. 8.
9. Quoted in *Selina, Countess of Huntingdon,* Seymour 1839, Vol. 1, p. 92.
10. *Whitefield's Legacy to Bristol and the Cotswolds,* G.H. Wicks, 1914. Also Watson, op. cit.
11. Wicks, op. cit.
12. *Two Calvanistic Chapels 1743–1811,* London Record Soc., 1975.
13. *Howel Haris – Reformer and Soldier 1714–1773,* T. Benyon, 19589.
14. Seymour, op. cit.
15. ibid. *Cheshunt College,* published by the college, 1968. *The Significance of Trevecca College 1768–91,* Dr. G.F. Nuttall, 1969.
16. Adams, Hogg, Vines and Croom:
    Seymour, op. cit. Belden, op. cit. Wicks, op. cit. Watson, op. cit. Stratford, op. cit. *Memoirs of the Life of Mr. Hogg,* Theological Mag. February 1801. *Memoir of the Life of the late Rev. J. Croom,* Evangelical Magazine, October 1806. *Rodborough Tabernacle – A Memorial of Nonconformity. Rodborough Tabernacle,* T.C.H.S., Vol. 10.
17. Wicks, op. cit.
18. ibid.
19. as 16.
20. ibid.
21. ibid.
22. Letter from the Revd. Dr. G.F. Nuttall, 1967, relating to William Jones, the Castle Combe weaver mentioned here.

More information on Calvanistic Methodism will be found in *A Forgotten Thread in Congregational History — The Calvanistic Methodists,* E. Welsh, T.C.H.S., Vol. 21.

References – Chapter IV

1. *Letters of George Whitefield,* 5 vols., 1771.
2. Manuscript book written by Alfred Bloodworth in 1864 and in Dursley Tabernacle archives.
3. Letters of Whitefield, op. cit.
4. *The Weekly History* and its successors – a Calvanistic Methodist magazine.
5. ibid.
6. ibid.
7. ibid.
8. ibid.
9. G.R.O. GDR 284.
10. G.R.O. QS 02.
11. *Two Calvanistic Methodist Chapels 1743–1811,* London Record Soc., 1975.
12. G.R.O. GDR 292A.
13. G.R.O. GDR 284
14. Evangelical Magazine, 1810, p. 159.
15. ibid.
16. Evangelical magazine, 1935, p. 179.
17. G.R.O. GDR 292A.
18. Property deeds of Dursley Tabernacle U.R.C.
19. ibid.
20. ibid.
21. Bloodworth, op. cit.
22. Property deeds of Chippenham Tabernacle U.R.C.
23. Bloodworth, op. cit.
24. *Whitefields Legacy to Bristol and the Cotswolds,* G.H. Wicks, 1914, p. 150.
25. *Bristol Congregationalism,* I. Jones, 1947, p. 62.
26. as 18.
27. Bloodworth, op. cit.
28. T.H.C.S., Vol. 10, p. 285.
29. ibid., p. 286.
30. *Worship and Theology in England 1690–1850,* Horton Davies, 1961, p. 77.
31. *A History of the Methodist Church in Great Britain,* ed. Davies & Rupp, 1965.
32. *Howell Harris's Visits to London.*
33. Letters of Whitefield, op. cit.
34. Bloodworth, op. cit.
35. In the Countess of Huntingdon Archives, Westminster College, Cambridge.
36. Wicks, op. cit. also biographies: *Life of Rowland Hill,* Sidney, 1834; *Life of Rowland Hill,* Jones and Sherman, 1849.
37. *Rowland Hill and the Rodborough Connexion 1771–1833,* Dr. G.F. Nuttall, T.H.C.S., Vol. 21.
38. Sidney, op. cit.
39. Bloodworth, op. cit.
40. Blunt, op. cit.
41. Seymour, op. cit.
42. *Gloucestershire Biographical Notes,* J. Stratford, 1887, p. 119.
43. Seymour, op. cit.
44. ibid.
45. *The Life of the Revd. Benjamin Parsons,* Paxton Hood, 1856.
46. ibid.
47. ibid.
48. Stratford, 1867, op. cit., p. 301.
49. Hood, op. cit.
50. as 48, p. 311.

51. *Memoirs of the Life and Character of the late Cornelius Winter*, William Jay, 1809.
52. *Milestones*, Dursley Tabernacle publication 1958.
53. Glos. Notes and Queries, Vol. 2, p. 618.
54. Stratford, 1867, op. cit.
55. King: Bloodworth, op. cit. Wicks, op. cit. G.C.L. cuttings book 1873–78. G.C.L. W1 143117 – 3 volumes of cuttings etc. entitled *Robert Raikes and the Sunday School. Robert Raikes – The Man and his Work*, Harris, c. 1890. *Bristol mercury*, 28 July 1880.
56. *Prison Reform in Gloucestershire*, J.R.S. Whiting, 1975.
57. Bloodworth, op. cit.
58. G.J., 3 February 1821.
59. Whiting, op. cit.
60. *A History of Gloucestershire*, Fosbrook, 1807.
61. Survey of Dursley, 1795, G.R.O. p. 124.
62. Bloodworth, op. cit.
63. ibid.
64. ibid.
65. ibid.
66. ibid.
67. Adrian Newth and relations: G.C.L. W1 143117 op. cit.; Bloodworth, op. cit.; Congregational Church year books for 1876 and 1899.
68. Bloodworth, op. cit.

References – Chapter V

11. *Cheshunt College*, published by the college 1968.
2. Evangelical magazine, June 1804.
3. *An Incidental Letter addressed to the Lord Bishop of Sarum . . . with some observations and reflections in favour of Village Preaching*, British Museum 4106-C58/10.
4. 1795 Survey of Dursley. G.R.O. p. 124, VE1/1. Also, *Memories of Old Dursley*, James Newth, 1910 (unpublished).
5. Manuscript notes by Alfred Bloodworth in Dursley Tabernacle archives.
6. ibid.
7. G.J. 5 October 1801.
8. Surman Index in Dr. Williams's Library, London.
9. Bloodworth, op. cit.
10. ibid.
11. *Dursley Methodist Church Centenary 1864–1964*, James Alderson.
12. Addendum to Whitmore's *Directory of Dursley*, 1882.
13. Bloodworth, op. cit.
14. Newth, op. cit.
15. *Recollections of Cam sixty years ago*, W.T. Turner, Glos. Notes and Queries, Jan–March 1904.
16. Surman Index, op. cit.
17. *Cheshunt College*, op. cit.
18. Dursley Tabernacle archives.
19. Bloodworth, op. cit.
20. Dursley Tabernacle Deeds.
21. Bloodworth, op. cit; also G.J. 10 January 1820.
22. Newth, op. cit.
23. as 20.
24. *Another Milestone*, published by Dursley Tabernacle, 1908.
25. Evangelical magazine, November 1809.

26. Bloodworth, op. cit.
27. as 24.
28. A list of those who contributed existed until at least 1900 but is now lost.
29. Bloodworth, op. cit.
30. ibid.
31. All information about the Tabernacle school comes from Bloodworth, op. cit.
32. Bloodworth, op. cit.
33. Information on North Nibley Tabernacle from the Revd. Richard Chidlaw.
34. Bloodworth, op. cit.
35. Unless stated information on St. James's school comes from Bloodworth, op. cit.
36. Newth, op. cit.
37. ibid.
38. G.C.L. RZ 1115(4).
39. Evangelical Magazine 1811.
40. Information on formation of Protestant Society and its activities from Evangelical Magazines through 1811 and 1812.
41. ibid.
42. ibid.
43. Dursley Tabernacle baptismal registers.
44. Bloodworth, op. cit. (Ichabod = The glory is departed).
45. Evangelical Magzines, 1813.
46. ibid, 1812 and 1814.
47. ibid, November 1812.
48. Bloodworth, op. cit.
49. as 18.
50. G.R.O. D2831/13.
51. Surman Index, op. cit.
52. St. James's Church registers 1804.
53. Original with Mr. Herbert Edwards, g.g. grandson of William; also Bloodworth, op. cit.
54. Bloodworth, op. cit.
55. ibid.
56. Surman Index, op. cit.

References – Chapter VI

1. Deeds G.R.O. D2719/2.
2. *Dursley Methodist Church Centenary 1864–1964,* James Alderson. Also Bloodworth, op. cit and G.R.O. D2719/2.
3. *Bristol Congregationalism*, Ignatius Jones, 1947, p. 62.
4. ibid.
5. W.T. Turner, op. cit.
6. ibid.
7. A plaque to Richard Trotman exists in the Tabernacle. A long obituary on him was printed in the Evangelical Magazine for May 1812. Unfortunately for us it takes for granted his life history and dwells at length on his piety and his end.
8. Evangelical Magazine, October 1813.
9. Jones, op. cit., p. 31.
10. The Christian Witness Magazine of 1850, p. 482 has a long article on this event.
11. Kingswood Tabernacle record books.
12. *From Whitefield's Tabernacle,* E.A. Bodey, Bristol Congregational Magazine, May, 1928.
13. Edward Gardner of Frampton-on-Severn, Glanville's birth place, intimate friend of Edward Jenner of Berkeley, man of letters and John's uncle.

14. Surman Index, Dr. Williams's Library, London.
15. G.J. 17 March 1866.
16. Addendum to Whitmore's Directory of Dursley, 1822.
17. Surman Index, op. cit.
18. Deeds of premises.
19. Surman Index, op. cit.
20. G.R.O. D586; see also *Pages of the Past – Dursley*, 1976, p. 39 et seq.
21. Surman Index; Evangelical Magazine, 1833, p. 317; Bloodworth, op. cit.
22. Bloodworth, op. cit.; Select vestry minutes, G.C.L. D 15406.
23. Miles report on 'Conditions of the Handloom Weavers', 1839.
24. ibid.
25. ibid.
26. ibid.
27. G.J. 13 July, 3 August 1839.

References – Chapter VII

1. G.J. 30 April 1842.
2. Frequent references to this co-operation in Evangelical magazines for 1808–11.
3. Newth, op. cit.
4. ibid.
5. G.J. 14 January 1865.
6. *Dursley Methodist Church Centenary 1864–1964*, James Alderson.
7. G.J. 25 January 1868.
8. Alderson, op. cit.; also *Listers – the First Hundred Years*, D. Evans, 1979, p. 97–8.
9. Alderson, op. cit.
10. Alderson, op. cit.; also county directories, and G.J. 23 December 1865.

References – Chapter VIII

1. G.J. 4 June 1842.
2. The Manchester Guardians of August 1841 have long reports.
3. ibid., quoted in Dursley Gazette of 12 December 1905.
4. Keene's Bath Journal, 2 June 1827.
5. G.J. May and June 1843.
6. ibid, 8 June 1844.
7. Stratford, 1867, op. cit.
8. G.J. 8 July 1854.
9. Dursley Gazette 17 november 1979.
10. ibid. 16 October 1976, quoting from Gloucester Chronicle of period.
11. 1851 census returns.
12. Property deeds of R.A. Lister & Co. Ltd.
13. Stratford, 1867, op. cit.
14. G.R.O. p. 124 VE2/2.
15. Surman Index, Dr. Williams's Library, London.
16. Dursley Gazette, 16 September 1911.
17. Memorial of John Waite of Southgate Congregational Church, Gloucester, in *Gloucestershire Biographical Notes*, J. Stratford, 1887.
18. ibid.
19. G.J. 6 march 1869.
20. G.C.L. R2115(4).
21. Property deeds.

22. G.J. 10 June 1865.
23. ibid., 25 March 1865.
24. Surman Index, op. cit.
25. G.J. 6 april 1867.
26. ibid., 18 July 1868.
27. ibid., 6 June 1868.
28. *Dursley Church in History*, Canon D. Daven-Thomas, c. 1964. Also Glos. Journals of period.
29. Newth, op. cit.
30. Whitmores Dursley Directory, 1882 addendum.
31. G.C.L. Hockaday Abstracts.
32. Dursley Gazette 13 June 1883.
33. ibid., 19 November 1881.
34. ibid.,
35. Two of the few are *Chapels and Meeting Houses*, K. Lindley, 1969; *The Fall of Zion –Northern Chapel Architecture and its Future*, K. Powell, 1980, published by SAVE Britain's Heritage, 3, Park Street West, London, N.W.1.
36. Dursley Gazette, 23 June 1883.
37. Dursley Parish Magazine 1878.
38. ibid.
39. Dursley Gazette 17 July 1880; also Whitmore, op. cit.

References – Chapter IX

1. Dursley Gazette 25 June 1887.
2. Whitmore's Dursley Director addendum 1882.
3. Dursley Gazette.
4. Whitmore, op. cit.
5. Court of Quarter Sessions list 1903.
6. Information from Mrs Nellie Head, Bristol.
7. Information from Mr & Mrs C. Pyle, Cam.
8. ibid.

References – Chapter X

1. Information from Miss K. Kemp, Minchinhampton.
2. Information from Mrs M. Henderson, Cam.
3. Printed in the April 1979 edition of 'Reform' from the March issue of Hillingdon's *Communicare* magazine.
4. Information from Mr Dobbs, Dartington Hall, Devon.

References — Addendum

1. All material from "Records of the Life of the Revd W.H. Havergal M.A" by his daughter, Jane Miriam Crane 1882.

Index

(Pages numbers to illustrations are in italic)